RETHINKING THE TRIANGLE

Washington-Beijing-Taipei

RETHINKING THE TRIANGLE
Washington-Beijing-Taipei

Editors

Brantly Womack
University of Virginia, USA

Yufan Hao
University of Macau, China

UNIVERSIDADE DE MACAU
UNIVERSITY OF MACAU

World Scientific

Published by

University of Macau
Avenida da Universidade
Taipa, Macau, China

and

World Scientific Publishing Co. Pte. Ltd.
5 Toh Tuck Link, Singapore 596224
USA office: 27 Warren Street, Suite 401-402, Hackensack, NJ 07601
UK office: 57 Shelton Street, Covent Garden, London WC2H 9HE

Library of Congress Cataloging-in-Publication Data
Names: Womack, Brantly, 1947–   author. | Hao, Yufan, author.
Title: Rethinking the triangle : Washington, Beijing, Taipei / Brantly Womack & Yufan Hao.
Description: New Jersey : World Scientific, 2015. | Includes bibliographical references and index.
Identifiers: LCCN 2015031986 | ISBN 9789814713122 (alk. paper)
Subjects: LCSH: United States--Foreign relations--China. | China--Foreign relations--United States. |
    United States--Foreign relations--Taiwan. | Taiwan--Foreign relations--United States. |
    China--Foreign relations--Taiwan. | Taiwan--Foreign relations--China. |
    Taiwan--International status.
Classification: LCC E183.8.C5 W655 2015 | DDC 327.73051--dc23
LC record available at http://lccn.loc.gov/2015031986

British Library Cataloguing-in-Publication Data
A catalogue record for this book is available from the British Library.

This edition is jointly published by University of Macau and World Scientific Publishing Co. Pte Ltd.
This edition is distributed by University of Macau only in Macau, Hong Kong and Taiwan.

In-house Editors: R. Raghavarshini/Dong Lixi

Typeset by Stallion Press
Email: enquiries@stallionpress.com

Printed in Singapore

Foreword

The idea for this book originated in a conversation at the University of Virginia's Miller Center between Admiral Joseph Prueher, Harry Harding, and Brantly Womack concerning the way forward in U.S.–China relations. Taiwan was of course an important part of the discussion, but it seemed to be a problem — and not a problem — at the same time. On one hand, Taiwan as a problem was the most visible symbol of the distance and suspicions between the United States and China. If the relationship became hostile, Taiwan would most likely be in the middle. On the other hand, Taiwan was not a problem now, and was becoming less of a problem. There was no crisis, and a crisis did not seem likely. As Admiral Prueher pointed out, even the continuing sales of American military equipment to Taiwan were driven by politics rather than by military considerations. Cross-Strait trade was booming, and both China and the United States were happier with President Ma Ying-jeou than they had been with his predecessor Chen Shui-bian. If we put on dark strategic glasses, then Taiwan was at the center of the Pacific "ring of fire" between China and the United States, but if we took the glasses off and looked at what was actually going on, things seemed much brighter.

This "problem-no problem" anomaly led to a new idea. Taiwan could be part of the solution rather than the problem. Peace and prosperity on Taiwan were not only to Taiwan's interest, but to the interests of China and the United States as well. If we viewed the triangular relationship as an inclusive, opportunity-driven one, then all three sides would benefit. Moreover, this was actually happening, driven by market forces and the prudent diplomacy of all three sides. Strategic thinking was lagging behind empirical reality. The Washington–Beijing–Taipei (W–B–T) triangle needed to be rethought.

In an inclusive triangle, better relations between any two sides would be beneficial to the third. This was certainly the case in economic interactions, but it could be true in security as well. Less cross-Strait tension means less chance of crisis intervention by the United States. Better U.S.-China relations mean less negative pressure on cross-Strait relations. Better U.S.-Taiwan relations — if we look beyond weapons sales — strengthen Taiwan's ability to contribute to cross-Strait relations. Moreover, these effects are not hypothetical. If we contrast triangular relations in 2000–2008, the presidency of Chen Shui-bian, with relations in 2008–2012, Ma Ying-jeou's time in office, there is clear evidence of the positive effects of inclusive interaction. Since 2008 tensions between China and neighbors north and south of Taiwan have increased, but cross-Strait relations have improved.

So rethinking the W–B–T triangle was a good idea. However, old ways of thinking die hard, and for 70 years the United States, China and Taiwan were used to thinking of their relationship in exclusive security terms. More than a bright idea was needed. Each partner in the relationship had to rethink its perspective. One side could not change the relationship alone — the other two would be suspicious. Moreover, the regional neighbors, especially Japan, would have to adjust to a new triangle close by.

Thus Miller Center hosted an international workshop in March 2013 featuring a well-known expert from each side of the triangle and also from Japan and Macau. The revised papers from the workshop provide the substance of this book. For the convenience of readers, we added to the papers, a comprehensive timeline of the triangular relationship as well as some of the key diplomatic documents.

The workshop was a success, and the participants decided to organize a series of international conferences on the general theme of rethinking the triangle. Each conference would include participants from each side of the triangle and from the region. The conferences would be held in the United States, Taiwan, China and Macau, but the focus of each would be on understanding the perspectives of the others. The American conference was held at the Miller Center in November 2013 and focused on Taiwan. The Taiwan conference was held on the island of Jinmen (Quemoy) in October 2014 and focused on China. The China conference was held in Shanghai in June 2015 and focused on the United States. The regional conference will be held in Macau in 2016 and will focus on the future of the triangle after the 2016 election in Taiwan. We hope that the research and participation involved in these conferences, together with this book, will make a significant contribution to a future-oriented understanding of the W–B–T potential.

Acknowledgments

Among the many people who have helped the project, Governor Gerald Baliles, the former Director of the Miller Center, deserves special mention. Governor Baliles was enthusiastic from the beginning, and under his leadership the Miller Center provided the venue and support for the workshop and the first conference. Admiral Prueher and Harry Harding provided distinguished and insightful commentary at the workshop. The workshop was funded by the Miller Center and University of Virginia's East Asia Center, Center for International Studies, School of Arts and Sciences and Politics Department.

The first international conference, "Taiwan Inclusive," was held at the Miller Center and was funded by the Chiang Ching Kuo (CCK) Foundation, the Taiwan Economic and Cultural Representative Office (TECRO), and University of Virginia's East Asia Center, School of Arts and Sciences, and Politics Department. Harry Harding and Chas Freeman provided distinguished commentary.

The second international conference, "The Rise of China and the Tangled Developments in East Asia," was held at Quemoy (Jinmen) University and was co-sponsored by National Chengchi University of Taipei. Professor Wang Jenn-hwan played a key role in organizing the conference, and Quemoy University was a gracious host.

The third international conference, "U.S. Rebalancing to Asia and Beyond," was hosted in Shanghai by the China Energy Fund Committee. Our special thanks goes to Jiang Chunyu, Director of China Energy Fund Committee International Center, and to Zhuang Jianzhong, the Center's Deputy Director.

Our heartfelt thanks to all those who participated in these conferences as presenters, chairs, discussants, and audiences. We hope that it was a stimulating experience for all.

Last and most importantly, our thanks to the University of Macau, the University of Macau Press, and World Scientific Publishing of Singapore for making this book possible. At the University of Macau we are especially grateful to Rui Paolo Da Silva Martins, Vice Rector for Research, the Publication Committee, and Dr. Wong Kwok Keung (Raymond), Director, and Clara Chung of UM Publications Centre. At World Scientific, the book has been in the capable hands of Dong Lixi, the Senior Editor for Social Sciences, and Ms. Raghavarshini managed its production. Carl Huang of the University of Virginia prepared the chronology for the book.

Contents

About the Authors

❧ **Professor Yufan HAO**, Dean of the Faculty of Social Science and Humanities and Chair Professor of Political Science, University of Macau. Professor Hao's publications include: *Sino-American Relations: Challenges Ahead* (2011), *Multiple Development of the Macau Economy* (2009), *Power of the Moment: America and the World after 9/11* (2002).

❧ **Professor Tse-Kang LENG**, Deputy Director and Research Fellow, Institute of Political Science Academia Sinica and Professor of Political Science National Chengchi University, Taiwan. Professor Leng's publications include *Dynamics of Local Governance of China during the Reform Era* (2010), *Globalizing Taipei* (2003) and *The Taiwan-China Connection* (1996).

❧ **Professor REN Xiao**, Director, Center for the Study of Chinese Foreign Policy and Professor of International Politics, Institute of International Studies, Fudan University, Shanghai. Professor Ren's publications include *New Frontiers of Chinese Foreign Policy* (2011), *U.S.-China-Japan Triangular Relationship* (2002) and *New Perspectives on International Relations Theory* (2001).

- **Takashi SEKIYAMA**, Director, Sasakawa Japan-China Friendship Fund, and Lecturer of International Political Economy, Department of International Studies, The University of Tokyo. Dr. Sekiyama's publication include *Cordination & Compromise* (2014), *The End of Japanese Yen Loan to China* (2011), *A History of Japan's ODA to China* (2008).

- **Professor Brantly Womack**, C. K. Yen Chair, the Miller Center and Professor of Foreign Affairs, Department of Politics, University of Virginia. Professor Womack's publications include *China Among Unequals* (2010), *China's Rise in Historical Perspective* (2010) and *China and Vietnam: The Politics of Asymmetry* (2006).

Introduction

Taiwan's future is with China, not against China. While this might seem to be a bold statement, for the past five years the diplomacy of Washington, Beijing, and Taipei has been based on this unstated premise. If you doubt the statement, consider the alternative. For an island one-third the size of Cuba and one hundred miles from the world's largest army and its largest trading partner, hostility would be a situation of permanent and increasing crisis. And indeed Taiwan was in a situation of martial law from 1949 to 1987, 38 years. While the mentioning of Cuba suggests that prolonged hostility with a very strong neighbor is possible, the Cuban example would hardly suggest that it is desirable.

But if the politics of the three governments most involved assume that Taiwan's future is with China, then why is the statement startling? Why does the premise remain implicit rather than explicit? Common sense is usually not a surprise.

The basic problem with the triangular relationship of Washington, Beijing, and Taipei is that while the reality of the relationship dictates cooperation, the history of the relationship has been one of entrenched suspicion. Richard Nixon's historic visit to China in 1972 began the process of backing off from hostility, and since 1979

China's policy of peaceful reunification with Taiwan has played an important role. Especially since 2008 all three governments have actively pursued better relations. But the practical and incremental adjustments in the relationship have not led to a fundamental rethinking of the triangle. Post-Cold War cooperation has occurred within an increasingly ill-fitting Cold War strategic triangle.

The purpose of this book is to begin the rethinking of the triangle. The old triangle was rooted in the hostility of the Chinese Communist Party (CCP) and the *Guomindang* (*Kuomintang*, Nationalist Party, KMT) since 1927 and enmeshed in Cold War confrontation since the Korean War began in 1950. From the founding of the People's Republic of China (PRC) in 1949 there was a profound enmity between Beijing and the remnant KMT forces on Taiwan, and the United States shared Taiwan's anti-communist hostility. Taiwan felt betrayed when the U.S. normalized relations with the PRC in the 1970s, but it still depended on the U.S. as its security patron. Meanwhile, the PRC felt cheated when the U.S. continued to sell weapons to Taiwan after it agreed that Taiwan was a part of China. Each side feared the collusion of the other two sides. It was a bad partnership, one driven by anxieties about security.

But the facts of the relationship have been gradually transformed, and while the exclusivist security triangle forged by hostility can be explained by history it fits neither the present nor the future. Backing off and working around an inappropriate diplomatic framework is good, rethinking the framework would be better. Increasingly, all sides of the triangle benefit from the better relations between the other two sides. American companies such as Apple and Motorola contract with Taiwanese companies to produce products in China. American presidents are relieved when cross-strait crises are avoided. The United States is still the primary final destination of Taiwanese exports, but two-thirds of those exports consist of parts sent to China for final assembly. Thus, if the U.S. were to restrict Chinese imports it would hurt Taiwanese exports as well. Meanwhile Taiwan is China's largest investor, and its expertise in high-tech production contributes to China's economic growth.

So the actual Washington–Beijing–Taipei relationship is *already* an inclusive, opportunity-driven relationship. The rethinking that we propose is not of an idealistic future world even though it is future-oriented. At the present time, progress is made through the pursuit of opportunities, and success benefits all three sides. It is win–win–win. There are ups and downs, but it would take very bad luck and very bad leadership to cause the situation to reverse irretrievably. However unwise and unlikely a return to hostile exclusivism might be, the lingering shadow of the old security triangle exaggerates the danger and thereby increases the possibility.

But an inclusive triangle is not all smiles and happiness. It provides a better framework for managing problems, but it does not remove or solve them. The core problem is the ambiguous status of Taiwan. Each of the three copes with the ambiguity in its own way. The PRC appears most adamant, but since 1991 its unification offer to Taiwan has included Taiwan keeping its own government, economic system, and even its own army. This was further clarified in 1995 with the promise that no PRC troops would be stationed there. And the "one China" appears to be an entity that both the PRC and Taiwan could be a part of. On the other side of the strait, Ma Ying-jeou, President since 2008, has pledged both no unification and no independence, leaving Taiwan's *status quo* somewhere in the middle. The American stance has been termed "strategic ambiguity": Taiwan is recognized to be part of China in principle, but we sell arms and are (ambiguously) committed to the defense of Taiwan against forcible unification.

Even though there is room to negotiate in the diplomatic positions on Taiwan's status, domestic politics and public opinion in each corner of the triangle make a settlement difficult. Older Taiwanese were taught by the KMT to hate and fear the communists; younger ones have grown up with a democratic system that they consider superior to that of the PRC. Increasing cross-strait contact has increased familiarity but also a sense of difference. On the Mainland, Taiwan is seen as unfinished business of the civil war, postponed by American imperialist interference. To accept Taiwanese independence would be the last act of the Century of Humiliation that began with the Opium War. To regain Taiwan is an essential part of redressing humiliation. There is little consciousness across the strait of how internationally diverse Taiwan has become since 1895, and of how important this diversity is to Taiwan's identity and sense of security. The Taiwan issue is not so central to American consciousness. Taiwan is viewed more as a problem than a place, and the United States wants above all to avoid a cross-strait crisis. But the U.S. is not eager to see the problem solved. The American political culture of anti-communism and anxieties about rivalry with China make it difficult for the government to encourage cross-strait amity.

From these different vantage points spring a multitude of misperceptions and doubts. Many Taiwanese dismiss PRC offers of autonomy because "you can't trust Communists." Meanwhile greater contact with the Mainland (and one in 23 Taiwanese is now living there) both increases a Taiwanese sense of a different identity and convinces them that convergence is inevitable. Meanwhile, many in the PRC think that the only way to eliminate Taiwanese separatism is to break Taiwan's link with the U.S., symbolized by continuing arms sales. In fact, however, Taiwan must be reassured that unification will enhance its international status, and especially with the U.S. Lastly, unless the American attitude toward Taiwan evolves beyond the "Taiwan problem," American interest and involvement in Taiwan will decline as the cross-strait relationship improves and the likelihood of crisis diminishes.

Even a smoothly running inclusive triangle will have frictions. While all might be convinced that the triangle is in their general interest, they will each have specific interests that require negotiation. The differences will be enhanced by the asymmetry between Taiwan and its partners, while the rivalry between the U.S. and

China will be sharpened as China approaches and then passes the United States as the world's largest economy. While the prospect of a superpower conflict is exaggerated, the relationship of a rising power to an established power is fraught with tension, and the tension is magnified by cultural and political differences.

Beyond the three participants themselves, the old security triangle has been a key element of regional and even global security architecture. The rest of the world — and especially the neighbors — will be interested spectators as the triangle develops. As Takashi Sekiyama's chapter argues, Japan will be the most concerned not because it favors hostility in the triangle, but because it will be anxious that its special relationship with the United States might be weakened while united action with Taiwan makes China stronger. The concerns of South East Asia would be similar though not as acute.

A final concern on the part of the United States is a subtle but serious one. While the U.S. would be relieved to see a peaceful cross-strait relationship institutionalized, its special role in the triangle has been an important part of its global leadership. If instead of an inclusive triangle a special bilateral relationship develops in which the U.S. is merely a passive and distant observer then it will have accomplished a peaceful withdrawal from part of its leadership role. A peaceful withdrawal is better than a losing fight, but better still would be the active promotion of a collaborative arrangement to the interest of all.

Preview

Since we are exploring the possibility of an inclusive triangle, the core of the book is a chapter from the perspectives of each of the three main actors, the United States, People's Republic of China and Taiwan. These are not chapters about the three different perspectives, they are analyses from each of the three sides, although of course there is a range of outlook and opinion at each angle.

Together they provide evidence both of the possibilities for an inclusive triangle and of the difficulties that remain to be bridged.

The titles of the chapters already show important differences in perspective. What from an American vantage point is a "Washington–Beijing–Taipei triangle" looks like a "Beijing–Taipei–Washington" triangle from China and a "Taipei–Beijing–Washington" triangle from Taiwan. Each chapter differs in its approach as well as its perspective. In addition to the three core chapters, we have chapters presenting the perspectives of Japan and of South East Asia because of the regional significance of the triangle. Lastly a timeline for the triangle as well as some of the most important documents are included for reference.

The first chapter combines an American perspective with a general review of the history of the triangle and its asymmetric structure. It argues that the stability of the Cold War security triangle was premised on the overwhelming military capacity of the United States and the presumption of hostility. Both of these factors have changed. Since 2008 China's military capacity in its near waters has increased and at the same time all sides of the relationship have improved. If we persist in viewing the triangle in exclusive security terms it becomes more and more threatening, but in fact a serious cross-Strait crisis is increasingly unlikely. Thus our assumptions about the triangle must be reconsidered, and a new American position developed.

While some analysts have suggested that the U.S. abandon Taiwan because it is a risky distraction from the bilateral relationship with China, others have said that Taiwan should abandon the U.S. and negotiate cross-Strait relations simply on a bilateral basis. Both of these suggestions have serious drawbacks. What is suggested here is that the United States explore the possibilities of advancing an inclusive triangle that is stable, conducive to our economic interests, and furthers global leadership. Triangles are not easy to change because no one wants to risk taking the first step. However, the practical diplomacy of all sides is aligned with an inclusive triangle, and informal diplomacy and confidence-building can bridge the gap to a win–win–win triangle.

In the second paper, Ren Xiao of Fudan University details the progress that has been made in the last ten years of the cross-Strait relationship. But he begins by pointing out the deep concerns Beijing had in 2000–2001 with the combination of the election of Chen Shui-bian, whose party had advocated Taiwan independence, and the harsh tone of the early George W. Bush administration, which considered China a "strategic competitor." Nevertheless China made important adjustments in its terminology of unification, from unity under the PRC to unity of both as part of China, and the general direction of its foreign policy was formulated as "peaceful rise," which evolved by 2005 into the even milder term, "peaceful development."

The problematic reelection of Chen in 2004 began a period of crisis. Beijing's immediate policy goal shifted from unification to preventing separatism, and the 2005 Anti-Secession Law was the embodiment of the shift. But peaceful initiatives also increased. The leaders of three opposition parties (including the KMT) were invited for discussions in Beijing and new economic policies were tied to these visits. Although Chen continued provocative moves PRC policies became more differentiated. Meanwhile the PRC appreciated the U.S. moves to rein in Chen's brinksmanship and to encourage cross-Strait stability. Finally the "high danger period" of 2006–2007 yielded to optimism with the election of Ma Ying-jeou in 2008.

With Ma in power in Taiwan a flood of economic initiatives could be launched, with the Economic Cooperation Framework Agreement (ECFA) of 2010 as the capstone. At the same time the global financial crisis and China's continued growth during the crisis raised the significance of the China-U.S. relationship to new heights. Since 2008, all sides wanted stability. China wanted progress but dropped its timetable, Ma wanted economic progress but had to be cautious about political contact, and the U.S. was happy to be beyond the brinksmanship of Chen Shui-bian. However China remains concerned about a possible DPP return to power in 2016, and so it is reaching out to DPP politicians as well as supporting Ma's government. Hu's final political report, at the 18th Party Congress in October 2012, emphasized peaceful development and institution-building across the Strait. In Ren Xiao's words, Hu Jintao's guidance of PRC policy during crisis and into the new era is "surely one of the most important achievements during his tenure." Hu's accomplishment survived the 2012 change of leadership in all three governments, but the difficult tasks of peace and politics remain ahead.

In Chapter 3, Tse-Kang Leng of Taiwan's Academia Sinica explores the changes in Taiwan's domestic politics and opinion, which are rooted in more profound changes in culture and identity. As the previous chapter implies, Taiwan has been the biggest question-mark in the triangle, and it is because of the democratization of Taiwanese politics. As Leng puts it, Taiwan has been "the tail wagging two dogs." The question for the future of an inclusive relationship is whether culture can play a positive role in cross-Strait integration. Besides the shared Chinese historical culture there are important historical differences, and in any case culture and identity remain dynamic and responsive to changes.

Leng fleshes out the problem of culture by sketching the points of view prevalent in Taiwanese academia. Taiwanese academics use Western theories such as power transition theory and constructivism to anticipate changes in relationships, but they also perceive differences between Asian and Western approaches to sovereignty. In Taiwan, the enmeshment of the KMT's commitment to one China with its authoritarian "emergency" control created a situation in which democratization created a new populist center for Taiwanese political culture and at the same time problematized its identity with a larger Chinese culture. As the KMT's Lee Teng-hui shifted his personal political role from leader of the KMT to popularly elected president of Taiwan in the mid-1990s, he initiated "new policy lines toward a democratic but independent Taiwan instead of unification with the Mainland." Although there are clear differences between the brinksmanship of Chen Shui-bian and the economic cooperation of Ma Ying-jeou, they have in common that they must satisfy a Taiwanese public that is increasingly conscious of itself.

The U.S. plays a general role in the inclusive triangle of providing leverage for Taiwan as it seeks to preserve the autonomy of its identity and interests while converging with the Mainland. Continuing arms sales are a sign of U.S. support, and therefore Taiwanese are nervous about American arguments to stop the sales. Actions such as the inclusion of Taiwan in the U.S. Visa Waiver Program in 2012 are appreciated not only in themselves but also as gestures of support for cross-Strait stability. Nevertheless, even with U.S. support Ma has to be cautious about seeming too compliant or moving too fast in his dealings with Beijing. As Leng details, hesitancy regarding convergence stems from more than simple inertia. The DPP and KMT have different interpretations of sovereignty, and, more importantly, public identity continues to shift toward "Taiwanese, not Chinese" despite closer economic relations. While hardliners on both sides of the strait argue for dichotomous views of Chinese/Taiwanese culture, increasing people-to-people contact should continue to strengthen a civil society base for the relationship.

Chapters 4 and 5 provide perspectives on the triangle from the points of view of interested outsiders. In Chapter 4, Yufan Hao of Macau University addresses the basic question of the feasibility of an inclusive triangle. He points out that economic integration often causes problems and crises rather than creating common interests, and that China's growth relative to the United States creates strategic distrust. Underlying both of these trends is the importance of perception. Despite these perceptual difficulties, or possibly because of them, Hao considers the paradigm change from security triangle to inclusive triangle to be a necessary and important move. Viewing the relationships in terms of exclusive security concerns accentuates anxieties and distrust, while an inclusive vantage point highlights mutual interest. In effect, the choice of triangular paradigms is important not because one correctly predicts developments and the other doesn't, but rather because, given the importance of perceptions and expectations, each has a tendency to become a self-fulfilling prophecy, one pessimistic and one optimistic.

Southeast Asia has become more concerned about China's peaceful leap forward since 2008 and its more assertive foreign policy especially in the South China Sea. But as Hao points out, the changes in China's attitude do not involve an expansion of its previous claims but rather a more vocal defense of long-standing ones. Nevertheless, the recent conflict between Taiwan and the Philippines suggests that if the PRC and Taiwan coordinated their diplomacy in the South China Sea it would cause problems for Vietnam, the Philippines, and Malaysia.

The significance of the Washington–Beijing–Taipei triangle is more immediate for Japan than for Southeast Asia, and in Chapter 5 Takashi Sekiyama of Meiji University provides a careful analysis of the potential effects of a transformed triangle for Japan. He considers two additional triangular situations, Japan–PRC–U.S. and Japan–PRC–Taiwan, looking at the effects of changes in the Washington–Beijing–Taipei triangle on each. While Hao makes the general argument that economic engagement can increase friction, Japan's trade situation *vis-à-vis* China adds a special asymmetric note. Japan has lost China trade share to the United States, while at the same time China's importance for Japan has increased. Therefore Japan worries that a closer U.S.–China relationship will increase the leverage of each in their dealings with Japan. Likewise, while the U.S. presence might make China more amicable in its relations with Taiwan, if China and Taiwan form a united front in disputes with Japan, for example over the Senkaku/Diaoyu Islands, then Japan would suffer from a closer relationship. However, as long as Taiwan remains an autonomous actor then Japan could benefit from closer ties between PRC and Taiwan because Japan is already intimately involved in cross-Strait trade. Sekiyama gives the telling example that almost half the parts in the iPhones assembled by Taiwan's Foxconn in China are ultimately from Japan.

To generalize the vantage point of the triangle's Asian neighbors, while they recognize the benefits of a thick, stable relationship between the U.S., China and Taiwan, they are wary of the consolidation of such powerful actors. On the one hand, conflict between the U.S. and China would be their worst diplomatic nightmare. It would destabilize the region and cost it the benefits of the Asian production cycle that has transformed the region's economy. On the other hand, the formation of an inclusive triangle *from which the neighbors were excluded* would leave them isolated and more vulnerable. Especially in the case of Japan, isolation and vulnerability could in turn lead to Japan balancing against the triangle by re-arming. The hedging and balancing options open to other neighbors might be less dramatic than Japanese rearmament, but anxious neighbors could both increase friction in the regional environment and stimulate tension within the triangle.

The lesson to be drawn from regional ambivalence is that the inclusiveness of an inclusive triangle should not be confined to its members. The argument for the inclusive triangle was not based on threats from outside, but rather on the opportunities inside. The logic of an opportunity-driven triangle is "inclusion for," not "inclusion against." However, convincing outsiders that they are not excluded poses a complex and difficult challenge. Southeast Asia is less problematic because of regional institutions such as ASEAN and the ASEAN China Free Trade Area. However, in North East Asia the two Koreas and especially Japan must be convinced that better Washington–Beijing–Taipei relations do not jeopardize their interests.

In his classic work *The Structure of Scientific Revolutions*, Thomas Kuhn argued that one paradigm replaces its predecessor because the new one can credibly incorporate and explain realities that for the old paradigm were anomalies accumulating beyond the edges of its vision. Even in the natural sciences, the process of paradigmatic revolution is neither smooth nor quick. Everyone is habituated to the old paradigm, and in the past it fit quite well the mainstream of research. It is all the more true of political paradigms because they are structures of perception and interaction rather than models of interpreting natural phenomena. Nevertheless, in understanding social reality as well as in natural reality, the better framework is the one that offers more adequate guidance to present and future efforts.

The authors of this book share the premise of diplomacy since 2008 within the Washington–Beijing–Taipei triangle, namely, that interests in common should displace the fear of exclusion as the guiding thread of the relationship. It is difficult to deny the trend of better relations between Beijing and Taipei, between Taipei and Washington and (with respect to the triangle) between Washington and Beijing. The anomalies produced by the inclusive trend crowd the exclusive security triangle and make increasingly unrealistic its dire predictions about the dangers of relative gains and power shifts. By contrast, these new realities and their future prospects are at the center of attention for the new paradigm of an inclusive, opportunity-driven triangle.

Even if the paradigm of an inclusive triangle is accepted, however, there remain many puzzles to be solved and many concerns to be addressed, both inside and outside the triangle. A political paradigm is a framework for understanding the structure of social interactions, but the perceptions of all actors remain rooted in their histories and in their different identities. What we have presented is not a magic key that solves the problems of the Washington–Beijing–Taipei triangle, but rather the beginning of a reorientation that we hope will provide a more appropriate model for understanding and managing the continuing evolution of its interrelationships.

Part 1: Inside the Triangle

Chapter 1

The Washington–Beijing–Taipei Triangle: An American Perspective

Brantly Womack

University of Virginia

The day to day relationships of the United States, the People's Republic of China (PRC) and the Republic of China on Taiwan (ROC) have never been better.[1] Trade across the Taiwan Strait grows by leaps and bounds, and to a great extent it involves American companies and targets the American market. The PRC is Taiwan's largest trading partner and largest export market. Meanwhile the American relationship to the PRC grows thicker. Hillary Clinton wants a 1,00,000 Americans to study abroad in China,[2] and almost 2,74,439 Chinese are already studying in the United States, one-quarter of the total number of foreign students.[3]

---

[1] "PRC," "China" and "Mainland China" will be used interchangeably. For the post-49 period, "ROC" and "Taiwan" will be used interchangeably.

[2] "100,000 Strong Initiative," http://www.state.gov/p/eap/regional/100000_strong/index.htm. Accessed August 5, 2015.

[3] *Open Doors 2011* (Washington: Institute of International Education, November 2014).

The very scale of American concerns about trade deficits, jobs and debt owed to China underscores the extent of the economic connection. Lastly the United States–Taiwan relationship remains strong, with almost 21,266 students studying in the United States, seven times China's per capita rate. Although U.S.–Taiwan trade has been rather flat for the past decade at around $70 billion dollars, direct exports are estimated to be only one-half the value of Taiwan components reaching the United States as inputs to Chinese products.[4]

But the best of times is shadowed by the worst of security triangles. The PRC is outraged at the continuing American sales of advanced weapons to Taiwan despite the promise in 1982 to gradually reduce such sales,[5] and is deeply concerned about the American commitment to the defense of Taiwan as expressed in the 1979 Taiwan Relations Act. For its part, the United States is concerned that, despite China's turn to a policy of peaceful reunification in 1979, it still reserves the option to use force. The increasing sophistication of Chinese weaponry poses a grave challenge to the invulnerability of American naval forces operating off China's coast. On the other hand, Taiwan's current security dependence gives the United States tremendous leverage in its dealings with Taiwan as well as almost $20 billion in arms sales from 2008–2011.[6] Lastly, Taiwan worries about both its vulnerability to the PRC and the possibility of being abandoned by the United States.[7] In short, each fears the collusion of the other two. Thus at the same time that contacts are increasing, these security concerns are sharpening.

---

[4] Shirley Kan and Wayne Morrison, *U.S.–Taiwan Relationship: Overview of Policy Issues* (Washington: Congressional Research Service, January 4, 2013), pp. 26–29.

[5] US–PRC Joint Communique on Arms Sales, August 17, 1982. *Public Papers of Presidents of the United States, Ronald Reagan* (Washington: Office of the Federal Register, National Archives and Records Service, General Services Administration, 1983), vol 2, pp. 1052–1053.

[6] Shirley Kan, *Taiwan: Major US Arms Sales since 1990* (Washington: Congressional Research Service RL 30957, March, 2013), p. 56.

[7] See for example, Huang Tzu-wei 黄子維, Impacts of new PRC–US ties on Taiwan, *Taipei Times*, June 15, 2013.

And while these concerns are most pressing for Taiwan, they are also central for the United States and China as well. As Michael Swaine puts it, "the effective management of the Taiwan issue is the *sine qua non* of stable and productive United States relations with China."[8] And the impact reaches beyond the immediate triangle. A major conflict could pose, Swaine continues, "extremely negative consequences for United States interests and stability across the entire Asia–Pacific region."

But how real are the threats embodied in the security triangle, and what would be the best trilateral policies for handling them? I argue that the exclusivist mentality of the security triangle actually increases security risks by distracting us from the significance of improving relationships. Ideas matter, and the Washington–Beijing–Taipei (W–B–T) security triangle is an old idea that has become a bad idea. Together with Beijing and Taipei, we need to rethink the relationship in terms of present realities and future prospects. The relationship on the ground between Mainland China, Taiwan and the United States has become an inclusive one, one in which improvements between any two sides benefits the third partner. Better cross-Strait relations reduce security risks and offer a variety of opportunities. Better relations between China and the United States could be reassuring rather than alarming to Taiwan. Better United States–Taiwan relations could expand China's opportunities. Instead of being captured by the high adrenaline of catastrophic what-ifs that are vanishingly unlikely, we should have an overall conception of our interrelationship that fits reality, promotes our mutual interests, and leads to effective diplomacy.

I begin by reviewing the development of the exclusive strategic triangle, followed by an analysis of how asymmetric security triangles work. The narrative and structural analysis are then brought together in a critique of the security triangle's mode of thinking as

---

[8]Michael Swaine, *America's Challenge: Engaging a Rising China in the Twenty-First Century* (Washington: Carnegie Endowment for International Peace, 2011), p. 85.

applied to post-2008 realities. The next section develops the idea of an opportunity-driven, inclusive W–B–T triangle. This involves a discussion of its economic and societal dimensions as well as security, and concludes with the regional implications of an inclusive triangle. The third section elaborates American interests in the context of an inclusive triangle. The first interest, of course, is that the inclusive triangle is not simply a phase between periods of confrontation. Then comes our interest in economic connectivity, and finally our concern with our status as a global power. The final section addresses the problem of diplomatic transitioning from the security triangle to an opportunity triangle. Since all parties start from an attitude of suspicion, it is difficult for any party to make a move. Thus the first steps must be informal ones to develop mutual trust in the relationship, and they may well be prolonged. The United States will have to be careful to reduce Beijing's concern about American interference in domestic affairs, but its most delicate task will be to restructure its relationship to Taiwan. An inclusive triangle remains asymmetric, and the smallest partner has the greatest sense of vulnerability.

W–B–T security triangle

An analytic narrative

Although the security triangle did not reach its full form until the beginning of the Korean War in 1950, General George Marshall's mission to China (December 1945–January 1947) provides an instructive prolegomenon.[9] Marshall tried to mediate between the *Kuomindang* (KMT) and the Communists, but without success since both felt that their only security lay in the defeat of the other side. Marshall's fall back position was to support the KMT

---

[9]Tang Tsou, *America's Failure in China* (Chicago: University of Chicago Press, 1963), vol 2, pp. 349–554.

financially but not to involve American troops in the civil war. The historian Ernest May considers Marshall's decision not to become involved one of the crucial turning points of the Cold War because the United States could not have prevented the Communist victory in China and the transfer of American military supplies from Europe would have made the Berlin airlift unlikely and would have undermined the financing of the Marshall Plan.[10]

Four aspects of the Marshall mission have resonance for later triangles. First, American involvement was part of a broader strategic picture. During the war the United States had to make difficult decisions in allocating resources between the European and Asian theaters.[11] At war's end the United States became the first superpower, but one that had recently experienced its limits. Second, China loomed too large in American interests to be left alone. President Truman called Marshall out of retirement to mediate the Chinese civil war, and direct American military involvement was prevented only by Marshall's pessimistic prediction of the outcome. Third, the Chinese Communist Party (CCP) had become too strong for the United States to be able to achieve its desired outcome. Like his China hawk critics, Marshall believed that a communist victory in China would be a major advance for world communism. But he did not want to engage in a campaign that could not be won. His wisdom was demonstrated by the later American experience in Vietnam. Finally, the "you live I die" attitude of both the KMT and the CCP made mediation impossible.

The founding of the PRC on October 1, 1949 and the final retreat of the KMT to Taiwan shifted the framework of the triangle, and the outbreak of war in Korea in 1950 confirmed the basic pattern that lasted for the next 20 years. The PRC considered the

---

[10]Ernest May, 1947–48: When Marshall Kept the US out of War with China, *Journal of Military History* 66:4 (October 2002), pp. 1001–1010.

[11]Barbara Tuchman, *Stillwell and the American Experience in China* (New York: MacMillan, 1970).

liberation of Taiwan to be the final step of their civil war victory, one frustrated by United States presence. The KMT considered Taiwan as its temporary refuge and its base for retaking the Mainland. United States support for the KMT was codified in the Mutual Defense Treaty signed in December 1954. However, as Victor Cha argues, the purpose of the treaty was to control the KMT's adventurism as well as to defend Taiwan.[12] Taiwan was the "unsinkable aircraft carrier" in the general strategy of containing communism and a willing helper in first line American containment efforts in Burma, Vietnam, Tibet and elsewhere. But "unleashing Chiang Kai-shek" would create a no-win crisis for the United States, a replay of the last years of the civil war. At the same time that it supported the diplomatic presence of the ROC at the UN and waged war against what it considered Chinese dominoes in Vietnam, the United States used its naval power to preserve the *status quo* in the triangle.

Kissinger's secret visit to Beijing in 1971 began a transitional phase in the triangle that lasted until formal recognition of the PRC in 1979. The United States could appear to be above the cross-Strait fray by acknowledging that "all Chinese on either side of the Taiwan Strait maintain that there is but one China and that Taiwan is part of China."[13] However, the announcement was made in Shanghai, not Taipei. The U.S. emphasized the importance of a "peaceful settlement of the Taiwan question by the Chinese themselves," and began a reduction of American military presence in Taiwan. The global strategic significance of China was turned on its head — rather than containing world communism by opposing the PRC, the new relationship with China was seen as a restraint on the Soviet Union. Meanwhile the PRC accepted the Nixon offer of "one China, but not now" as an adequate beginning for normalization, which itself was a significant development in the PRC's cross-Strait policy. Taiwan remained unsinkable, but increasingly alone.

---

[12]Victor Cha, Powerplay: Origins of the US Alliance System in Asia, *International Security* 34:3 (Winter 2009–2010), pp. 158–196.
[13]"Shanghai Communique," February 27, 1972.

Normalization on January 1, 1979 began the longest phase of the security triangle, lasting until 2008. On the day of normalization with the United States, the PRC changed its policy toward Taiwan from "liberation" to "peaceful reunification." Although China retained its option of using force, this was a momentous change, and over the following 30 years it permitted a vast increase in cross-Strait economic and societal activity. The KMT's attitude moved from resistance to reluctant permission of contact to cautious acceptance of the "1992 consensus" on one China, but at the same time the democratization of Taiwanese domestic politics brought Taiwanese identity to center stage. A corollary was the emergence of the Democratic Progessive Party (DPP) and Taiwanese independence as a domestic issue, much to the distress of the PRC.[14] Cross-Strait security tension moved from its civil war focus on "which China?" to tension over Taiwanese autonomy and secession. The American position remained ambiguous, committed by normalization to official recognition of the PRC's claim to Taiwan and opposing Taiwanese independence, but on the other hand committed by the 1979 Taiwan Relations Act to maintaining forces capable of resisting a forcible takeover of Taiwan. Meanwhile the global strategic significance of the triangle shifted from the "China card" against the Soviet Union in the 1980s to China as a major power in its own right in the 90s, with the Taiwan crisis of 1995–1996 playing a major role in the American reorientation. Since the crisis, which was provoked by Taiwan's President Lee Teng-hui's visit to the United States and concluding with the visits of two aircraft carrier groups to the area, there has been no question of the importance of China in American strategic thinking.

The election of DPP candidate Chen Shui-bian in 2000 and his reelection in 2004 marked a major change in Taiwanese domestic politics that also had serious consequences for the triangular relationship. Chen and the DPP consider themselves the voice of Taiwanese in opposition to the all-China ambitions of the KMT.

---

[14]Shelley Rigger, *Why Taiwan Matters* (Lanham: Rowman and Littlefield, 2012).

While Chen did not risk a public declaration of Taiwanese independence, he made numerous gestures in the direction of trying to assert separate sovereignty. He provoked China into adopting the Anti-Secession Law in 2005. In contrast to the missile crisis of 1995–1996, the United States considered Chen's brinksmanship to be the source of cross-Strait tensions and publicly rebuked him. The State Department's Thomas Christensen made speech carefully laying out American policy and distancing the United States from Chen's initiatives, but triangular tensions remained palpable until Taiwan's 2008 election.[15]

2008 can be taken as the watershed of a new situation for security triangle.[16] Tensions throughout the triangle were lessened by the election of the KMT's Ma Ying-Jeou as President of the ROC. In its domestic struggle with the DPP, the KMT had to be cautious about appearing too friendly to the PRC, but it would benefit from avoiding crises and furthering economic prosperity. Ma's reelection in 2012 was an important popular confirmation of the KMT approach. However, two other factors increased strategic tension. The PRC's military modernization raised the possibility that the United States navy could be seriously damaged in the event of a military confrontation, and the shock of the global crisis of economic uncertainty raised China to the new status of global power. The American global posture has shifted toward rivalry with China, and the United States military is deeply concerned about threats to its invulnerability in the Western Pacific. As a result, the United States is even more committed to avoiding a cross-Strait crisis because it is concerned that it may not be able to intervene successfully.

---

[15] Thomas J. Christensen, Deputy Assistant Secretary for East Asian and Pacific Affairs, "A Strong and Moderate Taiwan," speech to U.S.-Taiwan Business Council Defense Industry Conference, Annapolis, Maryland, September 11, 2007, http://2001-2009.state.gov/p/eap/rls/rm/2007/91979.htm. Accessed August 5, 2015.

[16] Alan Romberg, *Across the Taiwan Strait: From Confrontation to Cooperation, 2006–2012* (Washington: Stimson Center, 2012).

Meanwhile in the shadow of the triangle…

Although politics and security have received the lion's share of attention under the security triangle, the transformation of Taiwan's socio-economy under United States patronage deserves attention. The United States encouraged land reform in the 1950s, which both increased agricultural production and created a base of support for the KMT among Taiwanese farmers.[17] The U.S. also encouraged and supported infrastructure creation and industrialization, providing more than $600 million in non-military aid from 1950–1965.[18] Of course, economic development served the strategic purposes of strengthening Taiwan and making it, along with Japan, South Korea, Hong Kong and Singapore, a showcase of non-communist success.

The Taiwanese economy had been international before. The Dutch in Taiwan had exported deer hides, and in the 1860s a Scotsman started the Taiwan tea industry. Under Japanese rule the ratio of trade to GNP rose steadily until the outbreak of the war in the late 1930s, and the ratio did not regain colonial heights until the 1970s.[19] But the exports of Taiwan before the 1960s were primarily agricultural products. In 1960, however, the government adopted the Nineteen Point Plan for Economic and Financial Reform to reorient the economy toward industrial exports. As Hsueh, Hsu and Perkins put it,

> The critical role of United States foreign aid in the 1950s made United States aid officials important players in the debates that led up to the 1960 policy reforms. Actions by the United States Executive Branch and pressures from the United States Congress also played an important role in Taiwan's exchange rate and trade liberalization decisions in the 1980s.[20]

---

[17] Neil Jacoby, *US Aid to Taiwan* (New York: Praeger, 1966), pp. 171–172.
[18] *Ibid.*, pp. 260–261.
[19] Wu Tsong-min, A Trade History of Taiwan, November 29, 2004, http://homepage.ntu.edu.tw/~ntut019/ltes/TaiwanTrade.pdf. Accessed August 5, 2015.
[20] Li-min Hsueh, Chen-kuo Hsu and Dwight Perkins, *Industrialization and the State: The Changing Role of the Taiwan Government in the Economy, 1945–1998* (Cambridge: Harvard University Press, 2001), p. 5.

The United States was the patron, advisor, model and target for exports, and thus Taiwanese drive on the right side of the road, use 110 watt electrical current, and American-style three-pronged electrical plugs. With the added dimension of educational exchange and emigration, a new American dimension has been added to Taiwanese culture.

Beginning in the 1990s, Taiwan's economy began to turn toward China, though primarily as a point of final assembly for products destined for the United States. By 2004 total trade with the Mainland exceeded total trade with the United States, and in 2010 Mainland total trade was twice its direct United States trade.[21] If we estimate indirect trade through China with the United States at twice direct trade, then the United States remains the overwhelmingly dominant final destination of Taiwanese products. However, the new pattern requires a healthy cross-Strait relationship.

Asymmetric security triangles

We normally imagine triangles as equilateral, but that is only accurate insofar as it shows the interdependence of the three actors.[22] Picturing a relationship such as that of W–B–T as a triangle implies that action between any two partners affects and is influenced by the third. Since the reaction of the third party is simultaneous, each actor must take both partners into account. If the third party's potential reaction is significant enough to limit the bilateral interaction then the triangle is a "hard" triangle. If the third party is influential but not decisive, then it is a "soft" triangle.

---

[21] Calculated from National Statistics of the Republic of China, http://eng.stat.gov.tw/mp.asp?mp=5. Accessed August 5, 2015.

[22] Lowell Dittmer, The Strategic Triangle: An Elementary Game-Theoretical Analysis, *World Politics* 33:4 (July 1981), pp. 485–516.

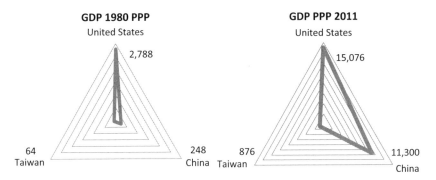

Figure 1:   Economy in 1980   Figure 2:   Economy in 2011

Source: International Monetary Fund, *World Economic Outlook 2012*, database.
Comparing 1980 and 2011 Economies (current US$ billion).

But for most triangles in international relations, and certainly the W–B–T triangle, the interrelationship is only half the story. The more interesting half lies in the differences of exposure.[23]

Figures 1 and 2 provide a graphic picture of the relative shifts in aggregate economic productivity between the United States, China and Taiwan.[24] In 1980 the American economy dwarfed both the Chinese and Taiwanese economies. The American angle of exposure to the triangle was minimal, China's was much larger, and Taiwan's was larger still. In 2011 relative exposures of the United States and China are becoming more equal, while Taiwan's exposure is roughly double. All economies have experienced considerable growth, but China is transforming its weight in the triangle, and the trend is not likely to change in the foreseeable future even as Chinese growth slows.

---

[23] Brantly Womack and Wu Yu-Shan, Asymmetric Triangles and the Washington–Beijing–Taipei Relationship, in Brantly Womack, *China Among Unequals: Asymmetric Foreign Relationships in Asia* (Singapore: World Scientific Press, 2010), pp. 371–404. Also Brantly Womack, *Asymmetry and International Relationships* (New York: Cambridge University Press, 2016), Chapter 3.

[24] The triangles are created by mapping respective GDPs on 120° radians from a central point. If the GDPs were equal it would produce an equilateral triangle.

How does an asymmetric security triangle work? If we assume a situation such as the 1980 triangle, the strongest power is in the pivot position because its weight plus either of the others is decisive. However, it also has little to gain or lose in the triangle, so it can justly be called a "reluctant pivot."[25] It is interested in avoiding crises because they require commitments, but it is less interested in resolution of conflict between the others because it would then lose its controlling position. The pivot is thus a *status quo* peace-holder, but not a peace-maker. The middle power is the frustrated one, since it can imagine being able to resolve its conflict with the third power if only the pivot would not interfere. The smallest is the anxious one since its fate is in the hands of the largest. The expected courses of policy therefore are that the smallest tries to bind the largest to the triangle while the middle power tries to break the relationship. The largest is thus the center of attention, and as long as the *status quo* prevails its position is high-profile, but low cost.

Imaginary risks and real costs

As the 2011 triangle suggests, the security situation is undergoing profound changes. Not only is China's Gross National Product (GNP) approaching that of the United States, but its military capabilities in coastal waters have increased markedly. The successful testing of an anti-satellite missile in 2007 began a broad series of Chinese military modernizations that put in doubt the invulnerability of the United States Navy in Taiwan's waters. These have included quiet conventional submarines, improved scud and intermediate missiles, stealth aircraft and anti-ship ballistic missiles. Since the Chinese leadership is well aware that they are raising the risk and cost of American involvement, their weighting of the United States factor in their cross-Strait thinking must change.

---

[25] Wu Yu-Shan, From Romantic Triangle to Marriage? Washington–Beijing–Taipei Relations in Historical Comparison, *Issues and Studies* 41:1 (March 2005), pp. 113–159.

Since Taiwan is also aware that they cannot defend themselves against the PRC alone, they are more likely to either become desperate or to yield to the PRC. The logic of the participants therefore changes. The pivot must choose between the prestige advantages of high profile and the increasing risk of high cost and perhaps failure. The smallest will desperately try to maintain the pivot's involvement or will break the triangle by yielding. The middle power is in a stronger position with both partners, and can decide to risk breaking the triangle.

With Taiwan's vulnerability as the primary focus, Aaron Friedman expresses the gloomy outlook of many security analysts: "Despite their vast cost, past success and impressive appearance, America's power projection forces in East Asia are in danger of becoming "wasting assets."[26] The Pentagon's "Air–Sea Battle" concept tries to maintain American invulnerability by expanding operations into China:

> "Attack-in-Depth": In traditional attrition models of warfare, forces attack the outer layer of an enemy's defenses and deliberately fight their way in. In contrast, under Air–Sea Battle, forces will attack adversary systems wherever needed to gain access to contested areas needed to achieve operational objectives.[27]

Since most of China's "adversary systems" are land-based, and rendering them ineffective would in some cases require attacks before launch, Air–Sea Battle implies preemptive strikes on the Chinese Mainland. Since the range of China's anti-ship ballistic missiles is at least 1,500 kilometers and the maritime exclusive economic zone (EEZ) it is committed to defend is only 500 kilometers offshore, a

---

[26] Aaron Friedberg, *A Contest for Supremacy: China, America, and the Struggle for Mastery in Asia* (New York: Norton, 2011), p. 224.

[27] General Norton A. Schwartz, USAF Chief of Staff & Admiral Jonathan W. Greenert, USN Chief of Naval Operations, "Air–Sea Battle: Promoting Stability in an Era of Uncertainty," http://www.the-american-interest.com/article.cfm?piece=1212 February 20, 2012.

preemptive strike could reach a 1,000 kilometers inland, and the overwhelming majority of China's population lives within a 1,000 kilometers of the Pacific. To see such a strategy as "promoting stability" requires dire prospects for stability under present strategy.

Of course, the prospects of a large asteroid hitting the world could lead to even gloomier thoughts and to more extreme measures. In both cases, the first question should be about the likelihood of crisis. Leaving the probability of asteroids to the astronomers, we can ask, are the political, social and economic trends of the triangle moving closer or further from confrontation? Does the increasing interconnection of the Taiwanese economy with the Mainland make it more or less likely to take desperate action? Under what circumstances is China likely to pursue a military option? Are there situations in which the United States could maintain profile and also reduce risk? An asteroid's impact with the earth is lose–lose for both, but the asteroid's course is set by physics. A crisis over Taiwan is lose–lose–lose, and the political communities as well as their leaderships have choices. Involved in Friedman's gloom is a near-asteroid certainty that China will challenge the United States when it has the capacity, and that Taiwan is only the proximate stepping-stone. Of course, if the United States prepares to contain China and moreover to "attack in depth," then it is to China's interest to develop the capacity to respond. However, Taiwan's security is an issue separable from such global concerns.

The most serious problem with the fixation on the security triangle is its exclusivity. It presumes that the interests of Washington, Beijing and Taipei are juxtaposed to the extent that if two actors "collude" the third is at risk. Thus peace is an unnatural interlude maintained by the decisive power of the reluctant pivot until that power can be challenged. As long as the PRC and the ROC were unalterably opposed, as long as mutually beneficial economic and societal interchange was marginal, the security triangle fit reality. But at present, and for the recent past, and for the future, the premise of exclusivity of interests needs to be rethought. If the interests of all sides can be inclusive, then the premise of the security triangle is in question. If the likelihood of military conflict diminishes to the vanishing point, then Friedman is quite right about "wasting assets." though not in the sense that to uses the term. Then the guns of all sides lack triggers, and the policy attention of all sides should turn elsewhere.

Imaging an opportunity triangle

Asymmetric inclusive triangles

I use the term "imaging" an inclusive W–B–T triangle rather than "imagining" it because it already exists. Substantial interactions that benefit all three parties are the daily reality of the relationship. What is missing is a general reconceptualization of relationship that is adequate and appropriate for its present and future.

It would be unrealistic to expect that turning attention to the positive effects of economic interactions would resolve the problems associated with a triangular relationship. Indeed, an interactive triangle opens up broader ranges of exposure and vulnerability than an exclusive security triangle. It should be recalled that the triangles in Figures 1 and 2 were of economic productivity, so the extreme exposure of Taiwan and the growing exposure of the United States were not simply military. As the smallest partner, Taiwan is proportionately more exposed to gains and losses, and most large, complex interactions are mixtures of plusses and minuses. Even a win–win–win situation has different implications for each side.

The essence of an asymmetric inclusive triangle is not unanimity of interests, but rather the assumptions that mutual benefit is possible, that individual benefit can be furthered by negotiation, and that the benefit of any two sides is likely to be beneficial to the third. In the realm of politics, it assumes that the three actors remain autonomous pursuers of their own interests while negotiating mutually acceptable arrangements. In the realm of security, it assumes that vulnerability can be reduced or structured through negotiation. In the realm of society and economics, it does not eliminate state control, but it does assume that the purpose of regulating interaction is to maximize mutual benefit rather than to limit contact.

These assumptions must be true for all participants in order for the triangle to be inclusive, but there are also concerns that are specific to each partner in an asymmetric triangle.

The smallest side is most exposed in an inclusive relationship and least in control, therefore it must be confident that its identity and interests will be respected. "Win–win" is not good enough. Unless its basic interests are acknowledged by its more powerful partners, it would be prudent to forego marginal advantage in order to minimize exposure. In the case of Taiwan this is an especially delicate problem because the implications of "one China" are ambiguous. Ever since Ye Jianying's "Nine Points" were announced in 1981 there have been significant public offers of areas of autonomy by the PRC, including retention of armed forces, domestic political autonomy, and economic and social autonomy.[28] However, these are offers contingent on reunification rather than recognition of the ROC. Moreover, armed force is threatened if Taiwan declares independence, as detailed in the Anti-Secession Law of 2005.[29] Under these circumstances, even in an inclusive triangle Taiwan retains an interest in its relationship to the U.S.

The situation of the two more powerful members of the triangle is complicated by China's economic growth relative to the United States. However, even when China reaches parity in terms of aggregate economic productivity its situation and interests will remain quite different from the U.S. China will be at one-fourth the American per capita GNP, and its technological level will be considerably lower. Moreover, its population will be aging rapidly, reducing its current labor advantage and raising welfare demands

---

[28] Xinhua, Ye Jianying Explains Policy Concerning Return of Taiwan to the Motherland and Peaceful Reunification, September 30, 1981. Available in Shirley Kan, *China/Taiwan: Evolution of the "One China" Policy — Key Statements from Washington, Beijing, and Taipei* (Washington: Congressional Research Service, 2011; RL30341), pp. 37–38.

[29] Anti-Secession Law, http://www.china.org.cn/english/2005lh/122724.htm. Accessed August 5, 2015.

on its budget.[30] Thus China's sensitivities to American global power are likely to continue even as it gains strength as a regional and as an economic power. It will have to be confident that the United States–Taiwan role is not part of a hard containment strategy aimed at challenging China or a soft containment strategy aimed at limiting China's influence. *Vis-à-vis* Taiwan, China needs to be confident that the concessions it makes to Taiwan's autonomy and welfare are not used to challenge its regional order.

Since 2008 the American position in the W–B–T triangle has become more complicated than that of an unwilling pivot. It is no longer decisive in the triangular relationship. The triangle is now soft rather than hard. However, it has strong interests in maintaining mutually beneficial relationships both with Taiwan and China, and these interests are furthered by a stronger cross-Strait relationship. Although the economic relationship with China is necessarily more important than with Taiwan, politically the status of Taiwan is important to America's global status. Just as China would avoid concessions that might lead to challenges of its regional order, the United States would avoid concessions that might lead to challenges of its global order. The only way to reconcile China's regional sensitivities and American global sensitivities would be in an inclusive triangle.

In sum, the W–B–T triangle rethought as an inclusive triangle involves a complex mixture of mutual deference and recognition. As the smallest, Taiwan would be deferential to China's "one China" policy in exchange for recognition of its autonomy, and remain deferential to the United States in exchange for recognition of Taiwan's special situation in East Asia. China would be deferential to the world order centered on the U.S. but only in exchange for American acknowledgment of its regional role. The U.S. can do that only if it is confident that China does not see itself as a global challenger. The requirements of Taiwan's autonomy and of the United States global role remain linked, but as part of a common relationship to China rather than as an exclusive security relationship.

---

[30] Brantly Womack, China's Future in a Multi-Nodal World Order, *Pacific Affairs* 87:2 (June 2014), pp. 265–284.

Inclusive progress

The discussion of an inclusive W–B–T triangle would indeed be bold if so much construction had not already occurred. The building is visible, but the intellectual foundations have been lagging. The shadow of the security triangle encourages exaggerated caution on all sides but it has not prevented progress. Most of the progress has been in each of the bilateral relationships, but there have also been important improvements in triangular inclusiveness.

At different times each of the three governments has played a key role in developing the reality of the triangle beyond its exclusivist form. In the 1970s American presidents and their advisors, from Kissinger and Nixon to Carter and Brzezinski, completed a diplomatic reorientation toward China and Taiwan that made possible an eventual inclusive triangle. While they were unsuccessful in achieving a direct American mediation of a peaceful cross-Strait reconciliation, normalization was a prerequisite for the next phase of interaction.

China's change of policy from liberation of Taiwan to peaceful reunification in 1979 was a fundamental contribution to better triangular relations. Although its offers for cross-Strait connections were initially rejected by Taiwan, and China was concerned about the continuing military relationship with the United States, China's persistence in permitting economic activity eventually undermined Taiwan's resistance and changed the economic underpinnings of Taiwan's cross-Strait policy.[31] China's patience and openness during the 1980s eventually bore fruit, though not the expected result of CCP–KMT accommodation.

Taiwan was clearly the dynamic force in the triangle from the mid-1990s to 2008, with mixed results. On one hand, and most obviously, Lee Teng-hui and Chen Shui-bian put the progress of

---

[31] Tse-Kang Leng, *The Taiwan-China Connection: Democracy and Development Across the Taiwan Straits* (Boulder, Co: Westview Press, 1996).

the inclusive triangle at risk. Lee tried unsuccessfully to divert the enthusiasm of Taiwanese businessmen from China to South East Asia, and his "pragmatic diplomacy," culminating in his visit to Cornell in 1995, provided the occasion for the last major crisis of the security triangle. His successor Chen Shui-bian, whose party, the DPP, advocated Taiwan independence in its 1991 Party Platform, was careful to avoid advocating independence in formal speeches but pushed the limits of Chinese and American patience. There is, however, an important contribution to the long-term potential of the inclusive triangle that is not obvious but nevertheless important. The DPP expressed the long pent-up alienation of Taiwan's native population against KMT rule, and the domestic side of its political effect was to bring the entire Taiwanese population into national politics. Since the "people from other provinces," the KMT supporters who came in 1947–1949, had suppressed domestic politics in service of returning to the Mainland, it was natural that an assertion of Taiwanese identity would emerge. With the rise and fall of Chen's presidency, Taiwan has become a political community capable of responding as a whole to strategic opportunities, and it has become more realistic about its cross-Strait options.

Credit for leadership in the new post-2008 era should be shared between Ma Ying-jeou and Hu Jintao. Every dimension of cross-Strait relations has improved, showcased by the signing of the Economic Cooperation Framework Agreement (ECFR) in June 2010. Just as important as the various measures to facilitate cross-Strait interaction has been the political restraint of both sides.[32] Ma Ying-jeou has moved cautiously, while Hu Jintao showed restraint and consideration. Hu's December 31, 2008 speech on the 30th anniversary of China's shift to a policy of peaceful reunification provided another landmark in flexibility in developing cross-Strait

---

[32] Alan Romberg, Shaping the Future, Part II: Cross-Strait Relations, *China Leadership Monitor* 39 (Fall 2012).

relations,[33] and after Ma's reelection China's positive assessment of the situation was reaffirmed by an authoritative article by Wang Yi, Director of the Beijing's Taiwan Affairs Office.[34] Developments since the 18th Party Congress in October 2012 have continued in a positive direction. Recent public opinion polls show two-thirds of voters support recent improvements.[35] The DPP is now reconsidering its 1991 call for independence.[36]

The United States has supported the improvement of cross-Strait relations, but it is caught in a security triangle dilemma. On one hand it is relieved that the threat of crisis that had been building during Chen Shui-bian's administration has diminished. American policy since 1972 has always supported the peaceful resolution of cross-Strait differences, so it cannot be unhappy with the current trend. Policies such as adding Taiwan to the visa waiver program in 2011 can be interpreted as implicit approval of Ma's cross-Strait progress.[37] On the other hand, the United States does not want Taiwan to feel abandoned, so it continues weapons sales.[38] It is rightly concerned that stopping military sales might undermine Ma politically, since his opponents could argue that he has traded a distant, reliable ally for partnership with a close and ambitious neighbor. Further to the right on the security side, Taiwan's current

---

[33]Hu Jintao, "携手推动两岸关系和平发展 同心实现中华民族伟大复兴 (Join hands to promote peaceful development of cross-Strait relations; strive with unity of purpose to advance the great renaissance of the Chinese people, Xinhua December 31, 2008. http://news. xinhuanet.com/newscenter/2008-12/31/content_10586495_2.htm. Accessed August 5, 2015.

[34]Wang Yi, "巩固深化两岸关系 开创和平发展新局面 (Consolidate and deepen cross-Strait relations, open a new situation of peaceful development), *Qiu Shi 2012*:8 (April 16, 2012). http://www.qstheory.cn/zxdk/2012/201208/201204/t20120412_150797.htm. Accessed August 5, 2015.

[35]MAC Poll Finds Support for Deeper Cross-Strait Ties, *Taiwan Today*, January 4, 2013.

[36]Alan Romberg, Following the 18th Party Congress: Moving Forward Step by Step, *China Leadership Monitor* 40 (Winter 2013), pp. 11–12.

[37]Richard Bush, *Uncharted Strait: The Future of China–Taiwan Relations* (Washington: Brookings, 2013), p. 216.

[38]*Ibid.*, p. 198.

cross-Strait compliance could be interpreted as a loss of faith in the American deterrence capacity, a credibility problem that could be addressed with military strategies like Air–Sea Battle.

The problem underlying the American diplomatic dilemma is that Taiwan is still seen as a problem rather than as an opportunity. As Chas Freeman has put it,

> "The danger that fighting will resume in the unresolved civil war that divided China is clearly diminishing apace with cross-Strait interdependence and rapprochement. Neither Beijing nor Washington has taken adequate account of this or of the extent to which it is reducing Taipei's deference to the United States and to American influence on Taiwanese attitudes and policies."[39]

As the "Taiwan problem" diminishes, Taiwan might simply disappear from the American radar. It is understandable that Taiwan feels that it might be abandoned if military sales stopped because there is little else left in the official and the media view of the relationship. For example, much of the *New York Times* discussion of working conditions at Foxconn factories building iPhones in China failed to identify Foxconn as a Taiwanese company.[40] The newspaper's "Learning Channel" featured a segment called "Connecting the Dots: Mapping Apple's Development and Manufacturing Process" which left the central role of Taiwan's contract manufacturing off the map.[41] Ever since the "China Lobby" of the 1950s Taiwan has nourished strong ties to the conservative side of the United States Congress, and now must rebrand itself as a stepping stone to China rather than as part of the wall of containment.

---

[39] Chas Freeman, *Interesting Times: China, America, and the Shifting Balance of Prestige* (Washington: Just World Books, 2013), p. 14.

[40] See for example *New York Times* June 2, 2010; June 7, 2010; May 21, 2011; February 17, 2012; February 20, 2012.

[41] Sarah Kavanagh, Holly Epstein Ojalvo and Katherine Schulten, "Learning Channel" featured a segment called Connecting the Dots: Mapping Apple's Development and Manufacturing Process, The Learning Network, *New York Times* January 31, 2012.

Beyond the triangle

Given the history of Sino–American confrontations in Korea and Vietnam, it is hardly surprising that the W–B–T security triangle is part of a larger heritage of zero-sum rivalry. When China began to expand its soft power in South East Asia, some observers viewed it as a plot to exclude the United States.[42] Despite an official attitude of engagement with China, many see the ability to counter Chinese influence as the measure of American leadership in Asia.

President Obama's "pivot toward Asia" has an ambiguity similar to that of the W–B–T triangle: does the dance include China, or is the American swing around China's periphery an attempt to isolate or even to contain China? Seen by China through the lens of a security triangle, the United States is colluding with China's neighbors. It appears that any improvement in United States–Asia relations is at the cost of China–Asia relations, and vice versa.

While China's neighbors currently benefit from the added attention and competitive wooing generated by Sino–American rivalry, having to choose between China and the United States would be their nightmare strategic situation. Not only would they face the cost of enmity with the side not chosen, but they would be the front line of vulnerability in a confrontation beyond their control. To assume that Vietnam, for instance, would leap at the opportunity to ally with the United States against China expresses the complacency of American parochialism rather than an appreciation of Vietnam's actual situation and of its experiences with both countries. Japan would be less vulnerable than smaller and less developed states, but even Japan would face an unwelcome triple choice between its biggest market, its strongest ally, or a new path of security autonomy. While China's neighbors are increasingly nervous about China's growth and the ambiguities of its long-term intentions, they, like Taiwan, have been major beneficiaries of China's peaceful rise.

---

[42] Joshua Kurlantzick, *Charm Offensive* (New Haven: Yale University Press, 2007); Jane Perlez, Chinese Move to Eclipse U.S. Appeal in South Asia [sic], *New York Times*, November 18, 2004.

In the long term, there is no good alternative to regional and global cautious cooperation between the United States and China. The goal of invulnerability will become too high for the American military budget, while China's target of area deniability still leaves China vulnerable. Moreover, China will soon face a sharply declining labor cohort. Rising wages and welfare costs will preoccupy its budget. Not only will China become old before it becomes rich, it will grow old before it becomes powerful, at least by American standards of global hegemony. The United States will remain the most advanced technological society, but China and the United States together will be an impressive but declining share of world population and productivity. Both the United States and China will face domestic political constraints that will make cooperation more difficult, in the United States, the polarization of the political spectrum, and in China the rise of a public voice that is stridently nationalistic. But if either tries to reinvent the Cold War, they will find that a globalized world lacks the required camps and camp discipline. Rather than taking sides, other states are more likely to try to reduce their exposure to great power rivalry.[43]

Rethinking the W–B–T triangle is arguably the most important single strategic step that the United States and China can take in order to realign for sustainable leadership in a globalized world. On one hand, it is important because it is a high-visibility, difficult problem that will not be dissolved by diplomatic moves elsewhere. The security triangle is the stone in the shoe of United States–China cooperation, and the prism through which larger scenarios of conflict gain their color. On the other hand, because it is a delimited problem it is easier to reconceptualize than more ambiguous or complex challenges. Credible progress in relations between Washington, Beijing and Taipei would not solve the problems of Northeast Asia or of global finance, but it would offer hope that even the most intractable difficulties can be overcome.

---

[43] Brantly Womack, China and the Future Status Quo, *Chinese Journal of International Politics* 8:2 (Summer 2015), pp. 115–137.

American interests inside a rethought triangle

Even in an inclusive triangular relationship each partner has its own interests. The major interests of the United States are first, that the triangle remains stable, second, that it generates marginal incentives for American participation, and third that it strengthens the American global position.

A transformation, not a phase

There has never been a PRC attack on Taiwan itself[44] and the ritual bombardment of the offshore island Quemoy (Jinmen) halted with the announcement of peaceful reunification in 1979.[45] In 1991 Ye Jianying's "Nine Points" included promises to allow Taiwan to maintain its own army and not to station PLA forces there.[46] As Jiang Zemin reiterated in 1995, Taiwan "may also maintain its armed forces and administer its party, governmental, and military systems by itself. The Central Government will not station troops or administrative personnel there."[47] The policy of peaceful reunification has now lasted longer than the previous policy of liberation.

Nevertheless, a transition from a security triangle to an opportunity triangle must be premised on the permanence of non-coercion. Is cross-Strait peace due to PRC and ROC policy or to deterrence by the security triangle? If policy, how stable is the policy commitment? The inclusive triangle must be more than just a phase if it is to be in the interest of all parties.

---

[44] The offshore islands Quemoy (Jinmen) and Matsu (Mazu) are considered by both the PRC and ROC to be part of Fujian Province.

[45] The last known shelling occurred in 1994 with an unauthorized bombardment by ROC artillery of a Mainland village. Four people were injured. After initial denials, the ROC apologized for the incident. Taiwan Apologizes After Troops Fire Artillery Shells Into China, *New York Times*, November 16, 1994.

[46] Ye Jianying on Taiwan's Return to Motherland and Peaceful Reunification, http://www.china.org.cn/english/7945.htm. Accessed August 5, 2015.

[47] As quoted in Richard Bush, *Uncharted Strait*, p. 224.

Since 2008 it can be argued that the primary grounds for a peaceful relationship has been cross-Strait policy. Economic and societal relations have blossomed, highlighted by **the Economic Cooperation Framework Agreement** (ECFA). The election of Ma Ying-jeou and especially his re-election strengthened Beijing's confidence in Taiwan's electorate. For its part, besides economic incentives the PRC has shifted its emphasis from "peaceful reunification" to "peaceful development" beginning with the KMT leader Lien Chan's visit to Beijing in 2005. According to Hu Jintao's report to the 18th Party Congress, reunification "in the common home of the Chinese nation" remains the goal, but "To achieve peaceful reunification, we must, above everything else, ensure peaceful growth of relations between the two sides of the Taiwan Straits."[48] Ren Xiao's chapter in this book provides a careful detailing of the evolution of the PRC's cross-Strait policy over the past decade.

Of course, the problem with policies is that they can change. Richard Bush describes three scenarios for the medium-term future of Ma's second term (2012–2016).[49] First, continuing the momentum of Ma's first term. He considers this less likely because established interests on both sides are likely to resist the sticky details of breakthroughs like the ECFA. Second, more likely, progress will stall, which would frustrate Beijing but not likely to lead to backtracking. Third, consolidation of gains. Rather than viewing these as discrete alternatives, they could be rearranged into a spectrum ranging from further progress to stalling, with consolidation in the middle. It is significant that neither unification (whatever that means) or Taiwan independence figure as likely alternatives.

Nevertheless, the trends since 2008 do not fully answer the question of the stability of peace. Official peace agreements cannot

---

[48]"Full text of Hu Jintao's report at 18th Party Congress Part X. Enriching the Practice of "One Country, Two Systems" and Advancing China's Reunification" Xinhua, November 17, 2012. http://news.xinhuanet.com/english/special/18cpcnc/2012-11/17/c_131981259_11.htm. Accessed August 5, 2015.

[49]Richard Bush, *Uncharted Strait*, pp. 118–136.

occur because the PRC does not recognize the ROC as a sovereign partner and views the United States as having no standing in a domestic concern. Instead of peace agreements there are declarations of contingencies for the use of force. The American–Taiwan Relations Act gives an ambiguous security commitment in the event of coercion against Taiwan. The PRC's Anti-Secession Law of 2005 commits the government to use non-peaceful means "In the event that the 'Taiwan independence' secessionist forces should act under any name or by any means to cause the fact of Taiwan's secession from China, or that major incidents entailing Taiwan's secession from China should occur, or that possibilities for a peaceful reunification should be completely exhausted."[50] It is worth noting that the Law requires minimizing damage in the use of force and guarantees the welfare of Taiwanese on the Mainland.[51] Taiwan has long given up retaking the Mainland, so its military option is purely defensive.

The PRC is the only party whose contingency on use of force would permit a first use. Fortunately, the use is restricted to matters related to secession, though the final condition suggests failure to meet a timetable of progress rather than movement toward secession. However, the Law was written at a low point in cross-Strait relations, and Hu Jintao's emphasis on peaceful development has been described as setting PRC policy "for the next five to ten years,"[52] in other words, for the term of his successor, Xi Jinping. Thus, assuming no secessionist act, peace in the Taiwan Strait is secured for the medium term. Moreover, Hu Jintao held out the prospect of reducing the apparent threat of armaments: "We hope the two sides will discuss the establishment of a cross-Straits confidence-building mechanism for military security to maintain

---

[50] "Anti-Secession Law," Article 8, March 14 2005. http://www.chinadaily.com.cn/english/doc/2005-03/14/content_424643.htm. Accessed August 5, 2015.

[51] *Ibid.*, Article 9.

[52] Ye Kedong, quoted in Alan Romberg, "Following the 18th Party Congress," p. 2.

stability in their relations and reach a peace agreement through consultation so as to open a new horizon in advancing the peaceful growth of these relations."[53]

Could Taiwan independence again become a powerful current in Taiwanese domestic politics? Ma Ying-jeou in his inaugural address of May 2012 promised "no unification, no independence and no use of force," a guarantee that would seem an adequate reciprocation of Hu's peaceful path.[54] There will be elections in Taiwan in 2016, however, and the DPP is likely to win. But even Chen Shui-bian was careful to avoid Beijing's redlines, and DPP leaders are currently discussing moderating their earlier cross-Strait positions. While China would be suspicious of the DPP in power and the DPP would be unlikely to do more than stall cross-Strait improvements, there is little likelihood of an interest in creating a crisis, or popular support for a crisis. The *status quo* does not stand still, and it has moved toward cross-Strait normalcy.

The implications of post-2008 developments for American triangular security concerns are clear. There is no likelihood of a military crisis in the mid-term, and the emergence of a future crisis is unlikely. Moreover, the possibility of a future crisis would be slow to emerge and tendencies in that direction would be likely to be reversed as crisis approached. Thus, as Admiral Joseph Prueher put it in 2011, "The complex U.S.–Taiwan relationship is political and should be examined outside of a military context."[55] If the security of Taiwan would be furthered by American participation in confidence-building consultations then they would be in accordance with the spirit both of the Taiwan Relations Act and the three joint communiques.

---

[53] Hu Jintao, "Report at the 18th Party Congress."

[54] "Full text of President Ma Ying-jeou's inaugural address," Focus Taiwan May 20 2012. http://focustaiwan.tw/ShowNews/WebNews_Detail.aspx?ID=201205200002&Type=aIPL Accessed August 5, 2015.

[55] Joseph Prueher, *The Way Ahead with China*, University of Virginia, the Miller Center, January 2011. http://web1.millercenter.org/conferences/chinaroundtable-report.pdf. Accessed August 5, 2015.

A security guarantee that both the United States and the PRC should make to Taiwan is that the security of Taiwan will not be linked to other possible venues of the Sino–American security relationship. Beijing's promise to allow Taiwan to keep its own army and not to station People's Liberation Army (PLA) troops there is already a major step in this direction. Taiwan is sui generis. The United States military should not consider its relationship with Taiwan as part of a larger presence in the Western Pacific.

Economic connectivity

The habit of thinking of Taiwan as a stone in the maritime wall containing China dies hard. With improving cross-Strait relations America's "Taiwan problem" shrinks, but the problem mentality should be replaced by an awareness of the "Taiwan opportunity." With growing confidence and development of the cross-Strait relationship Taiwan can be a stepping stone between China, the United States and Japan.

Taiwan's image in the United States is based on its contrast with China. "Free China *vs.* Red China" has been succeeded by "Democratic Taiwan *vs.* Authoritarian China." The problem with the latter pair is not that it is false but that it posits a dichotomy. In fact, Taiwan's autonomous political, legal and economic system — promised by the PRC to continue even with unification — gives it special advantages as a venue for relationships with China. Taiwan is experienced in dealing with Mainland opportunities and at the same time not enmeshed in its political and societal networks.

Especially the United States can benefit from Taiwan's distinctive connectivity. Sixty years of American patronage has given a thick American subculture to Taiwan's professional and academic circles. The United States is the largest foreign investor in Taiwan. Contract arrangements with American firms for manufacturing their products in China have been highlighted by Foxconn, with 1.2 million Chinese workers. The contract trilateral relationships have been interactive on many dimensions. American publicity has put pressure on firms like Apple to put pressure in turn on Taiwanese contractors to improve working conditions in China. With regards to cyber security and intellectual property, it would be easier for American firms to protect their production environment if Taiwan were a key link. The advantages of an offshore base out of the reach of PRC security would be enhanced by Taiwan's interest in establishing a reputation for electronic safety.

As the cross-Strait relationship matures, Taiwan's utility as an entrepot will increase. Taiwanese universities are rapidly expanding their relations with Mainland universities, and given their American structure and subculture they will be excellent institutional liaisons for the United States as well. Knowledge and innovation linkages can be added to Taiwan's existing information technology links. Taiwan provides an excellent interface for American universities because a major share of its professorate has American PhDs. International conferences in Taiwan are held in English.

Besides the United States–Taiwan–China connectivity, Taiwan is also the country most familiar and at ease with Japan outside of Japan itself. Thus it can offer a unique three-way fluency of communication, contacts, and venues for off-shore interrelationships. As Takashi Sekiyama's chapter details, already Japanese components are funneled into Taiwanese products before they head for final assembly in China.

While some areas of American business such at information technology are well aware of Taiwan's advantages in an opportunity triangle, Taiwan tends to be overlooked in the general American fascination with China and its potential, or remembered only as a problem. But the opportunity is not an either/or choice between China and Taiwan, but rather Taiwan's capacity to provide bi-directional and tri-directional connectivity.

A sustainable American global role

The security triangle poses a set of cruel choices for America's role in the Pacific. If a crisis occurs, it must choose between the humiliation of not backing a long-term protégé or a costly intervention that will put it in a long-term hostile relationship with the central country of East Asia. If it chooses intervention, it might win the sympathy of other states, but few would be willing to take its side. American credibility would depend on how well it did in the fight, and inevitably its capacity to fight elsewhere would be diminished. Moreover, its military budget would remain high, starving domestic programs. If the United States did not back Taiwan, then it would lose credibility as a patron. But a military crisis is highly unlikely. And yet the problems for America's global role are not over. If China and Taiwan successfully manage the cross-Strait relationship on their own and the United States remains in a dwindling security relationship with the "Taiwan problem," then it is sidelined from one of the most important diplomatic developments in East Asia. If the United States decides to cease military sales to Taiwan without reconfiguring the triangle, then it appears to be acknowledging China's superiority in its near waters. Thus America's non-crisis options within the security triangle are to abandon Taiwan or to be abandoned by it.

But the gloomy picture is a product of cloudly the lens of the security triangle. The United States has major contributions to make in an inclusive, opportunity-driven triangle, and these opportunities have strong resonances with a sustainable global role. The United States is the largest developed country and the center of a globalized world economy. But its capacity for leadership does not depend on domination, but rather on the common interest that all have in a predictable world order. Good global leadership is good global management, not domination. In an inclusive triangle, the American options are not siding with the PRC or siding with Taiwan, but rather cooperating with them both in a win–win–win context. There will be conflicts of interest, of course, and with Taiwan as well as with China. These differences must be negotiated rather than forced, and the unforced agreements will strength the relationships.

The W–B–T security triangle is only one prominent example of exclusive, security-based thinking that is inhibiting more reasonable and useful conceptualizations of the world situation in the 21st century. If the United States prepares for old wars it will miss new opportunities, and it will isolate and weaken itself.

Delicate diplomacy

In the abstract, a transition of the W–B–T relationship from an exclusive security triangle to an inclusive opportunity triangle may seem eminently reasonable, but the actual diplomacy of transition is more difficult. All sides are habituated to caution and to suspicion of bilateral collusion of their partners. In an asymmetric triangle, the gestures of the strongest are particularly subject to scrutiny. Moreover, in the W–B–T triangle there is the additional problem that the United States is viewed by Beijing as an interfering outsider and by Taipei as its sole security support.

Since 2008 the United States has supported Ma Ying-jeou in two apparently contradictory respects. First, it has demonstrated its approval of improving cross-Strait relations. Positive steps such as the inclusion of Taiwan in the Visa Waiver Program were linked to the sense of relief that the crises of the Chen Shui-bian days were over. Second, the United States continued arms sales, and at a higher dollar level than earlier. If the arms sales ceased, then Ma's opposition could claim that Ma had traded friendship with the United States for friendship with China. Beijing's objections to the continuing arms sales have been rather muted because Beijing also prefers Ma and the KMT to the alternatives. American formal diplomacy is thus hamstrung by the embedded security expectations of the triangle.

Track two and responsiveness

Given the difficulties of formal diplomacy and the sensitivities that all sides have concerning bilateral collusion, building an inclusive triangle requires more subtle and informal confidence-building. Non-governmental and track two efforts should be encouraged, especially those that involve participation from all three sides. Government research on relations with China and with Taiwan should refocus on the dynamic of inclusive opportunities (and their attendant problems) rather than simply on bilateral relations or on assumptions of the security triangle. Perhaps a trilateral Eminent Persons Group could be formed and asked to make recommendations, though not as a first step.

Just as importantly, the United States should be actively responsive to improvements and pending improvements in the cross-Strait relationship. The United States should be careful to respond in a way and to a degree that both sides find helpful. Neither side wants the United States to act as mediator. Mediation would be unacceptable to China because the cross-Strait relationship is domestic, and Taiwan would worry that, as a result of asymmetry, the outcome would be that the United States would side with China.

But given the present and future importance of the United States to each side there should be a mutual and continuing interest in the American attitude and an appreciation of useful support. Areas of responsiveness obviously should include cross-Strait peace accords and the question of continuing American arms sales, but efforts should be made to emphasize responsiveness in economic and societal areas as well. Ultimately it is up to the United States whether or not it is sidelined by cross-Strait rapprochement.

Highlight the inclusive in relations with Taiwan

With regards to Taiwan, the public and official mentality in the United States is still set by the "Taiwan problem." Even American approval and encouragement of Ma Ying-jeou's cross-Strait initiatives are mostly derived from their effect of lessening the likelihood of crisis rather than from the opportunities that they present. If an appreciation of an opportunity-driven triangle is not developed, then the American consciousness of Taiwan will simply dwindle as cross-Strait relations evolve. Fortunately there is enough inclusive activity in place in the United States–Taiwan relationship so that in fact the inclusive side should thrive, but the official and media framing of the relationship is important. If the future of Taiwan is with China, then at some point the current United States–Taiwan security relationship must be scaled back and re-defined. In 2011 discussion of curtailing weapons sales was solely in terms of United States–China security relations and it was described as "abandoning Taiwan."[56] In fact, however, as Joseph Prueher observed, the issue of arms sales is primarily political rather than military. The United States needs to adjust its understanding of the cross-Strait political context or else it will face the political embarrassment of appearing to abandon Taiwan, or perhaps the greater embarrassment of being abandoned by Taiwan.

While highlighting inclusive relations moves away from the inertial American focus on security, there are American economic interests for which the new triangle is important. The Asian production cycle, a multinational investment and manufacturing pattern with the American market as its major consumer target, was in part a product of United States pressure on Japan, South Korea and Taiwan in the late 1980s to balance their trade with the United States. In order to reduce their American import profile and at the same time to take advantage of cheap assembly labor in China, all three began to transfer high-value components, especially electronics, to China for final assembly by foreign-owned factories. In the case of sophisticated merchandise, the label "Made in China"

---

[56] Nancy Tucker and Bonnie Glaser, Should the United States Abandon Taiwan? *Washington Quarterly* 34:4 (Fall 2011), pp. 23–37.

should be interpreted "Last seen in China." China has become the world's largest trading nation in part because the components coming from Japan, South Korea and Taiwan are counted twice, first as imports and later as part of the value of finished exports. Thus the World Trade Organization (WTO) estimates that China's exports are only 67% Chinese value added, while the exports of Japan are 84% domestic value-added, the largest of any non-raw material exporter.[57] In electronics, 74% of China's export value is derived from intermediate imports.[58] The WTO does not estimate Taiwan's value-added, but it is likely to be closer to Japan's than to China's.

To the extent that trade balances matter for the United States, a greater awareness of multi-source linkages is important for analysis and for regulation. In trade relations with the United States, Taiwan is already a part of China because it is supplying the parts to China. United States trade policy has to become more sophisticated in order to deal with the hybrid realities of globalized products.

Respect Taiwan's voice

Possibly the most difficult dimension of an inclusive W–B–T triangle for all parties is the external status of the government of Taiwan. While its control over domestic affairs has been acknowledged since 1981 in Ye Jianying's Nine Points, the relationship of a non-independent Taiwan to the rest of the world is ambiguous. To use Hu Jintao's terminology, what are "reasonable arrangements under the special condition that the country is yet to be reunified?"[59] Even more interesting but more distant, what would be Taiwan's realm of external autonomy after unification? Surely the threshold of unification should expand Taiwan's global options rather than shutting its outside doors, otherwise why would Taiwan cross the threshold

---

[57] Paul Schreyer, *The OECD-WTO Trade in Value-Added Database* (Geneva: WTO, January 16, 2013), p. 11.

[58] *Ibid.*, p. 15.

[59] Hu Jintao, Report to the 18th Party Congress.

willingly? Taiwan understandably wants to be confident of its external future as well as of its internal future. "One country two systems" is only the beginning of a PRC answer to these questions because it addresses Taiwan's autonomy within a larger sovereignty but not its external relationships. And among these the United States will remain the most important.

There is no ready-made formula for Taiwan's external relations. Clearly it cannot enter into relationships that presume sovereignty except as the ROC, but what should be the rights and privileges of domestic autonomy? Taiwan entered the WTO as an "autonomous customs area," and it is a member of other international bodies under various names indicating a sub-sovereign entity. The United States rightly supports Taiwan's inclusion, but not as an indication of sovereignty.

Because of the ambiguities surrounding Taiwan's international status, it is important for the United States to respect Taiwan's voice in international affairs. A major part of transition away from a "Taiwan problem" mentality is to listen to what Taiwan has to say in matters of mutual and regional concern. Two important current examples are the Diaoyudao/Senkaku dispute in the East China Sea and the Spratly dispute in the South China Sea. Taiwan should have a special voice in both of these.

It should be recalled that the Chinese claim to the Diaoyudao/Senkaku islands is based on the claim that Japan seized them along with Taiwan in 1895. Thus they should have been returned to the ROC with Taiwan in 1945, and the United States was mistaken when they returned control to Japan in 1971. Taiwan is the closest inhabited land to the islands and the major user of the surrounding waters for fishing. Ma Ying-jeou asserts the Chinese claim, but he has also offered a peace initiative involving bilateral talks between the three parties followed by trilateral talks.[60] The group of former senior United States government officials sent to Tokyo and Beijing

---

[60]Meg Chang, Ma proposes East China Sea peace initiative, *Taiwan Today*, August 5, 2012.

in October 2012 to discuss the dispute should have included Taipei in their itinerary. Patriotic fervor is as high in Taiwan as it is in Japan and China, but Taiwan is better positioned to aid in a face-saving solution, and that is the intent of Ma's initiative.

Similarly in the South China Sea, Taiwan's continuous occupation of Taiping Island, the largest island in the Spratlys, is possibly the strongest leg of the Chinese claim.[61] Taiwan is therefore in a position to contribute to a solution, and it should be included in discussions. In both of these cases the United States — and the PRC — should respect Taiwan as an autonomous stakeholder and one interested in negotiating a solution acceptable to all sides. Moreover, precisely because Taiwan is different from the PRC its activities and claims do not seem as ominous to neighbors. It is thus in a useful, quasi-third party situation, and respecting its views could help manage these problems and contribute to adding substance to Taiwan's non-sovereign status.

Beyond the maritime territorial disputes, the United States should make special efforts to include Taiwan in all discussions in which voice rather than sovereignty is the entry ticket. Because no other major governments have Taiwan's peculiar diplomatic status it is easy to overlook their inclusion. Although the PRC's visceral reaction might be negative, due to the lingering influence of its side of the security triangle, it also must adjust to a new policy regarding Taiwan's international presence.

Rethinking the basic logic of a relationship is not easy. The sequence of progress of the United States-China rapprochement in the 1970s, China's peaceful reunification policies in the 1980s, and the re-invention of Taiwanese politics over the past 20 years constitute one of the most positive diplomatic trends of the past half-century. But rethinking a triangle is even more complex. Fortunately an inclusive, opportunity-driven W–B–T triangle does not have to

---

[61] Brantly Womack, The Spratlys: From Dangerous Ground to Apple of Discord, *Contemporary South East Asia* 33:3 (2011), pp. 370–387.

be imagined out of thin air. The thick reality of inclusion is already present. The shadow of the security triangle can be seen in the fears, suspicions, and inhibitions of the participants, but its empirical grounding has faded to a trace. It is time to put the reality of present and future interaction into an appropriate framework.

Chapter 2

The Beijing–Taipei–Washington Triangle: A PRC Perspective

Ren Xiao

Fudan University

Since the military failure of the *Kuomintang* (KMT) on the Chinese mainland in 1949 and its retreat to the island of Taiwan, the interactions among the People's Republic of China (PRC), Taiwan, and the United States have been going on for over 60 years. The three actors interacting with one another formed a triangle and have evolved intricate relations throughout the years. This continued into the PRC's Hu Jintao period of 2002–2012, the decade this paper aims to look at from the PRC perspective. After a brief overview of the last years of the Jiang Zemin period, I will analyze the difficult situation facing Hu caused by Chen Shui-bian's coming into power in Taipei, and Hu's adoption of a peaceful development doctrine that he employed as the guiding principle for the cross-Taiwan strait relations. This had a long-term impact and helped stabilize the triangular relationship. Since March 2008 with the election of Ma Ying-jeou, stability and peace have prevailed in the Taiwan Strait region. This paper explores these processes to see how transitions occurred and how they influenced the triangular relationship. After an elaboration of the post-2008 developments across the strait, this paper will come to its conclusions.

The nature of a triangular relationship

Triangular relationships are not uncommon in world politics. For example the strategic Washington–Moscow–Beijing triangle mattered greatly during the Cold War. In a triangular relationship, the three actors are involved in often complex and delicate behaviors of responding or reacting to one another. Within it, there are three bilateral relationships and the third actor is often sensitive to or suspicious of the developments in the relationship between the other two. Moreover, the third actor can more or less affect the perceptions or considerations of the other two. Complex interactions often characterize a triangular relationship.

There are conditions or constituent elements for a triangular relationship. Obviously, not any three states can form such a relationship, For example, if we consider Thailand, Malaysia and Egypt, there are three bilateral relationships between three states, yet they are not sufficiently interactive to be a meaningful triangle. In general, a triangular relationship worthy of analysis has two preconditions. One, the three actors that constitute a triangular relationship are mostly active forces, either at global or regional level. Two, each of the three bilateral relationships has explicit or implicit impact on the third party. There exist continual interactions of checking or balancing behaviors. Only when the two conditions are met can a triangular relationship be identified. Typical of this include the Britain–Germany–Russia triangle in late 19th and early 20th centuries and the great United States–USSR–China triangle during the 1970s and 1980s, as well as the more recent United States–China–Japan triangular relationship.

Further, assuming there are three states A, B and C in a triangular relationship, country A's policy behavior naturally has much to do with either its own calculation or country B's behavior. Besides, a policy decision may also result from country C's behavior and/or due to A's relationship with C or B's behavior toward C. Likewise, similar phenomena can be observed with respect to country B's or C's act. For Brantly Womack, "In many cases bilateral relationships are influenced by third-party interactions but not determined by them," and he calls these "soft" triangles. In a "hard" triangle, a major determinant of each of the three bilateral relationships is the simultaneous effect of the relationship to the third party.[1]

We can distinguish two ideal types of triangular relationships in global or regional clusters. One is strict or standard, under which the overall distribution of power among the three actors is more or less even and they form a quasi equidistant triangle. The other is more broadly identified triangle in which, compared to the first kind, distribution of power is more uneven but the interactive mechanism is still strong. Each side is sensitive to or wary of developments in relations between the other two actors.[2] Even though this may be a patron-client relationship, the "client," though disadvantaged, can still play a proactive role. The Washington–Beijing–Taipei (W–B–T) triangle falls into this second category, namely, what Womack calls an "asymmetric triangle," in which there is disparity between the strong and the weak. Womack has developed a theory of asymmetric triangles, and he points out, "An asymmetric relation usually

---

[1] See Brantly Womack, Asymmetric Triangles and the Washington-Beijing-Taipei Relationship, in his *China Among Unequals: Asymmetric Foreign Relationships in Asia* (Singapore: World Scientific, 2010), 371–404.

[2] For a detailed theoretical analysis of triangular relationship in international politics, see Ren Xiao *et al*, *Zhongmeiri sanbian guanxi* (China–U.S.–Japan Triangular Relationship), Hangzhou: Zhejiang People's Publishing House, 2002, Chapter 1. See also Lowell Dittmer, The Strategic Triangle: An Elementary Game-Theoretical Analysis, *World Politics* 33:4 (July 1981).

does not result in total domination of the weak by the strong, as the weak is struggling for its very survival and is thus more attentive to the relation, while the strong has a wide range of interests, and can live with different ways of coexistence with the weak."[3] The balancing force of the third party adds uncertainty for both of the original parties. In the case of W–B–T, United States did this kind of balancing, while PRC's approach transitioned from a strategy of "liberating Taiwan" to coexisting with it. Womack concluded by distancing from realism's assumption that relative power decides all. "The highest card does not simply win the game, and therefore international politics does not reduce to great power competition and the advent of challengers."[4]

At least starting from the 1946–1947 George Marshall Mission and its mediation between the KMT and the Chinese Communists, shortly after Japan's unconditional surrender and the end of the Pacific War, the triangular relationship has evolved and undergone a number of changes over several decades. When the KMT had lost the civil war in 1949 and had to flee the mainland for Taiwan and other smaller islands, the United States was prepared for all of them to be taken by the new PRC. However, the tide was dramatically reversed by the outbreak of the Korean War in June 1950 and the United States military intervention, including its sending in the Seventh Fleet to the Taiwan Strait. This was later consolidated by the conclusion of a Mutual Defense Treaty reached between Taipei and Washington. Against the backdrop of the changing balance of power in world politics, United States and China achieved rapprochement in 1972 with President Richard Nixon's historic visit to Beijing. Another major change came in January 1979 when United States and PRC normalized their diplomatic relationship and the United States Congress enacted the Taiwan Relations Act to guide its post-1979 relations with Taipei. With these the triangular

---

[3] Brantly Womack, *op. cit.*, at 384.
[4] *Ibid.*, 404.

relationship entered a new stage. PRC made a strategic about face and started its far-reaching reform and opening-up drive. It has experienced a great transformation and has eventually become the world's second largest economy, though daunting tasks remain. With the collapse of the Soviet Union, the United States–China quasi alliance, if it ever existed, disappeared. The strategic glue that combined the two dissolved, and they transitioned to a relationship of being neither allies nor enemies. As PRC continues to grow and rise to great power status, United States is making strategic counter moves in the form of a "strategic rebalancing" to the Asia–Pacific, to ensure that its predominance is not affected and that it can maintain power and influence.

As a legacy of the Chinese civil war, Taiwan and the Mainland, geographically separated by the Taiwan Strait, have coexisted over the years. While Taiwan does not enjoy much diplomatic recognition, it keeps extensive relations with many countries in the world. For Beijing, the "one China framework" is firm internationally, in the sense that Taiwan is not widely recognized as an independent sovereign state. Without a peace agreement that formally ends the civil war and given that the sword of Damocles is hung over the island, "Taiwan independence" is widely believed a dead end. However, neither can it be denied that it is a political entity and an important actor in the web of relations of East Asia. It keeps wide-ranging economic and social relationships with many states in the world. Though the smallest actor and sandwiched between PRC and United States, the world's two major powers, Taipei sometimes played an active role, though not necessarily always a welcome one, and it could force Beijing and Washington to react or respond, sometimes strongly. It also acted passively on other occasions.[5] Those interactions together constitute a complex triangular situation.

---

[5]For an excellent detailed study, see Alan D. Romberg, *Rein In at the Brink of the Precipice: American Policy Toward Taiwan and U.S.–PRC Relations* (Washington, D.C.: The Henry Stimson Center, 2003).

Peaceful unification *vs.* peaceful independence

During the latter part of Jiang Zemin's 13-year tenure, driven by a desire for achievement and a sense of urgency, Jiang tended to have kind of a timetable for a peaceful reunification with Taiwan. For Jiang, the solution of the Taiwan issue could not be delayed indefinitely. This is stated in the report he delivered at the 16th Party Congress held in November 2002, shortly before his formal retirement. But that wish to work out a timetable proved to be an extremely difficult job, especially against the backdrop of the worrying political developments in Taiwan. In 2000, largely due to the cleavage in the ruling KMT, Mr. Chen Shui-bian, the candidate of the opposition Democratic Progressive Party (DPP), was elected and became the new leader of Taiwan. As was well known in Taiwan and the PRC, the DPP had a political program for "Taiwan independence." It had adopted the Party Charter on Taiwan Independence in October 1991. Eight years later, the DPP's Resolution on Taiwan Future viewed "Taiwan (not the Republic of China) as a sovereign state."[6]

Chen's election was a sea change in Taiwanese politics that posed a serious challenge to the PRC leaders on the Mainland. Not long after, George W. Bush entered the White House as the new United States President. During his campaign, Bush referred to China as a "strategic competitor," which cast a shadow and was a harbinger signaling a rocky road ahead for the United States–China ties. The mid-air collision between a Chinese fighter jet and an American reconnaissance plane off China's Hainan Island in 2001 highlighted the potentially adversarial relationship between the two powers. Against this backdrop, the Bush Administration approved a package of arms sales to Taiwan, an issue that continued into the later years. Bush even stated in April 2001 that United States would

---

[6]Ma Ying-jeou, Taiwan's Approach to Cross-Strait Relations, in The Aspen Institute, *U.S.–China Relations: Fifth Conference*, Vol. 18, No. 1, (Washington, DC, 2003), pp. 29–37. Ma was Mayor of Taipei at the time.

do "whatever it takes" to help Taiwan defend itself, an alarming deterrence posture for Beijing.

Hu Jintao succeeded Jiang and became the new General Secretary of the CCP at the 16th National Party Congress in November 2002. Prior to that, there had been some adjustments in Beijing's policy toward Taiwan, and the change from the old to the new "three sentences" had occurred. The long-held old three sentences states "There is only one China in the world; Taiwan is an inseparable part of Chinese territory; and, the Government of the People's Republic of China is the sole legitimate government representing the whole China." In July 2001, Beijing, *via* Vice Premier Qian Qichen, came up with a new statement claiming "There is only one China in the world; both the Mainland and Taiwan are a part of one China; and, China's sovereignty and territory are inseparable." The latter comprise the "three new sentences." The expression that both the Mainland and Taiwan are a part of China sounded more equal and acceptable, and thus broadened the political foundation for the growth of cross-Strait relations. Obviously, Beijing moderated its tone and revealed more flexibility.

According to the overall estimate of the 16th Party Congress, the first two decades of the 21st century were a period of strategic opportunity that China should grasp. During this period, a lot more should and could be achieved and this was a historical moment China must not lose. In fact, "two decades" was artificially decided. Initially, it was "first decade" but this seemed too short for a document like Party Congress political report and was later changed to "two decades." The key here is not the number of years but rather China believed it had a strategic opportunity in front of it. Presumably, the biggest reason seemed the world remained to be in a peace and development era, and there was no likelihood for China to be involved in a major war in the foreseeable future. This ensured that China could continue its modernization drive and go on to build an all-round well-off society (*xiaokang shehui*). The second reason seemed to be the changing world since the 9/11 terrorist attacks had shocked the United States who soon started its counter-terrorism war and this would not end any time soon. As a result, America's pressure on China was somewhat alleviated. Moreover, to effectively combat international terrorism, Washington urgently needed cooperation from other major powers, including China. Meanwhile, it was argued in China's policy research circles that a period of strategic opportunity was not static and it could either be shaped or lost. This had to be understood as seizing an opportunity, otherwise there would be a risk. In fact, on the Taiwan issue, when the DPP had risen to power, there emerged more challenges than opportunities for Beijing. However, the threats from Taiwan did not appear to be very dangerous or imminent.

Around this time in 2002–2003, there emerged a major thesis that China should pursue a "peaceful rise." This was first formulated by Mr. Zheng Bijian and his team, who argued that China should inform the world it would neither pose a threat nor would collapse as some outside observers speculated. Rather, it should and would pursue a peaceful rise. In summer 2003, "China's new development path of peaceful rise" was officially launched as a fresh large research project, aiming to "answer a fundamental question for the humankind," namely, whether a major power can rise peacefully by participating in rather than detaching from economic globalization. This was driven by the reality that there was an emerging big question about the direction China was heading, a question that was hovering in the mind of many strategists and observers around the world.

Starting from late 2003, PRC leaders began to use the term "peaceful rise" and to sell the idea in their important speeches. On December 10, 2003, Premier Wen Jiabao delivered a speech at Harvard University while visiting the United States, in which he argued, "The overriding trend of the present-day world is towards peace and development. China's development is blessed with a rare period of strategic opportunities. We are determined to secure a peaceful international environment and a stable domestic environment in which to concentrate our own development, and with it, to help promote world peace and development." "China is a major power carrying out reform and opening up as well as peacefully rising."[7] The same month, Hu Jintao gave a speech on 26 December at an event commemorating the 110th anniversary of the birth of Mao Zedong. Hu made a call that China "should take a development path of peaceful rise."[8] Those were the earliest occasions that top Chinese leaders adopted and used the term "peaceful rise," signaling a new thinking of the new Chinese leadership. The message was clear: China wanted to take and could take a new path of peaceful rise, which was different from the old path taken by Germany and Japan in the first half and the Soviet Union in the second half of the 20th century. For Zheng, the architect of the peaceful rise theory, in today's China, reform, opening up, and peaceful development have been deeply rooted in people's life and the Chinese culture. This in turn has created an irreversible environment for China's strategic path for peaceful rise.[9] No doubt, to reassure the outside world was a key component of this thinking, but there was more than that. The peaceful rise thesis was a serious effort both to try to be theoretically persuasive and to sort out a number of important issues for itself. As many as sixteen concrete topics were put on the list for further studies, including how peaceful rise relates to issues like sustainable growth, energy consumption and environment, China's sovereignty and security, the Taiwan issue, international and regional systems, international order, and so forth.

The term "peaceful rise" and the ideas related to it soon aroused enormous discussions and debates within China, and there appeared

---

[7]Wen Jiabao, Turning Your Eyes to China, speech at Harvard University, December 10, 2003, available at http://www.news.harvard.edu/gazette/2003/12.11/10-wenspeech.html.

[8]胡锦涛在纪念毛泽东诞辰 110 周年大会上的讲话, available at http://www.gov.cn/test/2009-11/27/content_1474642_3.htm.

[9]Zheng Bijian, *Peaceful Rise — China's New Road to Development*, (Beijing: Central Party School Publishing House, 2005), p. 18.

a number of controversies. China's Foreign Service wanted to keep a low profile, and they advocated being careful regarding the use of "peaceful rise." China's military raised the Taiwan question and how this would be handled. For them, Beijing had to be always prepared for the worst case scenario. The result was a compromise. Around late 2004 and early 2005, "peaceful rise" became the more modest term "peaceful development," but in essence the two are the same thing. The change of term soothed those critical people and helped lower the temperature of arguing over "peaceful rise." As a result, "peaceful development" became widely accepted. Instead of "demise,"[10] as Bonnie Glaser and Evan Medeiros argued, "peaceful rise" transformed itself. It was firmly established and institutionalized. The debate bore fruit as it became internalized in the mind of Hu and the Chinese leadership, and from then on, to a great extent, peaceful development informed Beijing's Taiwan policy.

But across the strait Taiwan was not quiet. Since a new general election was approaching in 2004, the DPP government and Chen Shui-bian attempted to resort to a referendum and to combine it with the election. For both Beijing and Washington, this was a dangerous step of trying to alter the *status quo*. President Bush publicly expressed his opposition to Taipei's referendum plan and he also rebuked Chen for his intention of trying to unilaterally change the status quo. During Premier Wen's visit to Washington in December 2003, the United States side once again expressed this position very clearly. This became something Beijing and Washington had in common. In the meantime, the White House reiterated that Bush's commitment to helping Taiwan defend itself remained effective, a gesture to keep a balance across the Taiwan Strait.

Dramatic events occurred right before the election day in 2004. It seemed the KMT had a good chance of retaking the ruling party

---

[10]Bonnie S. Glaser and Evan S. Medeiros, The Changing Ecology of Foreign Policy-Making in China: The Ascension and Demise of the Theory of 'Peaceful Rise', *The China Quarterly* 190 (June 2007), pp. 291–310.

status. However, its fortune was reversed due to a mysterious shooting in the evening before people went to the polling stations. Reportedly, Chen Shui-bian, the DPP candidate and incumbent, was wounded. The KMT immediately requested to postpone the election to allow for investigating the shooting incident but was in vain. The election went ahead and it was announced that Chen won by a small margin of 23,000, less than two tenths of a percent of the total vote. The stake was high, and Beijing was hoping for KMT to gain power but did not have any effective leverage to exert influence. It had to accept the reality and to wait another four years for a possible major change, a time period full of unknowns and uncertainties. Beijing had good cards at hand but unfortunately they could not be played because of the continuation of the Chen administration.

Those were seemingly bleak and hopeless years. Whither Beijing's Taiwan strategy? Bureaucratic inertia appeared to be hindering a workable and effective policy toward Taiwan, and a new strategy seemed badly needed to offer direction or guidance for the road ahead. In 2000, the warning Premier Zhu Rongji gave right before the election clearly did not work, and worse, it backfired. The 1996 missile firing had been another bad example of miscalculation. Lessons had to be learned. Contrary to its wish, pro-independence Chen prevailed.

A hard won turning point

It was Hu who firmly believed that peaceful development would work and had to prevail across the Taiwan Strait. Contrary to his image of being seen as indecisive, Hu was determined on this and he orchestrated a change of course. On March 4, 2005, at the Chinese People's Political Consultation Conference, Hu released his four proposals for the cross-Strait relations in the new period, and they were later incorporated into the 17th Party Congress Report he delivered in October 2007. At the core are essentially the "four nevers," namely, "never waver with respect to upholding the one

China principle; never give up the efforts for peaceful unification; never change the guiding principle of putting hopes on the Taiwanese people; never compromise on opposing the separatist movement for 'Taiwan independence'."

As the last of the four nevers suggests, Hu had to address the unacceptable possibility of separatism. This was a reflection of the thinking "both hands have to be hardened" (*liangshou dou yao ying*). While the soft hand needs to become softer, the hard hand needs to be made harder. Given that the separatist forces in Taiwan were making moves one after another, on the Mainland calls had been repeatedly made to make use of the "legal weapon" (*falv wuqi*) to defend China's territorial integrity, even though this kind of initiative triggered voices of opposition from Taiwanese society. Nevertheless, Chen's reelection in March 2004 that resulted from the mysterious shooting incident meant that Beijing had to face a possibility of the DPP's long-term holding on power, and the Taiwan independence movement had to be contained. This prompted Beijing to move ahead with a major "hard" step. On March 14, 2005, the National People's Congress (NPC) unanimously passed the Anti-Secession Law, which won a long applause by the NPC delegates which demonstrated the deeply-held public sentiments on the Mainland. At this stage, the goal for Beijing was not reunification, which seemed still remote, but rather deterring Taiwan from moving away further in the direction of *de jure* independence.

In the meantime, "softer" measures were also taken. After all, Beijing had more in common with the opposition political parties in Taiwan with whom the Mainland at least could have dialogues. Through behind-the-scenes communication, those party leaders received formal invitations from Beijing. Opposition party leaders' consecutive landing on the Mainland turned 2005 into a year of dizzying visits by the KMT Chairman Lien Chan in April, the People First Party (PFP) Chairman Soong Chu-yu (James Soong) in May, and the New Party Chairman Yu Muming in July. The CCP General Secretary Hu met with them consecutively and the political parties released three joint statements in which the Mainland was able to announce a series of generous measures that were favorable to the Taiwanese economy (*hui Tai*), especially the farmers. The measures included opening up the Mainland market for the agricultural products from Taiwan by offering zero tariff treatment; being more open to the issue of Taiwan's "international space" for it to participate in more international activities in the future. In the Hu-Lien communiqué, the two major political party leaders agreed to first discuss the issue of Taiwan's participation in the activities of the World Health Organization (WHO). The visits turned the tide and made a huge difference in the mood of the cross-Strait relationship.

The consecutive visits to the Mainland by Lien and Soong, the major opposition party leaders, largely reversed the downward spiral trend of the cross-Strait relations and improved the atmosphere. They brought about unprecedented vitality to the long stalled cross-strait relations. The meetings between political party leaders and the joint statements they released showed a possibly benign cross-Strait prospect if the steps were taken. Previously, it was widely held on the Mainland that Beijing had landed itself in a passive position (*bei dong*) vis-à-vis Taiwan over the past decade. The relationship was allowed to be disrupted or driven by Lee Teng-hui's "two states" and Chen Shui-bian's "one country on each side" comments, provocative moves to divert the positive direction. For example, Wang Daohan, President of the Mainland's Association for Relations Across the Taiwan Strait (or ARATS, founded in December 1991), planned to visit Taiwan and hold another meeting with his Taiwanese counterpart Koo Chen-fu in 1999. The visit was unfortunately cancelled by Beijing because of Lee's provocative "two states" remarks. Lee's was certainly a deliberate act. By 2005 people believed that Wang's visit should have happened as planned so as to gain the initiative. Another opportunity was lost.

With the visits by Lien' and Soong' there was an important and tactical shift of emphasis on Beijing's part from the one China principle to the "1992 consensus," which was adopted in the joint statements. Previously, Beijing insisted that only when Taiwan first recognized the "one China" principle, could the cross-strait consultation or negotiation be resumed. The "1992 Consensus," meaning "one China, respective explanation," was more ambiguous or flexible and thus could be more widely accepted. Also, it was achieved when the KMT controlled political power and was reached in 1992 between Beijing's ARATS and Taipei's Strait Exchange Foundation (SEF). Beijing's adoption of the "1992 Consensus" by no means meant it gave up the one China principle. Rather, the adoption meant Beijing was demonstrating more flexibility which allowed more likelihood for the two sides to seek common ground. After all, both the KMT and PFP acknowledged "one China," however it was explained, which was clearly more desirable than either "two states" or "one China, one Taiwan." The "1992 consensus" derived from the practical needs to handle the growth of cross-Strait relations.

Given that exchanges between the mainland and Taiwanese societies were growing rapidly, concrete issues such as document examination and cooperation combatting crime urgently needed to be addressed. In March 1992, SEF sent its representatives to ARATS for the first ever consultation between the two organizations. Later the two further coordinated through communication and decided to hold a meeting in Hong Kong in October for an agreement on document examination, and they encountered the political one-China issue. The two sides failed to reach an agreement during the Hong Kong meeting but later they agreed to interpret the one-China principle flexibly. In this spirit, Taipei stated: "In the process of jointly making efforts to seek national unification, the two sides of the Taiwan Straits both insist on the one China principle, yet they have different interpretation of the meaning of one China." By contrast, Beijing stated: "The two sides on the straits both insist on the one China principle and try to seek national unification. But during the consultations between the two sides of the Straits on concrete matters, they do not need to settle the political meaning of 'one

China'."[11] This was later famously summarized as "one China, respective interpretations" (*yige zhongguo, gezi biaoshu*), and was referred to as the "1992 Consensus." This paved the way for the historic first Wang-Koo talks held in April 1993 in Singapore. "The '1992 Consensus' was the result of hard bargaining between the SEF and ARATS in 1992. Fragile as it is, it nevertheless has the important function of 'managing' instead of 'solving' the sensitive and intractable 'one China' question."[12]

The recognition of the "1992 Consensus" by leaders of the major political party leaders of both sides showed the potential for it to serve as an important foundation for future cross-Strait dialogues or negotiations, and in effect made preparations for the post-2008 cross-Strait relations when the KMT regained political power.

Having learned that visits by the opposition leaders might help dissipate the existing cross-Strait impasse and reduce tensions, the United States Administration expressed its approval right before Lien's visit, arguing this kind of visit would be useful for lowering the degree of cross-Strait tensions and serve as an opportunity for cross-strait dialogue. It also urged that dialogues be started at the official level. "With the United States State Department viewing Lien's trip as a 'positive development,' Chen had little choice but to declare his support for the visit."[13] This largely prompted Chen to shift attitude from negative criticism to being supportive, at least in appearance. The establishment of party-to-party bridges, which was unprecedented over the past 56 years, opened a possible avenue of peaceful development in the Taiwan Strait region.

---

[11] Su Chi and Cheng An-kuo, eds., One China, with Respective Interpretations — A Historical Account of the Consensus of 1992 (*"yige zhongguo, gezi biaoshu" gongshi de shishi*), (Taipei: National Policy Foundation (*Guojia zhengce yanjiu jijinhui*), 2002), pp. 4–5.

[12] Ma Ying-jeou, Taiwan's Approach to Cross-Strait Relations, in The Aspen Institute, *U.S.-China Relations: Fifth Conference*, Vol. 18, No. 1, (Washington, DC, 2003), pp. 29–37.

[13] See Erich Shih, After the Lien and Soong Visits: Chen's New Predicament, *China Brief* 5:13, (Washington, DC: Jamestown Foundation, 2005).

From danger to opportunity

Throughout Chen's eight years in power, the Taiwan authorities made one move after another and eventually resorted to dangerous adventurism. Those included statements ranging from denying the "1992 Consensus" and suggesting the formulation "one country on each side" to initiating a referendum, proposing to amend the constitution, changing the official name (*zheng ming*) of the government, and so forth. Beijing felt enormous challenges from Taipei. Those developments also made Washington increasingly worried.

In early 2006, Chen Shui-bian made further moves. In his New Year message, Chen stepped back with regards to Taipei's policy toward cross-Strait economic and trade relations by changing "active opening-up, effective management" (*jiji kaifang, youxiao guanli*) to "active management, effective opening-up" (*jiji guanli, youxiao kaifang*), a more negative attitude toward cross-Strait economic relationship. In the meantime, Chen announced he would move in the direction of having a "new constitution" by holding a referendum. Just over a month later, Chen made public his desire to terminate the National Unification Council and the National Unification Guideline, openly breaking his "one without" promise made in 2000. Those were apparently new provocations which further exposed Chen as a Taiwan independence fundamentalist. For Washington, the plan for termination was a "surprise" without a prior "consultation" with the Bush Administration. By contrast, Ma Ying-jeou, Chairman of the KMT, seemed much more reliable as he wrote that "The KMT ... believes that neither unification nor independence is likely for Taiwan in the foreseeable future and that the *status quo* should be maintained."[14]

Washington's reaction to Chen's plan was quick and strong. At a time when a hard counterterrorism war was still going on, the

---

[14]Ma Ying-jeou, Taiwan's 'Pragmatic Path', *Wall Street Journal* (February, 2006).

United States was stuck in Iraq, and the Iran and North Korea nuclear problems were stalled, Washington by no means wanted another crisis across the Taiwan Strait. Moreover it needed cooperation from Beijing on a number of issues, especially Norh Korea. The same day Chen announced his plan, President Bush was briefed and the Department of State spokesman made an unequivocal statement on United States policy, reaffirming that United States did not support Taiwan independence and opposed either side on the Taiwan strait to change the *status quo*. Particularly important was his observation that Chen Shui-bian's desire to join the United Nations in the name of "Taiwan" was a move to unilaterally alter the *status quo*. Washington also had a motivation to constrain PRC by preemption and setting the tone early to deter escalation. The United States reactions demonstrated that Washington and Beijing did have some space to cooperate on blocking Taiwan independence. Meanwhile, United States also wanted to keep cross-Strait developments under control. The United States reactions were a continuation of its policy to seek a dynamic cross-Strait balancing favorable to United States national interests. In 2003, when Chen Shui-bian planned to hold a referendum regarding the cross-Strait relationship, Washington rebuked Chen in front of the visiting Chinese Premier. In 2005, when PRC passed the Anti-Secession Law to provide legal basis for containing Taiwan independence movement, Washington expressed its opposition and openly criticized it when the law had been passed. Richard Bush pointed out, "These episodes led Washington to worry about the two sides would ignore its appeals for restraint and miscalculate themselves into a conflict, which then might entrap the United States in a war with China. It, therefore, employed an approach of 'dual deterrence,' conveying both warnings and reassurance to Beijing and Taipei."[15] Meanwhile, United States was keeping pressure on Taipei

---

[15]Richard C. Bush, Taiwan and East Asian Security, *Orbis* 55:2, (Spring (March–June) 2011), pp. 274–289.

to implement the program of purchasing the expensive arms from the United States sooner rather than later.

Beijing could not feel unhappier given the developments within the island in 2006–2007. In early 2006, Chen Shui-bian proposed to apply for joining the UN in the name of "Taiwan," and began to push it and make preparations for related steps and a referendum. Knowing that this was an impossible mission, Chen obviously had a political motive behind his attempts, trying to empower Taiwan independence movement but risking pushing the cross-Strait relations to the brink of the precipice. Facing the waves of provocative steps Chen Shui-bian and the DPP were taking, Beijing's nerves became more and more sensitive and tense, and eventually came to the conclusion that the Taiwan situation was entering into a high danger period (*gao wei qi*).

Nonetheless, during this same period, the Mainland was continuing to take measures deemed favorable to the Taiwanese people. During the Cross-Strait Economic and Trade Forum held in April 2006, Beijing announced 15 measures in favor of, for example, the selling of the Taiwanese agricultural products to the Mainland and the increase of tourists from the Mainland.[16] Those were the Mainland's unilateral commitments. A year later, Beijing further announced another set of 13 new measures involving direct air flight, education and investment. On the basis of the first four cities (Beijing, Shanghai, Guangzhou and Xiamen) being picked as the sites for direct charter flights, the Mainland would add six more including Chengdu, Hangzhou, Nanjing, Shenzhen, Dalian and Guilin. At the same time, Beijing pointed out that leaders of the Taiwan authorities repeatedly uttered extreme Taiwan independence rhetoric, were tightening "legal independence" movement through so-called "constitutional reengineering" (*xianzheng gaizao*), and were pushing the separatist activities such as "de-sinicization" and "rectifying the name for Taiwan." The danger deriving from

---

[16]*Renmin ribao* (People's Daily), April 16, 2006, p. 1.

"Taiwan independence" was growing, and this was the most serious, most dangerous, and most urgent issue facing peace and stability across the strait. The Mainland was determined, capable and prepared to stop "Taiwan independence" or any major incident leading to "Taiwan independence."[17] On July 24, 2007, in response to the return of the UN membership application by the UN Secretary General, Beijing claimed that the continual escalation of the Chen authorities' "Taiwan independence" activities were further pushing the cross-Strait relations to the brink of danger. At the same time, the next day (25 July) the Mainland and the KMT reached consensus on ten proposals to protect the legitimate rights and interests of people on both sides.[18]

Amid such a volatile and disturbing context, the 17th Party Congress was held in Beijing in October 2007, and Hu delivered his political report. The theme of the part on the Taiwan issue was in fact peace, calling for "firmly grasping the peaceful development theme of the cross-Strait relationship, sincerely seeking welfare for the compatriots on both sides and seeking peace for the Taiwan Strait area."[19] It also called for the following, namely, "on the basis of one China principle, formally ending the cross-Strait hostilities, reaching a Peace Agreement, and building a framework for cross-Strait peaceful development." In fact, this was a program of putting people first and peace as the priority.[20] For Beijing, the *status quo* was one China, of which both the Mainland and Taiwan are a part. In a fairly long period of time, Beijing's Taiwan strategy was to defend this *status quo*. As long as this was not challenged, peace across the strait could be guaranteed. The posture was a defensive one.

---

[17] Jia Qinglin's words at the third cross-Strait economic, trade, and cultural forum, see *Renmin ribao* (People's Daily) April 29, 2007.

[18] See *Renmin ribao* (People's Daily) July 26, 2007.

[19] Hu Jintao, 17th Party Congress report, (Beijing: Renmin chubanshe, 2007).

[20] Huang Jiashu, *Jiedu Hu Jintao duitai xin lunshu* (Interpreting Hu Jintao's New Discourse on Taiwan), *Zhongguo pinglun* (China Review) No. 120, December 2007.

Into 2008, warnings continued to come from Beijing. In January, Chen Yunlin, head of the State Council Taiwan Affairs Office, published an article in which he claimed that 2007 was a year the trial of strength between "Taiwan independence" and anti-"Taiwan independence" was unprecedentedly fierce while exchange and cooperation across the Strait were increasingly deepened and broadened. Thanks to Chen Shui-bian's pushing the envelope for a "UN membership referendum," peace in the Taiwan strait was facing a serious crisis.[21] When the Chen Shui-bian authorities decided to hold a referendum for joining UN in the name of Taiwan, Beijing warned that this was a serious step of seeking to change the *status quo* (both the Mainland and Taiwan being a part of China) and to move toward "legal independence" of Taiwan, and thus was a "Taiwan independence referendum" in another form.[22] Chen and his supporters were wrong if they thought the Mainland would swallow the bitter pill simply because of the upcoming Beijing Olympics were in summer 2008.

Amidst the tense atmosphere, Thomas J. Christensen, United States Deputy Assistant Secretary of State responsible for Chinese affairs also cautioned against the Taiwan authorities and raised warnings. Speaking at the United States–Taiwan Business Council Defense Industry Conference in Annapolis, Maryland on September 11, 2007, he stressed the importance of the political relationship by pointing out plainly, "a moderate approach by Taipei to relations across the strait will reduce the challenges faced by Taiwan's armed forces. ... [A]s much as we oppose Beijing's threat to use force, we also take it seriously, and Taipei cannot afford to do otherwise. It is for this reason that Taiwan's security is inextricably linked to the avoidance of needless provocative behavior. ... Responsible

---

[21] Chen Yunlin, *Weihu Taihai diqu heping wending, zhengqu liangan guanxi guangming qianjing* (Safeguarding peace and stability in the Taiwan strait area and striving for a bright future for cross-Strait relations), *Liangan guanxi* (Cross-Strait Relations) 1, 2008.

[22] See the Central Taiwan Affairs Office Statement, *Renmin ribao* (People's Daily), (February 3, 2008).

leadership in Taipei has to anticipate potential Chinese red line and reactions and avoid unnecessary and unproductive provocations."[23] It can be seen that Washington became impatient and made it very clear Taipei should not provoke the Mainland and any provocation would unnecessarily harm Taiwan's security. Political relationship was the key here. Cross-Strait peace is fundamentally a political issue rather than a military one.

Given what happened four years earlier during the 2004 elections, both Beijing and Washington followed very closely what was going on in Taiwan. Fortunately, as it turned out, the election went ahead smoothly. Both the referendum and the DPP candidate failed, and the KMT and Ma Ying-jeou won the election on March 22, 2008. Everybody was relieved. For Beijing, it was a victory of fighting "Taiwan independence" and was a win–win outcome. The "high danger period" (*gao wei qi*) was over and a new phase began.

Peaceful development a new reality

The second shift of political power, this time from the DPP to the KMT, became a major turning point for the cross-Strait relationship. Soon after the election, Hu Jintao greeted Vincent Siew, Ma Ying-jeou's deputy-elect, during the 2008 Bo'ao Forum for Asia while the latter was attending in his capacity as Chairman of the Cross-Straits Common Market Foundation. The two came very close to a consensus of building trust, shelving the disputes, seeking common ground while keeping difference, and jointly striving for a win–win situation. In May, Hu and Wu Boxiong, Chairman of the KMT, met in Beijing. Hu proposed to resume contact and consultation between the SEF and the ARATS as soon as possible to work out solutions on equal footing for various cross-Strait issues in a pragmatic

---

[23] Thomas J. Christensen, A Strong and Moderate Taiwan, speech to United States–Taiwan Business Council Defense Industry Conference, Annapolis, Maryland, September 11, 2007, http://www.state.gov/p/eap/rls/rm/2007/91979.htm.

manner. High on the agenda were the weekend charter flights that people on both sides cared much about and the arrangements for the Mainland tourists to travel to Taiwan.

Within 24 hours the SEF received an invitation for consultation from Beijing. The institutionalized consultation between the two organizations quickly resumed after a long moratorium of nine years, and within a year they held three important consultation meetings in Beijing, Taipei and Nanjing consecutively. Nine agreements were reached on cross-Strait charter flights, shipping, postal service, and the Mainland tourists visiting Taiwan, and so forth. Also, a principled consensus was reached regarding capital from the Mainland being invested in Taiwan. By December, the long-awaited three direct links of transport, trade and postal services (*san tong*) had fully materialized.[24]

Too many potential energies had accumulated during the past eight years and too much time lapsed. Finally Beijing was able to play out the cards it had held for too long — those measures it believed could benefit ordinary Taiwanese people including farmers, increase links across the strait, and entice the Taiwanese society. Diplomatic truce could now be carried out. Beijing decided to freeze its relations with those small countries that diplomatically recognized Republic of China on Taiwan (ROC)/Taiwan, even if they proactively sought a diplomatic relationship with PRC, so as to save face for Taiwan and to avoid igniting bad feelings from the island. An arrangement was made with the WHO on a case by case basis which allowed Taiwan to participate in the World Health Assembly. On the part of Washington, there was also relief regarding the reduced tension and prevailing peace across the Taiwan strait. According to Richard Bush, "… Having supported cross-Strait dialogue as a means to reduce tensions and exploit opportunities for

---

[24]"*Kaichuang liangan guanxi heping fazhan de qianjing — liangan guanxi yinian jian*" (Forging a Peaceful Development Prospect for the Cross-Strait Relationship), *Renmin ribao* (People's Daily) (June 6, 2009), p. 1.

cooperation, Washington has endorsed the progress that has occurred. … As a result, Washington has been able to retreat from dual deterrence and return to its prior approach of fostering a positive environment."[25]

Economically, Taiwan suffered from political infighting during Chen's eight years in office. Once hailed as an "Asian tiger" alongside the other three, Hong Kong, Singapore and South Korea, the fall of Taiwan's economic status was obvious. With regard to the four important indicators, i.e. economic growth rate, GDP, export growth rate, and export volume, during the Chen period, all fell to the bottom among the four little dragons.[26] The London-based *Financial Times* reports, "Indeed, of the four, the island faces the slowest annual growth, forecast at just 4%. It also trails in terms of per capita income, which stands at some US$15,000."[27] By 2008, the Mainland had already become Taiwan's largest trading partner and investment destination. When the domestic demand was shrinking considerably, economic growth was sustained largely because of Taiwan's huge trade surplus *vis-à-vis* the Mainland.

The regional economic landscape was also changing, and not to Taiwan's advantage. As was scheduled, from January 1, 2010 on, PRC and Association of Southeast Asian Nations (ASEAN), formed a free trade area. China–ASEAN FTA's taking effect meant that PRC and Southeast Asian countries were to comprehensively implement liberalization of trade in goods and to adopt zero tariff. That would pose a real challenge to Taiwanese export products since they would immediately become disadvantaged in either the Mainland or Southeast Asian markets. This would to a great extent impact Taiwanese industries such as textile, petrochemical,

---

[25] Richard C. Bush, Taiwan and East Asian Security, *Orbis* 55:2, (Spring (March–June) 2011), pp. 274–289.

[26] For concrete statistics, see *Jingsuan Taiwan cong sixiaolong zhishou lunwei qimo de genyou* (Calculating Taiwan's fall from the top of the four little dragons to the bottom), *Jingji ribao* (The Economic Daily) (Taiwan) Editorial, April 6, 2006.

[27] Kathrin Hille, Straitened times, *Financial Times*, March 26, 2008, p. 13.

mechanics and auto parts.[28] A major economic agreement with the Mainland seemed urgent. The idea dated back to the 2005 "five visions" agreed by Hu and Lien Chan, then KMT chairman, the third of which was to facilitate comprehensive economic exchanges and to establish cross-Strait economic cooperation mechanisms. It was not possible for this to be carried out during the Chen Shui-bian years, but now the option was right on the table.

During the fourth consultation between the SEF and ARATS held in December 2009 in the city of Taichung, the two sides agreed to target an economic cooperation framework agreement in their next meeting scheduled for the first half of 2010. On June 29, 2010, cross-Strait Economic Cooperation Framework Agreement (ECFA) was formally signed. ECFA consists of two parts, early harvest and follow-up programs. Early harvest concerns trade in goods. Listed in the early harvest program there were 539 Taiwanese products to be exported to the Mainland, and 267 Mainland products to be exported to Taiwan. According to ECFA, the tariff level for all those products would be lowered to zero in three years. The two would reach the overall goal of zero tariff comprehensively between them in 10 years time. Taking into account that, on the Taiwan side, ECFA would be submitted to the Legislative Yuan to deliberate and pass, Beijing accepted the article of allowing the agreement to be terminated by either side if desired. By doing so, Beijing helped to reduce the political burden on the Taiwan authorities.[29] In August 2012, the cross-Strait investment agreement and customs cooperation agreement were also signed during the eighth Chen Yunlin-Jiang Bingkun talks, signaling the successful completion of ECFA's first phase. By January 1, 2013, all 806 products that were on the

---

[28] Shu Hanfeng, *Yi 'jingji hezuo jiagou xieyi tuidong liangan heping fazhan'* (Pushing Cross-Strait Peaceful Development by 'Economic Cooperation Framework Agreement'), *Wenhuibao* January 12, 2010, p. 10.

[29] Zhou Zhongfei, *ECFA houxu jieduan fazhan xinsikao* (A Study of the Development of ECFA's Follow-Up Phase), in *Shanghai Taiwan yanjiu* (Shanghai Taiwan Research), Vol. 12, (Shanghai, December 2012).

list of ECFA's early harvest program realized zero tariff. This was not a small achievement in the cross-Strait relations.

Since May 2008, the cross-Strait relationship has become much more regular. Progress has been made in a variety of areas. Peaceful development became a new reality and has borne fruit. The PRC's successful hosting of the Beijing Olympics in 2008, plus the 2010 Expo in Shanghai, was a boost of its international status and influence. The rise of China was no longer just a possibility but rather a reality. Meanwhile, the global financial crisis originated in Wall Street was spreading. Against this backdrop there came the G2 theory, which argued that the United States and China could form a group of two powers to coordinate and make arrangements for world affairs. The concept was invented in the United States. Around the time the fourth China–United States Strategic and Economic Dialogue was held, C. Fred Bergsten, Director of the Washington, DC-based Peterson Institute for International Economics, published an article in *Foreign Affairs* in summer 2008, proposing that China and the United States should form a 'G2' to share the leadership of the global economy and make China partially take over the status of Europe. To be an economic superpower, a country must be sufficiently large, dynamic, and globally integrated to have a major impact on the world economy. Three political entities currently qualify: the United States, the European Union and China. Inducing China to become a responsible pillar of the global economic system (as the other two are) will be one of the great challenges of coming decades.[30] He gave the following facts for his argument: The United States and China were the two most important countries in the world economy; the two were the driving forces of world economic growth; China and United States were the world's respective biggest creditor and debtor, and had the largest surplus or deficit in the world respectively. They might setup a

---

[30]C. Fred Bergsten, A Partnership of Equals: How Washington Should Respond to China's Economic Challenge, *Foreign Affairs* (July/August 2008).

problem-solving framework to make their bilateral trade and world trade more open.

More generally than Bergsten who laid stress on the health of world economy, Zbigniew Brzezinski, a leading American strategist, was also a vocal advocate for the G2 concept. For him, an informal G2 was needed, and he promoted the idea by arguing for its importance in promoting cooperation at the global level. "The relationship between the United States and China has to be a comprehensive partnership, paralleling our relations with Europe and Japan. Our top leaders should therefore meet informally on a regular schedule for personal in-depth discussions not just about our bilateral relations but about the world in general."[31] In addition, for the World Bank's American President Robert Zoellick and its Chinese Chief Economist Justin Yifu Lin who wrote on the eve of April 2009's G20 summit in London, "Without a strong G2, the G20 will disappoint."[32] As the G20 London summit was approaching and took place, this issue became a hot topic that attracted much attention.

But others fiercely disagreed and refuted this view. For example, Elizabeth Economy and Adam Segal of the Council on Foreign Relations called this a "The G-2 Mirage."[33] For these two analysts, a heightened bilateral relationship may not be possible for China and the United States, as the two countries have mismatched interests and values. Washington should embrace a more flexible and multilateral approach.

For PRC, this was something which needed to be dealt with seriously. Beijing had its concerns. One, "G2" would give the world

---

[31] Zbigniew Brzezinski, The Group of Two that could change the world, *Financial Times*, January 14, 2009, see http://www.ft.com/intl/cms/s/0/d99369b8-e178-11dd-afa0-0000779fd2ac.html#axzz2Hk9pJBCY.

[32] Rocert Zoellick and Justin Yifu Lin, Recovery Rides on the 'G2', *Washington Post*, March 6, 2009.

[33] Elizabeth C. Economy and Adam Segal, The G-2 Mirage, *Foreign Affairs* May/June 2009.

an impression that United States and China would try to rule the world together. This was contrary to China's advocacy for more democracy in the management of world affairs. Two, other powers, such as European Union, Russia, India and Japan, as well as the developing countries, which China regarded as the "basis" of its foreign relations, would not be happy. It would be unwise for PRC to unnecessarily make them nervous. Three, there were analysts who still believed that it was a trap or conspiracy on the United States part to mislead China and to induce it to make mistakes. China should not fall into this trap.[34]

Eventually, during the China–European Union summit held in May 2009, Beijing went ahead to openly reject the "G2" concept. Premier Wen told reporters at the end of the China–European Union summit in Prague, "Some say that world affairs will be managed solely by China and the United States. I think that view is baseless and wrong." It is impossible for a couple of countries or a group of big powers to resolve all global issues. "Multipolarization and multilateralism represent the larger trend and the will of the people." China is committed to an independent foreign policy of peace and pursues a mutually-beneficial strategy of opening up, according to Wen. "China stands ready to develop friendly relations and cooperation with all countries and it will never seek hegemony."[35] Beijing's rejection after deliberation speeded up the disappearance of the G2 theory in the United States.

Over the years Taipei was always extremely sensitive to the developments in the Washington–Beijing ties and worried about Washington's making concessions to Beijing at Taipei's expense or simply betraying Taiwan. It had reasons to feel this way. There was a loss of the UN membership in 1971 which even Washington could

---

[34] See Cai Weiwei, *Zhongguo yuanhe bu rentong G2 shuo*, (Why China does not affirm the G2 theory), *Zhongguo shehui kexueyuan bao* (Chinese Academy of Social Sciences Review) June 2, 2009, p. 1.
[35] Wen rules out 'G2' proposal, *The Global Times*, May 22, 2009.

not control. There was the "Nixon shock" in 1972. There were United States decisions of terminating diplomatic relationship with, withdrawing United States troops from, and abrogating the Mutual Defense Treaty with Taiwan. Whenever United States appeared to need Beijing's cooperation, Taipei immediately became worried.

However, with a more stable and positive cross-Strait relationship, Taipei was less worried than before. This was demonstrated when United States President Barrack Obama traveled to Beijing for his first China visit in November 2009. In fact, the United States–China joint statement that resulted from Obama's visit did not harm Taiwan in any way. Recent improvement in the United States–PRC ties was not made at Taipei's expense. In January 2010, Washington announced its new arms sales to Taiwan. One explanation stated, "The United States Administration, for domestic political reasons, must offer arms to Taiwan (The large difference between what is approved and what is actually transferred is another subject)."[36] This, like what happened before, triggered strong reactions from Beijing, who expressed its resolute opposition and threatened to sanction the American arms producers that lobbied for the arms deal. Yet the threatened sanctions did not materialize. Beijing simply raised such a possibility for future interactions.

A healthy *status quo*

By the end of 2008, which marked the 30th anniversary of the famous January 1, 1979 "Letter to the Taiwanese Compatriots," Beijing had the reasons to become more confident to reaffirm its peaceful development doctrine toward Taiwan through a Hu Jintao speech on 31 December. Hu acknowledged that cross-Strait relations now had a rare historic opportunity (*nande lishi jiyu*). The important speech came up with a new identification of the status

---

[36]Miller Center of Public Affairs, *A Way Ahead with China: Steering the Right Course with the Middle Kingdom* (Charlottesville, 2011), p. 24.

quo, which was seen not as a secession of Chinese territory and sovereignty, but as a continuing political confrontation left over by the Chinese civil war of the 1940s. Thus, reunification is not a remaking of sovereignty and territory, but rather an end of political confrontation. A second major signal was that Beijing became more open toward the possibility for Beijing and Taipei to explore the feasible ways for both economies to connect with the economic cooperation mechanisms in the Asia–Pacific region. A third important innovation involved more directly addressing Taipei's concerns by stating, "We know the Taiwanese compatriots" feeling toward participating in international activities, and take sorting out relevant questions seriously. On the issue of Taiwan's participating in the activities of the international organizations, reasonable arrangements can be made through pragmatic cross-Strait consultations, under the premise of avoiding "two Chinas" or "one China, one Taiwan."[37] In fact, the speech set the guidelines for Beijing's future policy toward Taiwan.

Given Taiwan's political system and party politics, Beijing has to be prepared for a general election there every four years, and there is a possibility that DPP, the major opposition party, would regain political power one day. The current positive trend might not be "irreversible." With a political party that has adopted a Taiwan independence guideline and a "resolution on Taiwan's future," Beijing shares much less and holds opposite long-term goals by way of reunification *vs.* independence. However, a major political party that possesses nearly 40% popular support can by no mean be ignored and has to be taken seriously. This had become a bottleneck, and contact was on and off. The DPP people could come to visit the Mainland. Beijing emphasized that "For those who

---

[37] Hu Jintao, *Xieshou tuidong liangan guanxi heping fazhan, tongxin shixian zhonghua minzu weida fuxing* (Jointly pushing for peaceful development of the cross-Strait relations, and accomplishing the great revival of the Chinese nation), *Renmin ribao* (People's Daily), January 1, 2009.

proposed, engaged in, and followed 'Taiwan independence,' we welcome them to return to the right direction of pushing for cross-Strait peaceful development." Beijing became aware that it had to do something (*zuo gongzuo*) and get along with the DPP in some ways. Hsieh Ch'ang-t'ing (Frank Hsieh's) visit to the Mainland turned out to be part of this.

Hsieh was the former Chairman and one of the leading figures in the DPP, and he was relatively more moderate. Through prior arrangements, Hsieh traveled to Beijing in October 2012 in his capacity as chairman of a private foundation. He was well treated at least in terms of protocols. Dai Bingguo, State Councilor for Foreign, Taiwan, Hong Kong and Macao Affairs, Wang Yi, Head of the State Council Taiwan Affairs Office, and Chen Yunlin, President of the ARATS, all held meetings with Hsieh. Though on a private visit, Hsieh's was the first such visit by a leading DPP figure and thus was an important one that set a precedent. Whereas both sides knew they held different positions on cross-Strait political relationship, Hsieh's "constitutional one China" (*xianfa yizhong*) has in it "one China." At least this was the common ground that could be sought. The United States welcomed Hsieh's visit, stating that cross-Strait communication was conducive to mutual understanding and useful for the long-term cross-Strait stability. The problem was that the visit was not welcomed within the DPP. A setback soon came for Hsieh the next month as he failed to be assigned the chairmanship of DPP's "Chinese Affairs Committee" responsible for dealings with the Mainland. This typically emboldened the infighting within the DPP. Hsieh's more moderate "constitutional one China" could not be tolerated, let alone accepted, within the party. DPP's electoral defeat in January 2012 once again demonstrated that its Mainland policy was inconsistent with popular wishes for peace, stability and people's welfare. While a rethinking is badly needed, Beijing and DPP have a long way to go to come closer for a "normal" relationship.

The outbreak of the crisis over Diaoyu Islands in 2012 high-lighted another thing the two sides on the Strait had in common. They both strongly and consistently argued Diaoyu (or Diaoyutai as is called in Taiwan) were Taiwan's offshore islands and those were inalienable part of Chinese territory. For many years, fisher-men from Taiwan went fishing in the Diaoyu waters but since the early 1970s they were increasingly constrained, harassed, or even expelled by Japan whose acts angered Taiwanese fishermen. In order to defend fishing rights, there occurred 13 standoffs between Taiwanese and Japanese coast guard ships from May 2008 to November 2012. Not surprisingly, Japan's "nationalizing" Diaoyu provoked many people on both sides of the Strait. Ma Ying-jeou himself participated in the movement of defending Diaoyu as early as in 1971, and he knew very well about the issue since Diaoyu was the topic of his dissertation at Harvard. According to an address Ma gave on September 27, 2003 as President of the inter-national law association in Taiwan, since Diaoyu were Taiwan's offshore islands, in line with international law, legally they were reverted to the Republic of China at the end of the Second World War, together with other territories Japan occupied or annexed. He also held that efforts were worthwhile to keep the issue alive for the fishing right and sovereignty to be sorted out in the future.[38] In September 2012, Taiwanese activists for defending Diaoyu landed on the island and erected both flags of ROC and PRC. Later that month, after Japan's "nationalization," as many as 75 Taiwanese fishing boats, escorted by coast guard ships, entered into the Diaoyu waters and exchanged water shooting with the Japanese coast guard ships. At least in appearance, a picture emerged as if Taiwan and the Mainland were jointly taking actions in defending territorial integrity. Meanwhile, Ma Ying-jeou went ahead with an

---

[38]Ma Ying-jeou, *Diaoyutai wenti jianxi* (A brief analysis of the Diaoyutai issue), speech before the second symposium on the Diaoyutai islands, September 27, 2003.

"East China Sea peace initiative," the core idea of which was "sovereignty is inseparable while resources can be shared." The emphasis was to shelve the dispute while not impacting on sovereignty claim.[39] This actually was not something new but was what Beijing long advocated, and it did not yield positive results thus far. Starting from 1996, Taipei and Tokyo began and conducted 16 fishing negotiations which stalled since February 2009. Taipei's moves prompted Tokyo to suggest reopen their fishing negotiations in a way to avoid Taipei and Beijing joining hands on Diaoyu. While Beijing hoped to draw closer cross-Strait relations, Taipei stated that it would not collaborate with the Mainland to defend Diaoyu. It appeared more desirable to demonstrate its presence internationally and domestically to soothe the Taiwanese fishermen and alleviate pressures from them.

The United States factor also existed here. While carrying out a strategy of rebalancing to the Asia–Pacific, Washington urged Japan to share more burdens in security and defense, and wanted Seoul and Tokyo, its two allies in East Asia, to manage their territorial dispute over Dokdo/Takeshima and get along one another. With regard to Diaoyu, Washington has listed it as a place the United States–Japan security treaty applies, but has not gone so far to try to mediate between Tokyo and Taipei.

PRC's Hu Jintao period ended with the 18th Party Congress held in November 2012. As always, the political report he delivered has a particular part on Hong Kong, Macao and Taiwan affairs, which incorporated key elements of his December 31, 2008 speech regarding Taiwan. For the first time, the "1992 consensus" was written into a Party Congress report. It is stressed that a common identification with the one China framework is at the core of the consensus which serves as a political basis of cross-Strait relations, though it is interpreted in different ways. The report set to

---

[39] *Dujia zhuanfang Ma Ying-jeou* (Interview with Ma Ying-jeou), *Yazhou zhoukan* (AsiaWeek) November 18, 2012.

reinforce "institution-building" (*zhidu jianshe*), which was a new focus. Broadly speaking, regular meetings or contacts across the Strait were established through institutions, including the annual high level contact during Asia–Pacific Economic Cooperation (APEC) leaders' meeting, the KMT– The Chinese Communist Party (CCP) party to party channel, high level contact during the annual Bo'ao Forum for Asia, the Strait Forum held in Fujian annually, and of course, regular consultations between SEF and ARATS. Building on these, ECFA institutionalized the cross-Strait economic relationship and the two sides are likely to open an office in each other's place. The report repeated the call for negotiating a military and security confidence-building mechanism to stabilize cross-Strait situation. Given its sensitivity and high politics nature, the call has not yet received positive feedback from Taipei. This also requires a strong leadership capability on Taipei's part, which currently is a problem for Ma Ying-jeou. The approval ratings show he is weak and a weak leader is less likely to make bold moves. While retiring, the legacy Hu left was a healthy one, surely one of the most important achievements during his tenure. An overall situation of peaceful development across the Taiwan Strait will hopefully continue until the 2016 election. At this time, there is no reason for Beijing to change its current policies toward Taiwan. The same is true for Washington. *Status quo* sustains, though this is a dynamic *status quo*.

In 2013, there are three important items on the cross-Strait agenda. First, the two sides will continue to move ahead with the ECFA follow-up negotiations, and they are supposed to complete trade in services consultations and to speed up talks on a dispute resolution agreement. Second, ARATS and SEF will proceed with plans to open cross-Strait offices. The setup of offices are conducive to timely and conveniently handle the concrete matters that have sprung from the cross-Strait interactions so as to better serve and safeguard the rights and interests of cross-Strait people. Third, a cross-Strait currency settlement mechanism will start operation.

Taiwan has definitively regarded the development of an offshore RMB center as an objective, and the establishment of a currency settlement mechanism will greatly facilitate this goal.

Conclusion

This paper has analyzed the interactions between and among Beijing, Taipei and Washington over the past decade from a PRC perspective. Under Hu's leadership, it was a decade in which China further rose to great power status and became the world's second largest economy. During this period, China encountered a number of crises, ranging from the Severe Acute Respiratory Syndrome (SARS) epidemic to global financial crisis, among which Taiwan under Chen Shui-bian was probably the biggest challenge. The decade also saw the articulation of the peaceful rise/peaceful development thesis which attempted to answer the major question what path China should and would take in the future. The Hu–Wen leadership adopted the peaceful development theory and tried to apply it to cross-Strait relations, at a time when Chen was taking steps to drift to Taiwan independence and going all the way to the so-called UN membership referendum, which prompted Beijing to anticipate the coming of a "high danger period." It took Beijing a long time to realize that winning the hearts and minds of the Taiwanese people was the key and it had to become more patient and allow more time. The peaceful development thinking persisted and was practiced with respect to relations with the major opposition parties of Taiwan. It eventually bore fruit with the 2008 election of Ma Ying-jeou, a result that served the interest of all three sides. In this particular triangle, the smaller did challenge the larger sometimes but failed. However, this does not preclude future crises, again likely caused by the smaller, since the larger cannot impose its will on the smaller. In this regard, domestic politics factors in tremendously.

Looking at the triangle in a broader context and from the long-term perspective, some American analysts argue, "United States policymakers view China as the century's biggest strategic challenge for the United States, and this is the strategic lens through which they view cross-Strait relations."[40] This complicates the triangular relationship. Throughout the decade, Washington remained a key player whose policy had two sides. Overall, it wanted a "balance," defined by the United States Administration, across the Taiwan strait and a *status quo* maintained. On one hand, arguing that the military balance was shifting in Beijing's favor, United States Administration continued its arms sales to Taiwan which was both politically driven to counter balance the growth of military power on the Mainland and economically driven to gain benefits to please its domestic constituents. On the other hand, it wanted to constrain the provocations and dangerous moves from Taiwan at a time Washington was engaged in a strenuous counterterrorism war and Sino–United States cooperation increasingly became important in many other areas. Chen Shui-bian's ill-intentioned initiatives of holding referenda in Taiwan ignited wide-spread oppositions or concerns from the stakeholders in the region, including Washington and Beijing. Both wanted to avoid the risks of Taiwan's drifting toward independence which was counterproductive and potentially dangerous. Yet Washington's "one China policy" was different from Beijing's "one China principle." The former discouraged Beijing not to coerce Taipei, whereas it had many more challenges to grapple with throughout the world and Taiwan was not high on the agenda. As long as Taiwan is self-restrained and not seeking independence, the Mainland is not using force, and thus there is no trouble across the strait, Washington is happy to see the *status quo* continue.

For Beijing, since peaceful development doctrine proved to work for the cross-Strait relations, it has no reason to change policy. Pragmatism prevails and there is no rush for reunification for the

---

[40] Evolving Cross-Strait Relations and Challenges and Implications for the United States, *Sigur Center Asia Report*, 11, (Washington, D.C., September 2011).

time being. In other words, reunification is not the goal at this stage. Instead, the current objective is the promotion of the cross-Strait ties in various areas, helping make Beijing–Washington–Taipei an "inclusive triangle," as Brantly Womack argues in his article in this volume. The harder goals relate to the signing of a cross-Strait peace accord and the establishment of a military confidence-building mechanism. As the Ma Administration is weak, it must be cautious in addressing those goals Beijing has proposed. However, closer economic and people-to-people connections and more institutionalization of cross-Strait relations will likely move ahead with the implementation of ECFA and the creation of operating offices in each other's place. The nature of an inclusive triangle is, after all, not unanimity of interests, but rather opportunities of mutual benefit.

Among Washington, Beijing and Taipei, a delicate balance is maintained. In 2012, leadership changes occurred in all three capitals. Both Ma Ying-jeou and Barrack Obama were reelected, and there was a major leadership transition in Beijing from Hu Jintao and Wen Jiabao to Xi Jinping and Li Keqiang. The leaderships are expected to be stable for the next few years until the next Taiwan election in 2016. For the time being, no one desires to change the overall *status quo* and they all have formidable domestic agendas. Beijing and Washington both cooperate and compete in the Asia–Pacific region. In this inclusive triangle, while Washington and Taipei keep a "normal" relationship, Beijing and Taipei try to avoid troubles while a growing and better relationship benefits both. Beijing has demonstrated strategic patience and continues to try to win the hearts and minds of people on Taiwan which will take a long time to work.

Chapter 3

The Taipei–Beijing–Washington Triangle: The Taiwanese Aspects

Tse-Kang Leng

Academia Sinica and National Chengchi University

Introduction

This paper delves into the interplay of domestic politics and external relations in the context of the triangular relationship among Taiwan, China and the United States. In some respects Taiwan plays the role of a tail wagging two dogs. Taiwan took advantage of the Sino–American rivalry and survived during the Cold War era of bi-polar confrontations. The Sino–Soviet split changed the global balance of power and prompted the United States to form an unofficial strategic partnership with China. Taiwan's drives toward democratization in the last decade of the 20th century created uncertainties over the eventual unification of China. Taiwan's domestic changes and policy shift away from national reunification led to a brief missile crisis in 1996. The pro-independence line of the democratically elected President Chen Shui-bian in 2000 further worsened cross-Strait relations as well as the mutual trust between Taiwan and the United States. Taiwan was thus labeled as a troublemaker in international society over fears it would bring about a war in the Taiwan strait between a rising China and the United States.

Taiwan's democracy serves as a double-edged sword in the triangular relationship. The success of Taiwan's democratic development sets a model for peaceful transition from authoritarian rule. However, the root of the instability in the Taipei–Beijing–Washington triangle stems from Taiwan's drive for a more autonomous position in cross-Strait relations. The power-centered realist approach suggests that the United States sacrifice democratic Taiwan to create a more constructive and cooperative mechanism for the remaining two major powers. From a more inclusive angle, the rise of Taiwanese identity and a mature civil society empower the non-state sector to make deeper engagements between the two sides of the Taiwan strait. Such social and cultural interaction will lay a foundation for integrating Taiwan and China into the broader global realm of social, economic and cultural cooperation.

This paper will focus on the complex impact of Taiwan's domestic change on the formation of the inclusive mechanism. The basic premise is that smooth cross-Strait relations will be the key factor to bring peace to the trilateral relationship. This paper will first introduce the crucial concepts of culture and identity in the linkage of domestic politics and foreign policy making, followed by analysis of Taiwanese academic perceptions on the new role of China and of Sino–American relations. In terms of domestic politics, this paper intends to re-interpret the impact of the changing nature of Taiwan's identity as well as the empowerment of a dynamic civil society. In addition to the social aspect of Taiwan's democracy, the last section of this paper will discuss whether culture could serve as a catalyst to link the two ethnic societies to achieve peace across the Taiwan strait.

Identity, culture and domestic politics of the triangular relationship

The shift of identity and value systems of Taiwan and China in the past decades are important factors in the discussion of triangular relationship. These changes may create uncertainties and anxieties for foreign policy makers. In the process of searching for a new status as a major power, some Chinese experts are tracing back to traditional strategic thought and the classical international system when China considered itself to be the center of the world.[1] American academics have also delved into the implications for the current international system of classical cases of the "Confucian long peace."[2] How to accommodate the new identity of a rising power with a long and glorious history and recent authoritarian legacy into the triangular relationship will be of interest both from a theoretical as well as a policy perspective.

Forces of globalization in culture, which serve as one of the most important external impetus to change domestic behavior, need to be integrated into the framework of analysis in the historical context. As the classical work of E.H. Carr demonstrates, norms will not stop states from engaging in acts of barbaric aggression, but historical experiences and perceptions of legitimacy nevertheless condition the way in which states interpret the meaning of each other's actions.[3] Historical experiences have influential impacts on the current perceptions and misperceptions of the actors involved in the triangle. However, history does not necessarily serve as the only

---

[1] Xuetong Yan, ed., *Ancient Chinese Thought, Modern Chinese Power* (Princeton: Princeton University Press, 2011).

[2] Brantly Womack, *China's Rise in Historical Perspective* (New York: Roman and Littelfiled, 2010); David Kang, *East Asia Before the West: Five Centuries of Trade and Tribute* (New York: Columbia University Press, 2010).

[3] Edward H. Carr, *The Twenty Years' Crisis, 1919–1939* (New York: Perennial, 2001). Reprinted edition.

independent variable to determine the destined clashes of interests. Instead, the three actors involved will undergo a "learning" or "socialization" process that will help them adjust and accommodate one another in the long-term historical trajectory. Some critical junctures and major events in history are important to understand the socialization and learning experiences.

The major advantage of the domestic interpretation of international politics is to grasp the potential of "governing" instead of "balancing" international power distribution. Even the hard-core realists do not reject the possibility of social learning and socialization in international society. The learning process also reflects the change of state behaviors with respect to contingency maneuvering, compromise and ideological adjustments. Through the lens of historical learning and socialization, researchers understand the changes of identity and the impacts on developing national interests. Scholars like Alex Wendt, Peter Katzenstein and Jeffery Legro focus their studies on the interaction among institutions, culture and identity.[4] History may shift the direction of a power constellation, but history per se is also the result of human construction and power manipulation. A persuasive discussion on the governance of power relations is rooted in the thorough understanding of the historical process of identity formation.

New forces of globalization create a dynamism of people-to-people cooperation. In the case of Taipei–Beijing–Washington triangle, such dynamism also helps states to escape from the rigid, power struggle-centered approach to foreign policy, and return to the original spirit of realism to balance morality, power and capacities. However, culture also serves as a type of "tool kit" from which decision makers can pick certain instruments to aid their political purposes. Through the non-state dimension of power management, mutual trust and avoidance of misperception could be realized in

---

[4]Peter J. Katzenstein, *The Culture of National Security* (New York: Columbia University Press, 1996).

the framework of global governance. Political leadership serves as a bridge to link domestic and international politics. The dynamics of this approach are embedded in a globalizing world characterized by forces of institutional change, ideological evolution and interest adjustment. The instrumentalism of culture and public diplomacy also serves as a major vehicle to enhance bottom–up forces of mutual understanding.

Taiwanese academic perceptions on the "China Factor"

Perceptions of the rise of China impact Taiwan's understanding of the trilateral relationship. In general, the Taiwanese academics have a more moderate view of the Chinese position in the global system. Mostly trained in American social science approaches, Taiwanese scholars attempt to link the study of the rise of China with contemporary international relations theories in the Western world. Some scholars attempt to adopt a more critical approach to review the sources of change and continuity of Chinese foreign relations. For instance, Lang Kao argues that the Chinese calculations on external affairs are rooted in the collective wisdom dating back to the pre-reform era. Pure materialist measurements on the Chinese capacities without incorporating historical lessons and memories will be missing a big piece of puzzle.[5] Chih-yu Shih and Teng-chi Chang adopt psychological approaches to review four key concepts of the rise of China, namely, the nature of the Chinese nation state, *Tianxia* (天下), Chinese civilization and Asian dynamism. According to Shih and Chang, these four dimensions provide a more comprehensive framework to understand the rise of China in the contemporary world than the Western power-centered approaches of realism. Shih and Chang provide a unique analysis of the concept of *Tianxia* and

---

[5]Lang Kao, Ruhe lijie zhongguo jueqi (How to understand the rise of China?), *Yuanjing jikan*, 7:2 (2006), pp. 53–94.

its implication for the rise of China. Echoing the original interpretation of *Tianxia* from the Chinese scholar Zhao Dingyang, Shih and Chang argue that the concept of *Tianxia* provides an approach different from the Westphalian tradition of international systems. China's policy of a "harmonious world" will be utilized to buttress the nation state in the jungle of power politics. The culture-based Chinese soft power will also be developed to satisfy market demands dominated by the Western world. Ironically, the current Chinese leadership's promotion of a "harmonious world" and "soft power" distorts the concept of *Tianxia* and leads the nation into the Westphalian system of nation states and power politics.[6]

Whether the rise of China will bring instability to the international system in general, and to Washington–Beijing–Taipei (W–B–T) triangle in particular, is also a major concern of Taiwanese scholars. Yu-shan Wu's study of power transition theory sheds light on the flexibility and constraints of a stable international system. According to Wu, stabilizing either the process of power transition or intentions after China gains its new status in the international system may decrease the possibility of war. In the context of Sino–American relations, United States foreign policy efforts to change the Chinese perception and intention on the issue of Taiwan to a more flexible position will be the key to avoid clashes of the two major powers. Furthermore, if international institutions provide enough space for interest engagements and articulation, the Chinese will accommodate international norms and values and this will eventually result in the peaceful resolution on the Taiwan issue. However, as Wu indicates, domestic politics and the impact of culture will constrain the willingness of existing powers to "open the door" to accommodate the new role of China in the international system.[7]

---

[6]Chih-yu Shih and Teng-chi Chang, Zhongguo jueqi de yiyi (The meaning of the rise of China), *Wenhua Yanjiu*, 8, pp. 193–212.

[7]Yu-shan Wu, Quanli yizhuan lilun: beiju yuyan? (Power transition theory: The prophet of tragedy?) in Tzong-ho Bao, ed., *Guoji guanxi lilun* (*Theories of International relations*) (Taipei, Wunan, 2011), pp. 389–416.

Recently, there have been noteworthy efforts by Taiwanese academics to use constructivism in analyzing foreign policy and international relations. Adopting the constructivist approach, Taiwanese scholars try to analyze the changes and continuity of the Chinese identity from "a third party role." In general, these Taiwanese academics take a more optimistic position on the rise of a new Chinese identity in international society. For instance, Kun-hsuan Chiu and Wei-en Tan argue that the Chinese theory of the "harmonious world" reflects the fact that the Chinese identify themselves as a "junior power" or "late comer" in the international system. The Chinese perceive the need to cooperate with the United States in the interdependent international system. The harmony-oriented Chinese self-identification presents China with a more active role in traditional as well as human security issues based on the principle of equality and mutual-benefits. Chiu and Tan even allege that the harmonious world thesis has been deeply embedded in the value system of Chinese leaders following the rise of China's comprehensive power in the international arena.[8]

The combination of classical and constructivist approaches of power politics on Chinese external behavior is also utilized by Yun-han Chu and Min-hua Huang in their work on the rise of China. Chu and Huang emphasize the conflicts and cooperation on ideas and culture, instead of power, as the central stage of Sino–American relations. They also presume the rationality of Chinese leaders in the reform era to revise the power or material-centered approaches to Chinese national security threats. Under such a logical inference, Chinese leaders tend to regard the "peaceful evolution" strategies from the Western world as a clear and present threat rather than a power imbalance in the international system. Such theses,

---

[8]Kun-Hsuan Chiu and Wei-en Tan, Zhongguo hexieshijie waijiao zhengce zhi yanjiu (A study on Chinese foreign policies of the harmonious world), in Kai-huang Yang, ed., *Hu Jintao zhengquan zhi xu yu bian* (*The Continuity and Change of the Hu Jintao Administration*) (Taipei, Wenjintang, 2007), pp. 257–290.

according to Chu and Huang, match the constructivist arguments that "identity comes before interests." Hence, the Chinese solution to cope with the United States threats is to search for China's domestic cohesion. By contrast, the United States policies toward the rise of China are to attract Chinese intellectuals and elite groups with cultural diplomacy, and thus lead China towards integration with Western civilization.[9]

In contrast to the more radical and plural opinions among the policy making circle and the general public, the above mentioned mainstream Taiwanese academics attempt to combine the Chinese logics of its peaceful rise with western theories. System level analyses and cultural approaches are adopted to explore how to live with a rising China. The following sections will introduce the impact of Taiwan's domestic politics on trilateral as well as cross-Strait relations.

Taiwan's domestic politics and triangular relationship under Ma Ying-jeou administration: The state-centered analysis

Discussions on the inclusive triangle have to include the important factor of Taiwan's domestic political change. In contrast to the other two pillars of the triangle, Taiwan's domestic politics create more unpredictability and uncertainty, especially in its policies toward the other side of the Taiwan strait. External policies are more or less the reflection of domestic political change. The traditional wisdom of democratic peace argues that the peaceful nature of democratic regimes will reduce the ambition to use military force in international affairs. However, the transitional democracies have less

---

[9]Yun-han Chu and Min-hua Huang, Tansuo zhong guo jueqi de lilun yihan (Exploring the theoretical implications on the rise of China), in Yun-han Chu and Qingguo Jia ed, *Cong guoji guanxi lilun kan zhongguo jueqi* (*International Relations Theories and the Rise of China*), (Taipei, Wunan), pp. 23–58.

coherent mechanisms of foreign policy making. In domestic politics, consensus on vital national interests is still in the process of formation; on diplomatic fronts, the new democracies may pursue "democratic crusading" to deviate from the political realism of international affairs. Young democracies may bring instability and uncertainty to the international and regional systems.

Ironically, it is political authoritarianism instead of democracy that has brought about the major policy shift to achieve compromise between Taiwan and China. Ye Jianying's nine-point proposal, released in the early 1980s, did not receive a positive response from Taiwan's authoritarian leader Chiang Ching-kuo. However, friendly gestures from the mainland side, such as new policy guidelines of "peaceful reunification" and "three direct links," did lay a foundation for the subsequent breaking of the ice. Chiang finally liberalized cross-Strait relations and opened the KMT party state in 1987, a few months before his death in 1988. The purpose of Chiang's breakthrough was not to achieve an independent and democratic Taiwan. The eventual goal of Chiang's mainland policy was still peaceful reunification of an integrated China.

The instrumentalism of using cross-Strait relations to consolidate domestic power can be found in the early years of Lee Teng-hui's leadership. The historic Koo-Wang talks, the 1992 consensus, and subsequent negotiations to normalize cross-Strait relations were implemented under the alliance between Lee and the older KMT veterans. The National Unification Council was established in 1990 to continue Chiang's line of peaceful reunification based on gradualism. However, the instrumentalism of peaceful reunification was abandoned as Lee gained legitimacy after the first direct presidential election in 1996. The pronouncements of "the sadness of being Taiwanese" and "special state to state relationship" by Lee further laid the foundation of new policy lines toward a democratic but independent Taiwan instead of unification with the mainland. The policy shift of cross-Strait relations was also utilized by Lee to undermine the KMT from within. Lee's sharp turn in the late 1990s

broke the long-held myth that the KMT was a political party representing the whole of China. The old KMT was labeled as an "external regime" which suppresses the Taiwanese people. In other words,
Lee's policy shift toward Taiwan independence in reality paved the
way for the first party turnover in 2000.

The DPP's victory in 2000, a milestone for Taiwan's democracy,
ushered in an era of uncertainty and turmoil for the Taipei-Beijing-
Washington relationship. The landslide victory for Ma in 2008 did
not mean the overwhelming support of his mainland policy of no
independence, no unification and no use of force. Rather, Ma's victory reflected the disappointment over Chen's brinkmanship strategy in playing the "democracy card" on the triangular relationship,
and the DPP's inability to globalize the Taiwanese economy without
engaging with China. The American attitude did not play an influential role in the 2008 election, but the strong United States–Taiwan
distrust did serve as the straw that broke the camel's back. For
instance, Thomas Christensen, then the Under Secretary of State,
provided strong opposition to Chen's attempt to join the UN under
the name of Taiwan.[10]

The return of power of KMT in 2008 stabilized the triangular
relationship. Ma Ying-jeou's basic policy line of "no unification, no
independence, no use of force" was utilized to strike a balance
between domestic politics and external relations. Ma's approach of
institutionalizing cross-Strait relations reflects his attempts to
enlarge and deepen the interests of cross-Strait interaction. It is also
an attempt to encourage bottom–up forces to create informal institutions and mechanisms. At the same time, Ma has stressed the importance of "never to interfere" but to change the way of thinking. The
Ma administration continued to mention Taiwan's democratic values, the rule of law, and an advanced civil society, what might be
called "political soft power."

---

[10]Speech to United States–Taiwan Business Council Defense Industry Conference,
September 11, 2007, Annapolis Thomas J. Christensen, Deputy Assistant Secretary of
State — A Strong and Moderate Taiwan http://www.ait.org.tw/en/officialtext-ot0715.html.

As to the "hard power" aspect of national defense, Ma continued to stress that Taiwan has the resolve to defend itself. In a videoconference with the Center for Strategic and international Studies in 2011, Ma elaborated on his "three lines of national defense."[11] According to Ma, the first line is to institutionalize cross-Strait rapprochement; the second line is to enhance Taiwan's international contributions; and the third line is to align Taiwan's defense with diplomacy. In addition to mentioning the importance of changing the mindset of national security, Ma expressed his plan to build the necessary structures that encourage the right conditions for growth in societal expectations. According to Ma, in order to institutionalize cross-Strait relations, Taiwan needs to create explicit principles, norms, rules and procedures around which the expectations of both sides can converge. This very convergence has created predictability and mutual understanding in cross-Strait relations, leading to stability across the Taiwan Strait and in the region as a whole. Ma emphasized that the idea of institutionalizing the cross-Strait rapprochement is not only to reduce the possibility of miscalculation, but to increase the cost of reversing this trend as well.

Some sensitive issues such as weapons procurement from the United States remain, but Ma tries to divert the security issue into different angles. First of all, Ma has regarded the issue of arms sales as an instrument for facilitating future negotiations across the Taiwan Strait. According to Ma:

"...For cross-Strait relations to continue advancing, the United States must help Taiwan level the playing field. Negotiating with a giant like the Chinese Mainland is not without its risks. The right leverage must be in place; otherwise Taiwan cannot credibly maintain an equal footing at the negotiation table."[12]

---

[11] Ma Ying-jeou, Building National Security for the Republic of China, President Ma's Remarks at the Video conference with the Center for Strategic and International Studies, Office of the President News Release, May 12, 2011.

[12] *Ibid.*

The defense and arms sales issues are thus linked with Taiwan's external relations and regional stability. Taiwan's defense links with the United States help preserve the *status quo* led by United States security arrangements. The self-defense capacities of Taiwan are utilized as an instrument to guarantee that Taiwan is a "trustworthy partner" who will act after "full consultation" with major powers. Arms sales from the United States, in Ma's own words, are the realization of an American presence in the Asia Pacific region. Ma argues that only a strong United States commitment by its credibility in East Asia can guarantee peace and stability in the region.[13]

However, pressures on Taiwan's new cross-Strait policies also come from the United States side. The Taipei–Beijing–Washington triangle has shown signs of change in American academic circles since the Taipei–Beijing détente that began in 2008. Two articles in *Foreign Affairs* reflected new thoughts on Taiwan's strategic status in a potential United States–China rivalry. In his article on the "Finlandization" of Taiwan, Bruce Gilley argues that Taiwan should reposition itself as a neutral power, rather than a United States strategic ally. In return, Beijing would back down on its military threats, grant Taipei expanded participation in international organizations, and extend the island favorable economic and social benefits. According to Gilley, Finlandization will allow Taiwan to break the cycle by taking itself out of the game and moderating the security dilemma that hangs over the Washington–Beijing relationship. Gilley argues that from a strictly realist perspective, there is no need for the United States to keep Taiwan within its strategic orbit, given that United States military security can be attained through other Asian bases and operations. Taiwan's Finlandization should be seen not as a necessary sacrifice to a rising China but rather as an alternative strategy for pacifying China.[14]

---

[13] *Ibid.*

[14] Bruce Gilley, Not so dire straits, *Foreign Affairs* (Jan/Feb, 2010), pp. 44–60.

A more straightforward hard-core realist interpretation of major power politics across the Taiwan Strait could be found in Charles Glaser's arguments. Glaser argues that given the fact that Washington has limited control over Taipei's actions, a crisis could unfold in which the United States found itself following events rather than leading them. Ongoing improvements in China's military capabilities may make Beijing more willing to escalate a Taiwan crisis. Given the risks, the United States should consider backing away from its commitments to Taiwan. This would remove the most obvious and contentious flashpoint between the United States and China and smooth the way for better relations between them in the decades to come. In Glaser's words:

> "...Territorial concessions are not always bound to fail. Not all adversaries are Hitler, and when they are not, accommodation can be an effective policy too. When an adversary has limited territorial goals, granting them can lead not to further demands but rather to satisfaction with the new status quo and a reduction of tension."[15]

Such reflections of great power politics would change, instead of maintain, the current *status quo* in the East Asian region. The change would not be for the better. Sacrificing Taiwan is not a feasible solution to ease a potential United States–China military confrontation. First of all, withdrawing United States support of Taiwan will certainly raise the anxieties of Japan, South Korea and other East Asian powers. The dynamics of the current East Asian system are fueled by multiple players. By contrast, the current self-restraint policies of Taiwan serve the interests of all the stakeholders by maintaining the stability of cross-Strait power accommodation and deflecting confrontation.

Secondly, proposals of "Finlandization" or "backing away from United States support" of Taiwan do not have domestic feasibility

---

[15] Charles Glaser, Will China's Rise Lead to War? Why Realism Does Not Mean Pessimism, *Foreign Affairs*. 90:2 (Mar/Apr 2011), pp. 80–92.

in Taiwan. The "Finlandization" proposal mistakenly presumes that opposition to Ma on cross-Strait relations is muted after Ma's 2008 landslide victory. Domestic consensus on sensitive political issues in Taiwan is slim. The so-called "Taiwan model" of development provides both negative and positive implications for future evolution in mainland China. The Taiwan model could not fit all the Chinese experiences and expectations, but it does provide an option for the ethnic Chinese region. From this normative aspect, the existence of Taiwan offers an alternative of peace and development other than great power politics and pure concerns of power struggles.

Beijing's high expectations for Ma to reverse the pro-independence line neglect the basic structure of Taiwan's domestic politics. By the same token, Washington's worries over Ma's pro-engagement policies promoting eventual unification in the short term are groundless. Roots of Ma's inability to boost economic growth through economic integration with China can be traced to the key era of the late 1990s. The watershed of the rise of China's comprehensive power and relative decline of Taiwan's global economic competitiveness occurred around 2000. Due to continuous political interventions on economic engagements with China, Taiwan's master plan to transform itself into an Asia–Pacific hub of global services finally came to a halt during this period. About the same time, China's entry into the World Trade Organization (WTO) provided a major stimulus to open the Chinese market to the world and promote Chinese external exposure beyond the export-led growth. The negative effects of the lost opportunity to institutionalize the relationship with the mainland were exacerbated by the eight years of self-isolation under Chen Shuibian. Economic interactions between the two sides resulted in quantitative growth, but such interaction also reflected the deepening of Taiwan's economic dependence on China.

In 2008, Ma inherited the heavy burdens of an economic slowdown and a decline in global competitiveness. The main driving force of cross-Strait economic interaction has remained the original equipment manufacturing (OEM) and original design manufacturing (ODM) type of Taiwanese investments in China. Major Taiwanese IT manu-facturers like Taiwan Semiconductor Manufacturing Company (TSMC) concentrate their efforts in the perfection of manufacturing process rather than initial design. Taiwanese firms do not control the upstream core technologies. Even though these OEM/ODM firms link United States technologies, Taiwanese know-how, and Mainland Chinese manufacturing capacities, the profit margin was getting slim. Companies like Foxconn had to squeeze their manufacturing costs which resulted in problems like sweat factories and labor disputes. In response, OEM manufacturers like Foxconn have tried to globalize their operations and seek new breakthroughs in international markets. But famous Taiwanese brand names, like Acer, Asus and HTC, are still rarities in the global marketplace.

Poor economic performance thus made it increasingly difficult for Ma to implement his mainland policies. Closer economic ties through official agreements have not enhanced the support for political engagement between the two sides. Even though the two sides of the Taiwan Strait have signed 18 economic agreements since 2008, including the ECFA, most Taiwanese remain skeptical over the normalization of political relations. The large contracted purchase from the Mainland side of agricultural products from Southern Taiwan did not win local support for the KMT or for uni-fication. For example, Xuejia District in Tainan, the biggest location of Taiwan's local Shimu fish farms, did not show any change of residents' party preference for the DPP or of their support for the independence platform after the lucrative deals with the Mainland buyers went through.

From a more inclusive aspect, the first term of the Ma adminis-tration shows that Taipei could simultaneously improve its relation-ship with Beijing and Washington once mutual trust is established. Simultaneous enhancement of mutual trust was demonstrated by Taiwan's inclusion in the United States Visa Waiver Program (VWP) in November 2012 at the same time that the ECFA was being implemented. In Ma's first term, after the opening of Taiwan to Mainland Chinese tourism, Mainland Chinese have made some 7.17 million visits to Taiwan from 2008–2012. In 2012, 200,000 visits to Taiwan were made by Mainland Chinese individually rather than as part of tour groups. Mainland tourists accounted for about 30% of all visits to Taiwan in 2012, thus Mainland China represents one of the largest sources of visitors to Taiwan. As to opening Taiwan to Mainland Chinese students, Taiwan still has a policy of "Three Restrictions and Six Prohibitions"[16] in place, but these restrictions, according to the government, will gradually be eased. At present, Taiwan only recognizes degrees from 41 Mainland Chinese schools. The goal in the future, however, is for Taiwan to recognize the degrees of all universities and colleges included in the Mainland's Project 211, which promotes educational excellence. Taiwan will thus recognize degrees from over 100 Mainland Chinese schools, and additionally it hopes to allow mainland Chinese junior college students to study in Taiwan in 2013.[17]

---

[16] It refers to the rules provided by the Ministry of Education in Taiwan to regulate students from Mainland China:

Three restrictions:

Restriction on school — only certificates or diplomas from top-ranked universities in Mainland China will be recognized.

Restriction on quantity — The number of Chinese students will be limited to 1% of overall local student recruitment.

Restriction on research fields — The research field of Chinese and Western medicine, pharmacy, national security and high technology will not be accepted currently.

Six prohibitions:

No extra credit will be offered to the Mainland students.

The process of local student recruitment will not be affected by Chinese student recruitment.

No scholarship opportunities for Mainland students.

Working off-campus is not permitted.

Taking tests for professional license is not permitted.

Working in Taiwan after graduating is not permitted.

[17] Ying-jeiou Ma, Gradual reconciliation in cross-Strait relationship; expansion of peace and prosperity, a speech delivered on February 18, 2013. http://english.president.gov.tw/Default.aspx?tabid=1124&itemid=29283&rmid=3048.

Ma's "East China Sea Initiatives," released in August 5, 2012, provide a more realistic proposal to cope with controversial sovereignty issues. Such practical interpretations of and applications to the sovereignty issue may have implications for the thorny political resolution for the sovereignty of Taiwan and Mainland China. Although not addressing directly the Taipei–Washington–Beijing triangular relationship, Ma stresses that while sovereignty is indivisible, resources can be shared. All parties involved should replace confrontation with dialogue, shelve territorial disputes through negotiations, formulate a code of conduct, and engage in the joint development of resources.[18] Ma further elaborates that his proposal calls for the recognition of the existence of controversies over sovereignty. Such recognition does not harm the stances of all parties involved on their claims of sovereignty. The purpose in shelving these controversies is to start negotiations; shelving does not equate to losing sovereignty.[19]

The hesitation on Ma's part to move forward on more sensitive political issues, such as peace talks, has created a certain degree of disappointment in Beijing. Hu Jintao's six-point proposal of 2008 and the 18th Party Congress Report of 2012 called for the negotiation of a peace agreement between Beijing and Taipei. Electoral constraints on Taiwan's more creative Mainland policy will be minimal until the end of 2014. The semi-presidential system in Taiwan causes political deadlock for the cabinet and premier, but it is the President who shoulders the major responsibilities on national security and external relations. The political culture in Taiwan under the democratic rule still places the major political responsibilities on the part of the President. Ma's political charisma waned after 2008, but he is still the key figure to explain to the public and to

---

[18]The Republic of China (Taiwan) Proposes: The East China Sea Peace Initiative, (Taipei, Ministry of Foreign Affairs, December 2012).

[19]President Ma met with delegates from the Project 2049 Institute, Press Release, Presidential Office, February 26, 2013. http://www.president.gov.tw/Print.aspx?tabid=131.

mobilize popular support for a more progressive Mainland policy. In other words, in addition to institutional aspects of cross-Strait economic and political relations, political leadership matters. In the last two years of Ma administration (2014–2016), leaders of the two sides of the Taiwan Strait need to develop new mechanisms of top-down initiatives of cross-Strait rapprochement to lay a more solid foundation for future cooperation.

Reinterpreting Taiwan's democracy and identity: The social aspect of cross-Strait and triangular relations

For a long period of time, the focus of Taiwan's democratic development has been concentrated on electoral politics and institutional reforms. The current democratic institutions, which are the result of political compromise after several rounds of constitutional amendments, reflect the partial reality of Taiwan's democratic politics. Under such institutional arrangements, electoral concerns will distort policy rationality and constrain any potential breakthrough in cross-Strait relations. Furthermore, the rise of Taiwanese consciousness has been politicized to distinguish different identities in the Mainland and Taiwan.

The empowerment of a robust civil society is a dynamic aspect of Taiwanese democracy. The dynamic civil society has been realized through the work of energetic NGOs, grassroots activities and community-building efforts. These bottom–up forces have put democratic wheels in motion and promoted social developments in Taiwan. The social dynamics in Taiwan will serve as a catalyst to recreate social linkages with the other side of the Taiwan strait. In addition to the complex social and economic impacts of opening Taiwan to Mainland Chinese visitors and tourists, institutionalizing of student exchanges have far-reaching impacts on integration at the grassroots level. Past studies on the shortage of spillover effects from economic integration to political cooperation focus on unilateral investments from Taiwan to China. After 2008, the social interaction based on student exchanges has been conducted in both directions.

Even though Taiwan's legislature has put in place various institutional hurdles for the incoming mainland Chinese students, dynamic young people from the mainland will certainly bring back seeds of understanding on the real aspects of Taiwanese society to China. Since these students will stay in Taiwan for a longer period of time for academic exchanges or to pursue degrees, their penetration capacities will be much greater than those of businesspeople. Bright or dark, the real face of a different ethnic Chinese society will be exposed to the young minds of the new Mainland Chinese. At the same time, mainland Chinese students provide the necessary stimulus for Taiwanese students to understand the mindset on the other side of the Taiwan strait. Such interaction lays a much more solid foundation for mutual understanding and learning than that which had existed prior.

Literature on the trilateral relationship mentions the change of Taiwan's national identity and deems it as one of the major sources of instability. Figure 1, a survey conducted by the Election Studies Center of National Chengchi University, demonstrates the decline of Chinese identity and rise of Taiwanese identity over the past 20 years. The data need further elaboration in order to understand the implications beyond the statistics.

The gradual shift of identity is the reflection of the change of socialization themes in Taiwan since democratization. On one hand, the education system under Taiwan's authoritarian era focused on the legitimacy of the Republic of China (ROC) on Taiwan government in Taiwan to represent the whole of China. Knowledge of Taiwanese history for school children was limited or even prohibited. Re-emphasizing domestic affairs is a means to return to the normal course of learning about one's own homeland. On the other hand, a more exclusive socialization angle, especially after the DPP came to power, was politically motivated to redefine the legitimacy

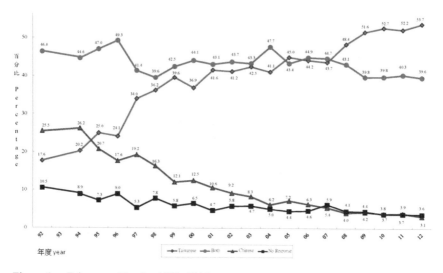

Figure 1:   Taiwanese identity 1992–2012

Source: Election Studies Center, National Chengchi University http://esc.nccu.edu.tw/modules/tinyd2/content/tonduID.htm.

of the ROC as limited only to Taiwan. Under the new educational scheme under the DPP, the Mainland was treated as a foreign and hostile country.

The choice of terms used to identify the other side of the Taiwan strait has undergone changes in Taiwan as well. Before the end of 1990s, the term "Chinese people" (Zhongguoren, 中國人) had more comprehensive cultural, ethnic and political implications. Recognizing oneself as Chinese did not mean identification with the PRC regime on the mainland. After the year 2000, however, the term "Chinese" began to have exclusive political meaning to refer to the PRC. In other words, the decline of Chinese identity after 2000 reflects the refusal to identify with the PRC. Still, despite this change in connotation, such a decline does not necessarily imply that Taiwanese tend to separate their cultural identity from the "Chinese" in a broader sense.

Another dimension that deserves further attention is the decline of "double identity" compared to "Taiwan identity" after Ma came to power in 2008. There are two possible explanations for this tendency. First of all, as Ma reopened the door for cross-Strait dialogue and China responded positively, the Taiwanese public sensed the need for a new stance to hold bilateral interactions. From a strategic point of view, a sharp and shining brand is necessary before striding toward the negotiation table. No other option would be better than the brand name of Taiwan. Secondly, Ma's victory in 2008 provided a unique opportunity for Taiwanese to embrace the new Taiwanese identity with confidence. Ma's platform is to develop a more inclusive definition of Taiwan to include indigenous as well as Chinese cultures. Being Taiwanese, under Ma's banner, signifies a new, broader horizon for embracing Chinese as well as local culture. Double identity encounters political hurdles of political loyalty, as the term "China" has become a political symbol instead of a cultural one.

Last but not least, the rise of Taiwanese identity does not mean the rise of radical drives for independence. As the preceding analyses show, the more comprehensive and strategic content of the new Taiwanese identity does not necessarily create instability for cross-Strait relations. The rise of Taiwanese identity does not equate to an abandonment of ROC legitimacy and a rush toward *de jure* independence. Figure 2 demonstrates the more prudent attitude of the Taiwanese people toward independence and reunification. For the past 20 years, radical attitudes toward immediate independence have consistently been a minority among the Taiwanese public. Tendencies toward independence have gained more support, but more than 60% of Taiwanese still prefer the *status quo*. The more significant tendency will be the rise in the attitude of "maintaining the *status quo* indefinitely" after 2007. Such a tendency is parallel with the sharper rise of Taiwanese identity and relative decline of double identity in Taiwan.

It has always been a puzzle to explain the substantial content of the term "status quo" in the Taipei–Beijing–Washington triangle. Ma's policy aims at guaranteeing to the United States that Taiwan

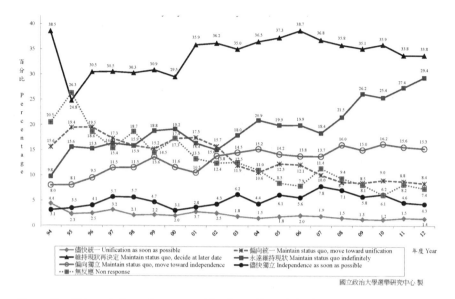

Figure 2:   Taiwan indeoendence *vs.* unification with Mainland 1994–2012

Source: Election Studies Center, National Chengchi University. http://esc.nccu.edu.tw/modules/tinyd2/content/tonduID.htms.

will not cross the "red line" toward *de jure* independence. Keeping the *status quo* across the Taiwan strait and providing no surprises to the United States will help stabilize the American strategic situation. However, the two major political parties in Taiwan differ in their interpretation of the *status quo*. For the KMT under Ma's administration, sovereignty of the ROC, according to the existing constitution, still covers the Mainland even though administrative capacities are limited to Taiwan and its offshore islands. Such a separation of sovereignty and administrative power provides the theoretical basis for "one China, different interpretations" under the 1992 consensus. The DPP rejects the KMT's argument on the sovereignty issue, and insists that both administrative power and sovereignty of the ROC are confined to Taiwan. The long-term goal of the DPP is to achieve Taiwan's independence, according to its party platform. The *status quo* is regarded as the consensus among

Taiwan, United States and China to maintain cross-Strait stability. In any case, preserving the *status quo* does not mean freezing the current situation as it is. Substantial steps based on political realism and flexible adjustments are required to maintain the changing stability.

Since the DPP lost control of the presidency in 2008 and became the opposition party its Mainland policy provides a contrast to Ma's policy guideline of "one China, different interpretations." From the DPP's viewpoint, Ma's policy is to downgrade Taiwan's sovereignty as a "region" under the authority of the PRC. The DPP insists that no government should exclude any possibility for Taiwan's future, including independence. It argues that Ma's policy will eventually lead to final unification with China. The DPP continues to promote its long-standing platform that Taiwan's future should be decided by the Taiwanese people themselves, as this is the natural right for people in a democratic country. In a Policy Briefing Session organized by the DPP headquarters, the DPP indicated the following principles regarding Taiwan's sovereignty:

(1) All options are open, with no foreclosure of any option;
(2) People on Taiwan have the right to make their own decisions;
(3) Decisions are to be made solely by the people of Taiwan.[20]

The DPP's platform of public sovereignty is buttressed by the argument that cross-Strait relations should be based on Taiwan's public opinion, not the goodwill produced by Hu Jintao's Six Points. Decisions on pertinent issues, such as the ECFA and Taiwan's future, must be approved by referendum. Such decisions could neither be made unilaterally by KMT, nor by the government in China.[21]

---

[20] DPP Headquarters Press Release, Policy Briefing Session for Diplomats and Foreign Representatives, September 26, 2008.
[21] DPP Headquarters Press Release, December 31, 2009.

The DPP's 2012 Presidential candidate Tsai Ing-wen expressed clearly that meaningful dialogues between the DPP and CCP are possible only if no preconditions are enforced. One such "precondition" refers to the recognition of the one-China principle.[22] On various occasions, Tsai has put forth her theory of "peaceful but different" and "peaceful and seeking commonality" to solve the cross-Strait puzzle. In Tsai's words, "peaceful" refers to peaceful development for Taiwan and China. The two sides of the Taiwan strait are different from one another, historically, politically, with respect to beliefs and within society. She argues that the KMT policies on cross-Strait relations are "peace aiming at unification, peace leading to unification".[23]

The real agenda for Tsai's theory on cross-Strait relations is actually peace without putting reunification as a pre-condition. By "acknowledging" Beijing's one-China principle, Tsai replaces Ma's compromise on "One China, separate interpretations" with her "Taiwan consensus". The gist of the Taiwan consensus is focused on Taiwan's democratic system and rejection of China's authoritarian one-party control. The "Taiwan Consensus," which was included in the "Ten-Year Political Platform of the DPP" in 2011, argues that the 1992 consensus was achieved by two authoritarian parties without conferring with the Taiwanese people. The DPP indicates that a new Taiwan consensus, through the democratic process in Taiwan, should be created before sitting down at the negotiation table. In other words, the 1992 consensus lacks legitimacy in the new democratic regime of Taiwan.[24] The Taiwan Consensus appeal has sent a strong signal to bind Taiwan's democracy with international drives to resist China's recent assertive foreign policy behaviors.

---

[22] DPP Headquarters Press Release of the 66th Meeting of Central Standing Committee of 13th National Committee, May 12, 2010.

[23] Tsai tackles cross-Strait relations, *Taipei Times*, February 24, 2011.

[24] Tsai Ing-wen's remarks at the American Enterprises Institute, September 13, 2011. Released by the Department of Foreign Affairs, DPP; for full text of the Ten Year Political Platform, please refer to http://10.iing.tw/2011/08/blog-post_9219.html.

In contrast to Ma's policies to search for a cross-Strait break-through as the first priority to proceed to globalization and improvement of relations with the United States, the DPP faces the challenge developing a new relationship with China and regaining the confidence of the United States. The official policy of the DPP was still to regard the U.S. as the most important and reliable partner to protect Taiwan's security. At the same time, the DPP has put strengthening international alliances as the bargaining chip to resist the pressures from the rise of China. It is DPP's calculation that Taiwan should ally with other Asian countries to cope with the hegemonic attempts of China. Under the current asymmetrical conditions, Taiwan needs to put cross-Strait relations in a multilateral rather than a bilateral context.

In January 2013, DPP Chairman Su Tseng-chang visited Japan. This was a controversial move considering the Sino–Japanese rivalry exacerbated by the ongoing dispute over the Diaoyu Islands. During his visit, Su promoted the idea of a "democratic alliance" incorporating the United States, Japan, South Korea and Taiwan to resist "other forces" that heighten the intensity of the East Asia region. Su put special emphasis on the continuous dialogues and cooperation among member states which enjoy the same universal values of democracy, human rights, liberty and the rule of law.[25]

Su's statement echoes Japanese Prime Minister Abe's arguments for "Asia's Democratic Security Diamond," which includes the United States, Japan, Australia and India. It also continues the policy line of former Taiwanese President Chen Shui-bian's "common value alliance" for Taiwan, the United States and Japan. The Mainland Chinese responses to Su's statement were loud and clear. In an editorial of a major newspaper, the Chinese side condemned Su's pro-Japan, anti-China policy and stubborn independence

---

[25]DPP Press Release, February 8, 2013. http://www.dpp.org.tw/news_content. php?sn=6478.

lines.[26] A very direct attack came from Yang Liqing, spokesperson of the Taiwan Affairs Office of the PRC's State Council. As Yang stated, Su's remarks in Japan "focus only on parochial personal interests and lose the basic spirit of Chinese nationality. Such flattery [of Japan] is shameless and will be condemned by all Chinese people unanimously."[27]

A different approach was adopted by the DPP Presidential candidate of 2012, Tsai Ing-wen. Tsai's concession speech in 2012 was well received in domestic and international circles. Instead of pushing Taiwan's democracy in the anti-China front, Tsai devoted herself to grassroots empowerment and community-building efforts to rebuild bottom–up support for her political future. In a recent report at the end of 2012, Tsai indicates that

> "...Some said that the hostile environment between political parties impeded political development in Taiwan. Today, one-party rule leads to the confrontation between the state and society, as the public opinions couldn't be heard by the Ma administration...
>
> "To achieve great political and social reforms not only requires the negotiation between ruling and opposition parties but also requires the re-empowerment of civil society, so that we can assist and supervise the government to realize reforms. ...If everyone began the process by paying attention to their communities and expanded that effort to public policies, the action and efforts would converge and ultimately become a power that could change the country."[28]

Because its time is limited, the Ma administration has to create strategic alliances to enhance the "democratic advantage" instead of deadlock. The existing forum of KMT–CCP talks should continue to serve as a platform of track 1.5 interactions between the two sides

---

[26] *Minjindang Meiri Kangzhong shi Sulu Yitiao* (DPP's alliance with Japan to confront China is a dead end), *Huanqiu Shibao*, February 7, 2013. http://opinion.huanqiu.com/editorial/2013-02/3626735.html.

[27] *Xinhua News*, February 5, 2013. http://news.xinhuanet.com/tw/2013-02/05/c_124327389.htm.

[28] Tsai Ing-wen, Xiegei 2013 de taiwan (a Letter to Taiwan of 2013), December 31, 2012. http://www.thinkingtaiwan.com/public/articles/view/408.

of the Taiwan strait. However, it is not practical to exclude the DPP from future negotiations with the Mainland side. The Ma administration should keep a neutral stance toward the new contacts between the DPP and Mainland China. The plural, if not opposing, viewpoints from the DPP will help demonstrate the complex domestic situation in Taiwan on sensitive political issues. If utilized smartly, these could be valuable bargaining chips for Taipei. Misunderstandings between the CCP and DPP will deter the KMT from deeper integration in the next stage as well as putting achievements at risk to a change of ruling parties. The political wisdom to neutralize or transform the pro-independence forces in Taiwan will have long-term impacts on more positive cross-Strait interactions.

Multiple faces of culture politics and inclusive cooperation

The preceding sections demonstrate the political and social aspects of Taiwan's domestic change and their impact on cross-Strait and triangular relations. This section will introduce the interplay of the state-centered approach and social dimensions of political change, utilizing the recent development of cultural interaction to discuss whether culture could serve as a fresh platform for win–win solution between the three actors involved.

Culture serves as the base of norms and a value system of foreign relations. It is also an instrument to perform certain functions in domestic as well as international politics. The Chinese government indicates that the peaceful development of China is based on its cultural tradition, economic globalization and changes in the international security environment. In a white paper on China's Peaceful Development released by the State Council in 2011, the Chinese government argues:

"The Chinese people have always cherished a world view of "unity without uniformity," "harmony between man and nature," and "harmony is invaluable." This belief calls for the fostering of harmonious family bond,

> *neighborhood harmony and good interpersonal relationships. Under the influence of the culture of harmony, peace-loving has been deeply ingrained in the Chinese character.*"[29]

It seems that the official line of the Chinese government presumes that Chinese culture is unitary and coherent. The Chinese government stresses the harmonious part of the culture, and uses it as a glue to achieve domestic unity. In addition to nationalism, the Chinese government tries to integrate traditional culture with the socialist ideology as the basis of regime legitimacy. Hu Jintao indicated in the 18th Party Congress Report:

> "...*We must create a new surge in promoting socialist culture and bring about its great development and enrichment, increase China's cultural soft power, and enable culture to guide social trends, educate the people, serve society, and boost development....*
>
> ... *We should continue to adapt Marxism to China's conditions in keeping up with the times and increase its appeal to the people.*"[30]

Furthermore, to alleviate the international skepticism on the rise of China, the Chinese government utilizes the rejuvenation of traditional Chinese culture as a useful tool to improve its international image. The Chinese government also promotes culture as a bridge to link Chinese domestic dynamics with economic globalization. At the same time, the Chinese government endeavors to integrate market forces to transfer the traditional culture into culture and creative business. As the 18th Party Congress report indicates:

> "*.....The strength and international competitiveness of Chinese culture are an important indicator of China's power and prosperity and the renewal of the Chinese nation. We should invigorate state-owned non-profit cultural institutions, improve corporate governance of profit-oriented cultural*

---

[29] China's Peaceful Development, Information Office of the State Council, the People's Republic of China, September, 2011, Beijing.

[30] http://news.xinhuanet.com/english/special/18cpcnc/2012-11/17/c_131981259.htm.

entities, and create a thriving cultural market. We should open the cultural
sector wider to the outside world and draw on cultural achievements of
other countries. We should foster a fine environment that enables a large
number of talented cultural figures, particularly eminent cultural figures
and representatives of Chinese culture, to distinguish themselves in artistic
pursuit. We should honor cultural personalities with outstanding
contribution."[31]

Culture industry has been utilized by the Chinese government as a useful tool to link market values and expand international influences — so-called Chinese soft power. According to the statistics of the Chinese Ministry of Culture, the Chinese cultural business contributes only 4% of the global market share, while the United States, European Union, Japan and South Korea shares are 43%, 34%, 10% and 5% respectively. Such a weak performance does not match China's status as the world's second ranked economic power. As shown in China's first Soft Power Blue Book, the basic situation of a "Strong West, Weak East" in an international cultural context has remained the same in the past decade. The Chinese government thus pushes hard to grasp the "voice power" in the global setting to resist the Western domination of the international mass communication channels. China also argues that cultural soft power must be backed up by an economic and military "hard power."[32]

The rise of China's cultural power is closely related to the domestic restructuring of its cultural bureaucracies. The Chinese analysts argue that the government's efforts to break down the Western monopoly over the international cultural system have to be buttressed by cultural diversity on domestic soil. Enhancement of international soft power is rooted in domestic reform of the cultural sector.[33] Lack

---

[31] http://news.xinhuanet.com/english/special/18cpcnc/2012-11/17/c_131981259.htm.
[32] *Zhongguo Ruanshili Lanpishu* (*The Blue Paper on China's soft power*), Beijing, Shehui kexue wenxian chubanshe, 2011.
[33] Qixue Zhang, "Zai duiwai jiaoliuzhong qieshi weihu guojia wenhua anquan (Protecting cultural security while promoting international cultural interaction), *Guangming Ribao*, April 11, 2012.

of coordination among competing governmental sectors leads to the fragmentation of policy innovation and implementation. These culture-bound bureaucracies include the CCP Propaganda Department, Ministry of Culture Affairs, Broadcast and TV General Bureau, Press and Publication Agency, Press Office of the State Council, Ministry of Commerce, National Commission of Development and Reform, Ministry of Finance, Ministry of Education, and Ministry of Foreign Affairs. Meanwhile the Chinese government has promoted the reform of corporatization of state cultural sector enterprises since the period of the 11th Five Year Plan. Over time, large state-owned cultural enterprise groups have emerged.

The Chinese government also attaches great importance to cultural factors in its Taiwan policy. In the 18th Party Congress report, Hu indicated that:

"We should expand cultural exchanges to enhance a common sense of national identity. We should encourage the compatriots on both sides of the Taiwan Straits to unite and pursue a common endeavor. The compatriots on both sides belong to the same Chinese nation and form a community of common destiny bound by blood ties."[34]

However, cultural exchanges must be based on the unchaged principle of One China and national unification. Cultural exchange is aimed at facilitating the process of peaceful reunification:

"Although the mainland and Taiwan are yet to be reunified, the fact that both belong to one China has never changed. China's territory and sovereignty have always been indivisible and no division will be tolerated. The two sides of the Taiwan Straits should uphold the common stand of opposing Taiwan independence and of following the 1992 Consensus. Both sides should increase their common commitment to upholding the one-China framework and, on this basis, expand common ground and set aside differences."

---

[34]http://news.xinhuanet.com/english/special/18cpcnc/2012-11/17/c_131981259.htm.

Sun Yafu, the Deputy Director of the Taiwan Affairs Office of the State Council, indicates that promoting cross-Taiwan Strait relations must be based on cultural dynamics. Economic and cultural development must reach a balance. Promoting the common culture will serve as a spiritual linkage to enhance common identity, and thus realize the rejuvenation of the Chinese nation.[35] More moderate Chinese experts notice the differences between Chinese and Taiwanese culture due to their different historical paths over the past decades. These differences are rooted in political struggles since 1949 across the Taiwan Strait. Basic values of traditional culture are shared by both Mainland China and Taiwan, but the mainland should not jump to conclusions about the omnipotence of the culture power in promoting unification.[36]

The hard-liners' version of the cultural explanation of cross-Strait relations could be found in the work of Xin Qi.[37] His major points are also echoed by like-minded Chinese experts on cross-Strait relations. Xin's explanation of Chinese culture is closely linked with political functions of national unification. Xin puts national unification as one of the core traditional cultural values in Chinese history. According to Xin, most of the heroes in Chinese history were those who fought for national unification. National unification is the pre-condition for harmonious development across the Taiwan Strait. The contingent and moderate policies adopted by the Chinese government are to promote national unification, instead of solidifying the *status quo* across the Taiwan Strait.

---

[35] Yafu Sun, "*Liangan guanxi heping fazhan ying bansui zhonghua wenhua dafayang* (*Cross-Strait relations must be based on glorifying Chinese culture*), Taiwan Affairs Office, January 19, 2011. http://big5.gwytb.gov.cn/newsb/201101/t20110124_1729871.htm.

[36] Xintian Yu, Liangan guanxi zhongde wenhua renshi wenti (Cultural understanding in cross-Strait relations), *Taiwan Yanjiu*, January 2010, pp. 1–6.

[37] Xin Qi is currently holding many Taiwan-related positions, including the Chairman of Association of Promoting Chinese Culture. He is regarded as one of the main supporters of the hard line of cross-Strait relations.

Xin's culture theory is the extension of his power-centered approach to cross-Strait relations. Against the current tide of re-evaluating republican (*Minguo*, 民國) cultural legacies on Mainland China, Xin devalues the humanitarian tradition of the May Fourth and *Minguo* period. To Xin, in order to refine Chinese culture, great efforts must be made to integrate traditional heritage with Marxism and Mao Zedong thoughts. Xin emphasizes the spillover effects of Chinese culture to the surrounding East Asian region. To Xin, if China does not promote or refresh its own culture, Chinese traditional heritage will be "stolen" by neighboring countries.

The power-centered cultural theory has specific implications for cross-Strait relations. Xin judges that regardless of political differences, Chinese nationality identification on the two sides of the Taiwan strait remains unchanged. In terms of respecting Taiwan's public opinion on independence and unification, Xin argues that the public opinion of 1.3 billion people on the Mainland will outnumber the 23 million who make up the population of Taiwan. The reality of the Taiwan strait, Xin emphasizes, is the large gaps in Gross Domestic Product (GDP) and diplomatic recognition between Taiwan and the Mainland. According to Chinese cultural tradition, the PRC is the "main legitimacy" while the ROC is a "subordinate legitimacy". The subordinate regime enjoys some administration power in specific regions, but the ownership and sovereignty of China remain unchanged. The tolerance of the main legitimate regime, as seen in the current PRC policies toward Taiwan, reflects the inclusiveness of traditional Chinese culture based on the motherland. Based on a common culture and national interests, the two sides of the Taiwan Strait should resist the intervention of foreign forces into the domestic affairs of the Chinese nation.[38]

---

[38]Qi Xin, Hongyang zhonghua wenhua chuantong, chixu tuidong liangan guanxi heping fazhan (Maintain Chinese cultural tradition, continue to promote peaceful development across the Taiwan strait), *Zhongguo Pinglun*, No. 178, October, 2012, pp. 20–24.

By contrast, in the context of cross-Strait relations the Taiwanese president Ma Ying-jeou's cultural statements could be understood from two main aspects. Ma argues that Taiwan will be the standard-bearer at the leading edge of Chinese culture. Among all the ethnically Chinese societies, Confucian values are practiced more widely and more seriously in Taiwan than anywhere else. The implication is that in terms of Chinese culture, Taiwan plays the legitimate role in maintaining and renewing the traditional value system of Chinese culture. Secondly, Chinese culture provides opportunities for the two sides to delve into traditional insights of co-existence. As Ma argued in his second inaugural address:

"In light of our common Chinese heritage, people on both sides should do their utmost to jointly contribute to the international community without engaging in vicious competition and the waste of resources. I firmly believe that Taiwan and mainland China are open minded enough to find a way to attain peace and co-prosperity."[39]

Ma's cultural statements demonstrate the instrumentalism of culture in cross-Strait relations. However, Ma stresses that Taiwan is the real successor of traditional Chinese culture. The "cultural legitimacy" also narrows the power gap between the mainland and Taiwan. The traditional wisdom of Chinese culture could be utilized to create a win–win situation of co-existence, but the relationship of the two sides must be based on equal footing. In other words, Chinese culture is developed by the Ma administration to enhance, instead of weaken, Taiwan's cultural supremacy when faced with the rise of China. The Taiwanese Culture Minister Lung Ying-tai also indicated in a speech at George Washington University that Taiwan provides an alternative and unique cultural option for the world with its democratic experiences. Lung expressed her hope that China will learn to acknowledge Taiwan's freedom of thought

---

[39] Ma Ying-jeou's inaugural speech, May 20, 2012.

and expression and adopt a softer position toward global society and to its people.[40]

The pro-Taiwan independence experts argue that the culture factor explains the difference, instead of integration, between China and Taiwan. Chinese culture is just one of the several major components of contemporary Taiwanese culture which incorporates Japanese, American, and indigenous heritages. Equating Taiwanese culture with Chinese culture was socially constructed during the KMT rule of the authoritarian era. Such efforts do not reflect the current situation in Taiwan.[41] Furthermore, the veteran independence supporter Gu Kuanmin introduces the traditional Chinese concept of brotherhood to describe current cross-Strait relations. Gu argues that since Chinese culture stresses that the elder brother should take care of his younger sibling, China should recognize Taiwan as an independent country and help Taiwan join the United Nations. In return, Taiwan will keep a close relationship with China based on brotherhood, and promises not to join any anti-China alliances in the world.[42]

Other Taiwanese experts also criticize Ma Ying-jeou's soft-power arguments and culture-based approaches toward China. Lin Cheng-yi, for example, postulates that the soft power must be based on hard power. The one-China precondition limits Taiwan's space for maneuvering or employing hard power. Such a retreat will eventually invalidate the utilities of soft power and cultural diplomacy. Michael Hsiao and Yang Hao also indicate that China's Confucius

---

[40] Soft Power in Hard Times: Minister Lung's DC speech emphasizes Taiwan's civil culture and right of international participation, Press Release, Ministry of Culture, August 29, 2012.

[41] Canhong Zhang, Wenhua: taiwan shehui de xindongneng (Culture: New dynamics of Taiwanese Society), World United Formosans for Independence (WUFI), June 5, 2012. http://www.wufi.org.tw/%E6%96%87%E5%8C%96%EF%BC%9A%E5%8F%B0%E7%81%A3%E7%A4%BE%E6%9C%83%E7%9A%84%E6%96%B0%E5%8B%95%E8%83%BD/.

[42] Kuanmin Ku, Xiongdi zhibang: zhongguo zengci yu liangan guanxi chuyi (Nations of brotherhood: A preliminary suggestion on cross-Strait relations), Xintaiwan Guoce Zhiku, October 29, 2012. http://traaworld.blogspot.tw/2012/10/blog-post_29.html.

institutions carry political, rather than cultural, purposes of international interactions. Such plans will weaken China's public diplomacy and eventually create negative effects on China's image building.[43]

In brief, this section demonstrates multiple faces of the utilities of cultural factors in cross-Strait relations. Taiwan and Mainland China share the same Chinese culture tradition, but such commonality is not enough to lay a solid foundation for inclusiveness. States of the two sides develop the instrumentalism of culture to connect political sovereignty and uniqueness. Therefore the function of culture provides mixed effects on deepening political cooperation between Beijing and Taipei.

Conclusion

Taiwan is the minor but key player in the triangular relationship among Washington, Beijing and Taipei. However, for quite a long period of time, Taiwan was labeled as a troublemaker and a deterrent to the development of a cooperative mechanism between China and the United States. Recent debates on the United States abandonment of Taiwan in order to stabilize the bilateral relationship between Washington and Beijing are the reflection of such policy concerns.

In the triangular relationship, Taiwan's policies toward the United States have been consistent over the past half-century. In terms of national security, the United States is the only protector of Taiwan and its survival under the military threat from China. Economically speaking, the United States provided the major market for Taiwan's exports which helped create an economic miracle

---

[43] Cheng-I Lin, Dongya jushi yu taiwan yinying (East Asian situation and Taiwan's policies), New Taiwan Think Tank, July 19, 2012. http://www.braintrust.tw/article_detail/1225; Michael Hsiao and Hao Yang, Kongzi xueyuan and zhongguo ruanshili (Confucius Institutes and China's soft power diplomacy), 2012, *Diyi Zhiku:* http://opinion.m4.cn/2012-07/1173500.shtml.

during the Cold War era. The United States served as the main source of technological know-how and talent flows for Taiwan to embrace the global division of labor in the high-tech sectors. At the same time, the United States also drew a "red line" against *de jure* independence for Taiwan to guarantee that the *status quo* across the Taiwan strait would remain under United States control and manipulation. Taiwan's heavy security and economic reliance on the United States in reality constrain the autonomy of Taiwanese leaders to make radical shifts in their policies toward China.

The more unstable aspect of the triangle is cross-Strait relations between Mainland China and Taiwan. This paper attempts to develop an "inside-out" explanation of the domestic linkages of Taiwan's policies toward China. It argues that the understanding of cross-Strait relations must be put in the context of historical evolution, changes of perceptions, and cultural and social interactions. The analyses in this paper demonstrate that the Taiwanese state is not a coherent unit of policy making. Both the KMT and DPP camps share the same goal to continue the long-standing relations with the United States, but differ in the basic policy lines toward Taiwan's future relations with the other side of the strait. The current KMT administration under Ma Ying-jeou adopts pro-engagement policies toward Beijing. However, Beijing is still suspicious about Ma's continuous hedging policies, arms procurements from the United States, and the ambiguous attitude toward talks on future political agreements. A more severe test on whether the cornerstone of cross-Strait stability can be maintained may occur in 2016 or 2020 if the DPP returns to power. Given the fact that DPP can likely count on around 40% of Taiwan's popular vote, its return to the center stage of Taiwanese politics is indeed a possible scenario for the future.

The state-centered analysis provides a more unpredictable picture on the cross-Strait side of the triangle. The social aspect of interaction, by contrast, provides a more optimistic estimation based on prudence and increased contact. As the preceding pages demonstrate, the rise of Taiwan identity does not equate to tendencies toward an independent Taiwanese nation. A dichotomous explanation between Taiwanese and Chinese culture loses explanatory power in Taiwan. The rise of Taiwanese identity must be put into the long-term evolution of Taiwanese history since the 19th century of the first Sino–Japanese war. By the same token, a new Taiwanese culture incorporates historical factors of Chinese, Japanese and American influences and heritages. The New Taiwanese identity and culture in turn empower a robust civil society in Taiwan.

It is unrealistic to expect cross-Strait peace to endure based simply on the KMT continuously holding power in Taiwan. Radical, pro-independence voices in Taiwan will sustain and should be acknowledged. One of the most salient achievements of the Ma administration was to make the first step toward institutionalizing social interactions of the two sides of the Taiwan Strait. Such efforts help China as well as Taiwan understand the reality of the two societies. However, Taiwan's "Sun Flower Movement", erupted in the spring of 2015 against the Service Trade Agreement with Mainland China, demonstrated the increasing anxiety on the political and social impacts of closer economic links. Such social atmosphere among the general public indirectly weakened the grass-root supports of the Ma administration and led to the landslide victory of the DPP in the local election in the end of 2014. The poor domestic economic performance, plus the general suspicion on deepening the cross-Strait economic relations, erodes the power base of the Ma administration.

The new social and cultural dynamics between Taiwan and China help the two sides come toward the middle ground of an inclusive relationship. Such institutionalized interaction does not mean the immediate integration of the two sides. The case of Hong Kong's social resistance toward Mainland Chinese visitors provides an alarming sign for the future management of cultural and social interactions. A mature civilian governance model will levy political constraints on political parties if they try to reverse the social trend of more cooperative development. Furthermore, the increasing complementary relations of the cultural industry between the Mainland and Taiwan link market factors with social integration. The cultural industry thus integrates economic interests, global culture, and domestic factors. The new cultural scheme will have far-reaching effects of social learning and understanding.

Part 2: Outside the Triangle

Chapter 4

Rethinking the Triangle: Possibilities and Pitfalls

Yufan Hao

University of Macau

Since the United States sent its Seventh Fleet to the Taiwan Strait after the outbreak of the Korean War in June 1950, there has existed a triangular relation between Washington, Beijing and Taipei. After 60 years of dynamic change in both global and East Asian regional contexts, the nature of the triangle has also substantially changed. Each set of bilateral economic relationships within the triangle has never been better, yet the increasing trust gap between the United States and China, the two bigger players in this triangle, has cast the third player and Asia more generally into uncertainty over the future direction of the triangle.

China's increasing economic and military capabilities have been the salient agent of change within the triangle. The spectacular performance of the Chinese economy over the last three decades has put China on the center of the world stage. With its GDP quadrupling in less than 16 years, China has become the world's economic powerhouse. Every day seems to bring new astonishing figures from China: China has become the largest trading state; China's foreign reserves exceed the two trillion dollar mark; China surpasses the United States to become the largest automobile market; China launches its first stealth jetfighter and its first aircraft-carrier, and so on. Within the span of a single generation, China has moved from near isolation to become the hub of the globalized economy, and from an obsolete and bloated military to a much more professional force possessing increasing degrees of high-tech excellence.

While China has become the world's fastest growing economy, the American economy grew by only 3% from 2008 to 2012. As China's influence has become increasingly expansive both within Asia and in other regions of the world, there is increasing concern in the United States that China may become the most fearful challenger to American interests. The media talk about China's thirst for global oil, and China's investment in strategically important regions of the world. Newspapers are full of stories about how China's economic achievement challenges United States manufacturers and service providers. Academia is talking about China's soft power offensive and China's neocolonialism. China's destruction of a satellite using one of its missiles in 2007 alarmed many military planners in the West. How should the United States respond to this newly emerged great power? Should Beijing be viewed as an impending adversary or a friendly competitor? Washington seems to have started another national debate over China just as it had 65 years ago over the former Soviet Union at the end of World War II.

As China's economic power grows, the economic relationship between Beijing and Taipei have also never been better, and Beijing has become Taiwan's largest trade partner and largest export market. Nevertheless, the fluidity of domestic politics in Taiwan has also cast huge doubts about future direction of cross-strait relations, and people widely speculate that the Democratic Progressive Party (DPP) may come back to power in 2016. Indeed, the best moment in the economic triangle is shadowed by the worst of the security triangle. Why has economic interdependence not brought expected improvement in the triangle?

To better understand this puzzle in the Washington–Beijing–Taipei (W–B–T) triangle is not only theoretically significant, but carries with it tremendous policy implications. Womack suggests that we view this W–B–T triangle from a new perspective. Since this asymmetric triangle has both security and economic dimensions, he believes that the security triangle has been more important and decisive to the whole triangle relationship, as it determines the fundamental stability of relations. However, the security triangle seems to have undergone significant changes over the last 30 years and has become increasingly unstable. In the 1980s, the United States, the strongest power within the triangle, was in the pivot position because its weight plus either of the other two was decisive, and therefore it was only interested in avoiding crises and maintaining its controlling position. The pivot was thus a *status quo* peace-holder. China as the middle power was the frustrated one, since it could imagine being able to resolve its conflict with the third power only if the pivot would not interfere. Taipei as the smallest player in the triangle was the anxious one since its fate was in the hands of the largest. The expected courses of policy, therefore, have been that the smallest tries to bind the largest to the triangle, while the middle power tried to break the relationship. The largest was thus the center of attention, and as long as the *status quo* prevailed, its position is advantageous with minimal costs.

Since 2008, the W–B–T security triangle has become fundamentally unstable and uncertain. Each leg of the triangle has become more complex in terms of security concerns. The rivalry in the relationship between Washington and Beijing has intensified globally, although each side recognizes that it needs the other in many facets of global governance. The drastic increase of China's economic and military power has profoundly changed the nature of the security triangle. As Womack notes, "Washington must choose between its advantages of high profile and the increasing risk of high cost and perhaps failure." Taipei has been trying desperately to maintain Washington's involvement for fear that they may break the triangle by yielding to China. China is in a stronger position with both the other two players and can decide to risk breaking the triangle.

Womack develops an alternative model of an opportunity-driven, inclusive W–B–T triangle. He argues that the exclusivist mentality of the security triangle actually increases security risks by distracting us from the significance of improving relationships. Therefore, the W–B–T security triangle should be revisited in order to change from the current "zero-sum mentality in this triangle relationship into a positive, constructive and inclusive mentality, the one in which improvements between any two sides benefits the third partner."

I agree with Womack's idea and his insightful analysis of the dynamic nature of this triangle. The W–B–T triangle indeed needs new and creative thinking. It is true that better cross-straits relations reduce security risks and offer a variety of opportunities. And better relations between China and the United States could be reassuring rather than alarming to Taiwan. Better United States–Taiwan relations could also further expand China's opportunities. It would be better that we should have an overall conception of interrelationship that fits reality, promotes mutual interests and leads to a win–win–win situation.

However, the reality also points in other possible directions. The mutual distrust between the United States and China may change their bilateral relations from the current benign competition to antagonistic confrontation, leaving Taiwan to either "abandon" Washington or "abandon" Beijing. If Taipei took such provocative action, Washington and Beijing may be dragged into a crisis over the Taiwan Straits that culminate in a lose–lose–lose outcome. Womack asks several important questions: Are the political, social and economic trends of the triangle moving closer to or further from confrontation? Does the increasing interconnection of the Taiwanese economy with the Mainland make it more or less likely to take desperate action? Under what circumstances is China likely to pursue a military option?

To answer these questions, we may need to examine if the economic interaction in the triangle is able to reduce tension and increase mutual trust in the long run. Or, whether the economic interactions between the three players have had virtually no impact on political and military trust within the triangle?

Does economic interdependence promote amity?

It is quite common to assume that economic integration may reduce the risk of military confrontation. Based on the assumption of classical liberalism, more extensive contacts between nations foster greater chances for peace because nations who rely upon one another economically cannot afford a war that may disrupt their daily life. Furthermore, more cultural contacts between nations may make people more sensitive to others' concerns. Beijing's policies towards Taiwan, Hong Kong and Macao are conducted under these assumptions.

China and the United States have become economically interdependent. China's trade with the United States was 14.7% of its overall trade in 2004. From 2003–2004, the volume of United States–China trade increased by 34% and the volume of United States import from China increased by 32%. According to the statistics of the World Trade Organization, China's exports to the United States were 17.1% of its total exports in 2011, and China's imports from the United States were 7.1% of its total imports in 2011. On the other hand, the United States' exports to China were 7.0% of its total exports in 2011, and the United States' imports from China were 18.4% in 2011. From 2001 to 2011, United States exports to China increased 5.41 times from $19.2 billion to $103.9 billion, while its imports from China grew 3.9 times from $102.3 billion to $399.3 billion. United States–China trade grew from $65 billion in 1996 to $343 billion in 2006 and to $503.2 billion in 2011. As a result, the United States suffered a trade deficit of $295.5 billion in 2011, a huge trade gap that has become a major concern in Washington.

Economic benefits tend to be mutual; however, Washington has begun to worry that China's mercantilist policy might undermine the American economy. Some special interest groups in the United States allege that China engages in unfair commercial practices, such as policies affecting exchange rates, intellectual property rights, subsidies, accumulation of foreign exchanges reserves and China-based cyber theft of American trade secrets and technology. On Chinese side, Washington is viewed as taking advantage of the United States dollar as a reserve currency, exporting inflation to China by "quantitative easing," and adopting various protectionist measures to undermine Chinese economic growth.

In April 2007, the United States Commerce Department applied duties on coated paper from China, reversing a 23 year-old policy of not placing duties on countries that do not have market economies. From 2001 to 2012, the United States initiated anti-dumping investigation 109 times and took anti-dumping measures 92 times against China in the WTO regime, and China initiated anti-dumping investigations 35 times and took anti-dumping measures 27 times against the United States. In WTO in the same period, the United States complained 15 times against China, and China complained eight times against the United States.

Huawei Technologies Co. Ltd., a Chinese private multinational networking and telecommunications equipment and services company headquartered in Guangdong, sought to purchase the 3 Leaf systems, but the bid was prohibited by the United States government due to security concerns. In 2012, The House Intelligence Committee said that after a yearlong investigation it had come to the conclusion that Huawei and another Chinese business, ZTE Inc., posed national security threats due to their close ties to the Chinese government, which, according to the committee, was heavily subsidizing the companies. The committee worried that the business of these two corporations in the United States may give the Chinese government the ability to easily intercept communications and could allow it to start online attacks to critical infrastructure, like dams and power grids.

In fact, the economic friction between Beijing and Washington has become a new source of tension in bilateral relations. Many in Beijing believe that China has become the scapegoat for American economic failure. Since China holds huge amount of United States treasury bonds, some Chinese experts use terms like "kidnapping," "cheating," "stealing" and "plundering" to refer to Washington's decision to devalue the United States dollar. China in fact has begun to diversify its import and export markets in an attempt to reduce its dependence on the United States. The trade dependences of the two went in opposite directions in the last decade. According to China's National Bureau of Statistics, China's international trade has been less dependent on the United States. Its total trade with United States decreased from 10.76% of its trade with the world in 2001 to 7.0% of its trade with the world in 2011. On the other hand, United States trade is more and more dependent on China. According to the United States Census Bureau, United States trade with China increased from 6.49% of its world trade in 2001 to 13.6% in 2011.

According to some historians, economic interdependence may not be a peace holder. For example, Japan depended on the American supply of raw materials during the 1920s and 1930s, and this dependence led to its attack on Pearl Harbor. John Lewis Gaddis once argued that the United States and the former Soviet

Union had a long peace during the Cold War that was the result of independence economically rather than interdependence. Gaddis further argues in his classic work "The Long Peace" that the distance and independence of the two superpowers provided the structural prerequisite for stability. The fact that there were so few opportunities for interaction between the United States and the Soviet Union provided little leverage to either in dealing with the other.

Tse-Kang Leng clearly articulates in his chapter the fact that the economic integration between Taiwan and Mainland China has not created any trust in the political and military arenas in cross-Straits relations. In fact, it complicated domestic politics in Taiwan and increased the differences in the basic policy between the KMT and DPP in their policy towards Taipei's future relations with Beijing. As he says, "The more unstable aspect of the triangle is cross-strait relations between Mainland China and Taiwan."

The same may be said of Beijing–Tokyo relations. The Sino–Japanese economic interdependence has deepened substantially over the last three decades, yet trade and mutual economic interests have done little to nurture trust between Beijing and Tokyo, or to ease the tensions of the territorial disputes. In his chapter Takashi Sekiyama argues convincingly that the steady improvement of Sino–Japanese economic relations has done little since September 2012, to prevent the sudden deterioration of bilateral relations due to sovereignty issues over the Diaoyu/Senkaku islands. Indeed, according to Japanese official statistics, trade between Japan and China grew six-fold from 1991–2011, while Japan–United States trade declined 20% during the same period. Japan has become quite important to China's foreign trade in 2012 as illustrated in Figures 1 and 2. Nevertheless, the image of China in Japan seems to have worsened over the last 10 years, as illustrated in Figures 3 and 4 below:

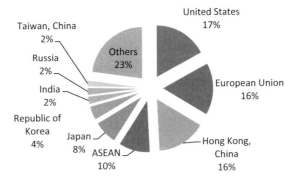

Figure 1: Mainland China's major exports destinations

Source: National Bureau of Statistics of China, Statistical Communiqué of the People's Republic of China on the 2012 National Economic and Social Development, February 22, 2013.

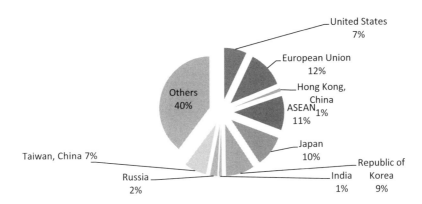

Figure 2: Mainland China's major imports sources

Source: National Bureau of Statistics of China, Statistical Communiqué of the People's Republic of China on the 2012 National Economic and Social Development, February 22, 2013.

Takashi tends to view the failure of economic interdependence to preserve good Sino–Japanese relations as a result of the decline of Japan's economic importance to China compared to the past, and he notes that this decline is particularly exemplified in the Japan's diminished share of China's trade. I would argue, however, that

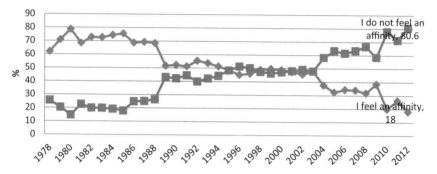

Figure 3:   Japanese affinity for China

Source: Public Relations Office of the Minister's Secretariat for the Cabinet Office （内閣府大臣官房政府広報室）, The Public Opinion Survey on Diplomacy （外交に関する世論調査）, http://www8.cao.go.jp/survey/h24/h24-gaiko/index.html, accessed on October 2012.

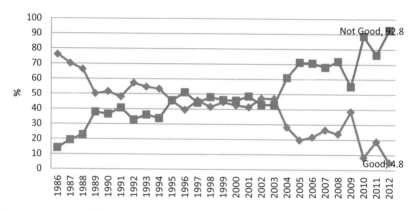

Figure 4:   Japan–China relations

Source: Public Relations Office of the Minister's Secretariat for the Cabinet Office (内閣府大臣官房政府広報室), The Public Opinion Survey on Diplomacy (外交に関する世論調査), http://www8.cao.go.jp/survey/h24/h24-gaiko/index.html, accessed on October 2012.

economic interdependence is simply a "light factor" that can easily be dwarfed by other political and security considerations.

A similar case is Hong Kong. Beijing has increased its economic "candy" to Hong Kong since its return to Beijing in 1997, with increasing bonuses given to the Special Administrative Region (SAR). In June 2003, the Government of the Hong Kong Special

Administrative Region and the Central Government of the People's Republic of China (PRC) signed the *Mainland and Hong Kong Closer Economic Partnership Arrangement* (CEPA), according to which qualifying products, companies and residents of Hong Kong enjoy preferential access to the Mainland Chinese markets. And in July 2003, the Beijing government initiated the Individual Visit Scheme to allow tourists from Mainland China to visit Hong Kong on an individual basis, not necessarily on business visas or in tour groups. However, Hong Kong has been moving in two interesting directions: economically more dependent on Beijing, while politically moving more decisively toward self-determined autonomy in its domestic politics.

Therefore, it is indeed difficult to say that economic integration will definitely lead to a harmonious relationship in the triangle. It is safe to say that the current trends have only produced mixed results. Economic incentive is obviously insufficient to improve mutual trust and to stabilize the triangle.

The contribution of an inclusive triangle

The question remains why economic interdependence couldn't reduce mutual distrust. The answer may lie in the structural change of the W–T–B triangle. Although 30 years of Sino–American relations have produced a mature relationship in which both sides seek to build a constructive partnership, the mutual distrust of long-term intentions has become more apparent lately and has increasingly become a central concern.

According to power transition theory, the threat posed by a challenging state is a function of its dissatisfaction with the existing international system created and maintained by the dominating power. Conflict, or even war, may occur when the dissatisfied challenger feel less "respected" and denied by the leading state's access to overseas resources. In today's international system, China and the United States fulfill roles of 'challenging power' and the 'dominating power' respectively, and the rapid expansion of China's influence in what is traditionally the American sphere of influence related to commodities markets and energy supplies reflects their structural contradiction. Yet the likelihood of war also depends on the posture of the dominant power, which can try to either contain or accommodate the challenger. At this moment, American elites are debating what kind of China policy might best serve American interests.

From the perspective of classic realism of international relations, the real issue here is the security dilemma. Since survival is the main motive of states, leaders of states tend to be distrustful of other states' intentions and, as a consequence, they always try to maximize their own security. China and the United States are now entering into a situation in which United States actions intended to heighten its security, such as "rebalancing," can lead China to respond with similar measures of military buildup, a response that may produce increased tensions that create conflict, even when no side really desires it.

Recently, people have realized the significance of perceptions in United States–China relations as the source of this fragility, and the study of mutual perceptions has achieved a prominent place in the scholarly literature on Sino–American relations. Indeed, what is perceived — though not necessarily a reflection of realities — has important impacts in determining a particular policy action. It is widely believed that the United States and China held ambivalent and contradictory mutual perceptions, and these perceptions, along with numerous stereotypes, have contributed considerably to the volatility of Sino–American relations for the last 100 years. However, some recent research seems to suggest that there has been a notable shift in Sino–American imagining of the other in recent years, and this shift has been towards the hardening of negative and demonized images. Due to this shift, a rise of anti-American nationalism in China and anti-Chinese sentiments in America has become noticeable.

Indeed, the increase of Chinese economic and military capabilities has begun to enable the Beijing leadership to secure many widely-defined core interests as a great power. Dai Bingguo, Chinese State Councilor for External Relations, defined China's core interests in three areas: First, China's political stability, namely, the stability of the Communist Party of China (CPC) leadership and of the socialist system; second, sovereign security, territorial integrity and national unification; and third, China's sustainable economic and social development.

China's long-term strategic goal is to catch up with developed countries by building "a prosperous and strong modern country" (*fuqiang de xiandai guojia*) with a high degree of internal harmony. China's national security and the CPC internal legitimacy depend on this strategic goal: To catch up with industrial countries not only in absolute economic terms, but also in technological and military terms as well by substantially improving its domestic economic structure and governing capability.

However, America cannot trust that China would be willing to be only a regional power. Based on Western historical experience, a country's ambition grows as its economic and military power expands. Meanwhile, China cannot trust Washington to refrain from containing China. Washington's efforts to promote democracy worldwide are viewed in Beijing as attempts to sabotage the CPC leadership in Beijing. The influence of American ideology, and especially the idea of the United States advancing human rights, is perceived as aimed to "westernize" and "divide" China. The fundamental sources of growing strategic distrust between the two countries, then, lie in their different political traditions, value systems and cultures, insufficient comprehension and appreciation of each other's policy making processes and a narrowing gap in power between the two countries.

President Obama's "pivot toward Asia" has an ambiguity similar to that of the W–B–T triangle; does the dance include China, or is the American swing around China's periphery an attempt to isolate or even contain China? Seen by China through the lens of a security triangle, the United States is strengthening its alliance with China's neighbors with the aim of containing China. It appears that any improvement in United States–Asia relations is at the likely cost of China–Asia relations, and vice versa.

The key question, then, is how to reduce the mistrust or distrust between the United States and China as well as in cross-Straits relations. Womack correctly notes that the inclusive, opportunity-driven W–B–T triangle is the solution. The reality of inclusion is already present and "the shadow of the security triangle can be seen in the fears, suspicions and inhibitions of the participants, but its empirical grounding has faded to a trace." It is true that there are positive developments on China side. China has chosen to cooperate with the United States during the financial crisis of 2008–2009, even though there are policy suggestions within China's policy study circle that Beijing should seize the opportunity to weaken the United States further. In that sense, China has tried to demonstrate its desire to "increase trust, reduce trouble and develop cooperation" an important move towards an inclusive triangle.

In terms of cross-strait relations, Beijing has also made efforts to ameliorate concerns on the Taiwan side. The "1992 Consensus" has been incorporated for the first time into the Party Report in the CPC's 18th Party Congress. As Ren Xiao details, Beijing also commits itself to "institution-building" in cross-Straits relations, which entails a promise not only to regular high-level meetings between *Kuomintang* (KMT) and CPC, but also indicates a possibility of opening an office in each other's capital.

It is also time to consider developing a deeper and more institutionalized relationship between Beijing and Washington, one that is firmly anchored in a strategic framework that accepts the reality of competition while encouraging cooperation, improvement of mutual trust and the establishment of a structure for negotiation of conflicting interests. That is why the idea of an inclusive triangle relationship deserves our serious attention.

This new framework for a relationship between China and the United States should recognize the reality of the two countries' strategic competition. Beijing and Washington should define key areas of shared interest and respect each other's strategic interests. China should respect America's global interests and promise not to challenge the existing global order led and maintained by the United States. In return, Washington should respect China as a leading regional power in Asia and its core interests, particularly in terms of the territorial integrity in the East China Sea and the South China Sea, as well as in the cross-straits relations. For this purpose, a regular summit between Beijing and Washington should be maintained annually and top leadership should be personally involve in handling issues in bilateral relations from a strategic perspective.

Misperception and distrust as factors in the triangle

In terms of cross-Strait relations, there are also misperceptions and distrust. As Ren's and Leng's papers illustrate that there is a perceptual difference as to whether Taiwan can be treated as a sovereign entity regarding to the nature of cross-strait relations.

The Taiwan issue has been the most disputed and disruptive issue in Sino–United States relations ever since the normalization of relations in 1979. On one hand, Taiwan benefitted economically from its interaction with the Mainland. On the other hand, China has made repeated offers to Taiwan with the hope that the island may be eventually be reunited with mainland. From 1995 to 2008, Lee Teng-Hui and Chen Shui-Bian have emphasized Taiwan's sovereignty, which concerns the Beijing leadership enough to engage in a military buildup in the mainland to deter Taiwan from drifting away. This, however, has only made Taiwan more anxious and produced more initiatives, including an attempted referendum for UN membership. Nevertheless, the issue seems to have become manageable in the last several years, since the enactment of the Anti-Secession Law by Beijing in 2005. America seems to have been well aware of the China's bottom line over the issue, and has joined China to keep the Taiwan issue within the *status quo*.

With United States assistance in this respect, Beijing has become less driven to rhetoric and over-reactions than before when facing the irritants initiated by the Taiwanese leaders. Beijing leaders seem to believe that the United States is simply not interested in supporting the *de jure* independence of Taiwan, even though they remain suspicious about the United States' intentions and are in principle unhappy with Washington providing sophisticated weaponry to Taiwan. In September 2007, despite Chinese protests the Pentagon announced possible sales to Taiwan of a dozen P-3C Orion anti-submarine, patrol aircraft, and SM-2 anti-aircraft missiles, altogether worth more than $2.2 billion. The United States continued the sale of advanced weapons to Taiwan, despite the improved cross-strait relations under the Ma Administration, a fact that has increased China's distrust of the United States' long-term strategic intentions. Washington's recent rebalance towards Asia further contributes to Beijing's sense of unease.

How to break this security impasse in the triangle, and transform the exclusive security one into an inclusive one? This is a difficult task, as all sides tend to be suspicious about any potential collusion in the triangle at its own expense. Womack suggests that we no longer view Taiwan as a problem and instead change our mindset to view it as an opportunity. People in the United States have begun to talk about reducing the United States security commitment to Taiwan as a policy option. Some believe that Taiwan itself has chosen to improve relationship with Beijing and, therefore, Taipei may need less weaponry from Washington. Others view that Taiwan has become more and more of a strategic liability to Washington and they argue that Taipei seems to have decided to accommodate to Beijing and rely much less on the United States. If so, it might be the moment for Washington to remove this longtime burden of providing for Taiwan's security. Should the United States reduce its security commitment to Taiwan? Many within the

Washington Beltway may not think so. In the last three decades Taipei remained sensitive to the developments in the Washington–Beijing ties, and worried about Washington's possible concessions to Beijing at Taipei's expense. However, after the 2008 election, Ma Ying-Jeou actively sought to engage China largely for the purpose of improving relation with Washington. This is because United States officials feared that Taiwan might spark a Chinese over-reaction, creating a crisis that may require United States intervention.

In his report delivered to the 18th Party Conference, Hu Jintao called for a peace agreement negotiation with Taiwan. This seems to be a major change in Beijing's cross-Strait policy, as Beijing used to oppose such an idea, arguing that Taiwan cannot be recognized as a sovereign partner and the United States should not interfere in China's domestic affairs. Should the United States encourage Taiwan to accommodate China's request? Since Beijing did not ask for unification at this stage and only asked for a peace agreement, this might be viewed as a positive step and a necessary instrument to stabilize the cross-Strait relations. It is also in the best interests of the W–B–T triangle and in American interests to encourage this development. In fact, the United States should use its influence to facilitate such an agreement, if not acting as a mediator. Some 60 years ago, Washington sent George Marshall to China to mediate the conflict between the CPC and the KMT during China's civil war. Why could not the Washington play a similar role at this historical juncture? Womack further develops the notion of negotiation within the triangle:

"The essence of an asymmetric inclusive triangle is not unanimity of interests, but rather the assumptions that mutual benefit is possible, that individual benefit can be furthered by negotiation, and that the benefit of any two sides is likely to be beneficial to the third. In the realm of politics, it assumes that the three actors remain autonomous pursuers of their own interests while negotiating mutually acceptable arrangements. In the realm of security, it assumes that vulnerability can be reduced or structured through negotiation. It should not be viewed as American abandonment of Taiwan, since the negotiation may enhance Taiwan's security rather than weaken it."

Washington is certainly a key player and able to move the relations into an inclusive triangle. However, at this stage, the United States seems unlikely to play that role. Many people in Beijing really doubt whether Washington would like to give up Taiwan and lose the leverage that Taiwan has provided Washington in its dealing with Beijing. Since most serious challenge for managing the W–B–T triangle remains to be the reduction of distrust among all players, Washington's possible involvement in Beijing–Taipei peace talks would substantially reduce Beijing's distrust of the United States' strategic intention.

There is a fundamental perceptual difference between Taiwan and Mainland China. Ren Xiao argues in his paper that, after overcoming the high danger period of Chen Shui-Bian, Beijing has taken practical steps with strategic vision to improving cross-Strait relations, and he believes that this has laid the foundation for cooperation. However, Leng articulates in his paper that domestic politics in Taiwan may continue to cast a lingering shadow on the future direction of the cross-Strait relations.

Current regional disputes and a transformed triangle

The recent development of conflict between Japan and China over a disputed chain of islands brought forth new elements in the W–B–T triangle. On September 10, 2012, the Japanese government decided to purchase from a private businessman three islets in a chain of disputed islands (the Diaoyu or Senkaku, Islands as they are called respectively in Chinese and Japanese) in the East China

Sea. Beijing sees the purchase as an affront to its claims and to the past tacit agreement to shelve the island dispute quietly. Despite Tokyo's attempts to calm the dispute, China sent patrol boats to the disputed area for the first time, an action that significantly escalated the two countries' worst dispute in recent years. Taipei has also claimed these islands and, therefore, strongly opposes Tokyo's unilateral action. During this crisis, Beijing and Taipei found a solid common interest and a common stance. However, Washington does not want to see the tacit alliance between Taipei and Beijing regarding this event. Ma Ying-Jeou is obviously under American pressure not to collaborate with China against Japan.

The possible change in the W–B–T triangle may very well have impact on Southeast Asian countries as well. The rise of China has brought forth structural change in East Asia and new challenges to Association of Southeast Asian Nations (ASEAN), an association that has so far tried to benefit from China's economic rise, but at the same time worries about China's growing power and the possible Chinese domination over the region. ASEAN as a regional interlocutor has responded to the rise of China by deploying a hedging strategy that seeks to benefit from the opportunities and manage the challenges by welcoming America's return to Asia as a balance to China.

However, China's recent territorial disputes with the Philippines and Vietnam in the South China Sea have made the situation in the region more fluid and uncertain. Beijing's leadership has begun to reexamine "the good-neighbor policy" that has been in place since 1978. That policy has been quite accommodative and concessive when it involves territorial disputes. For example, among the 230 reefs, islets, atolls and cays (most of them uninhabited), about 50 of them were occupied by China's surrounding countries since the 1970s. During the 1970s, China passively watched its neighboring countries occupy seven of them in the Spratly Islands without taking any action. In the 1980s, 19 more of them were occupied by surrounding countries, while China took only six, and in the 1990s, eight more were taken by the surrounding countries, while China has only occupied one. This concessive approach has been frequently criticized by increasingly powerful societal forces within China. China seems to have readjusted its diplomatic approach and has become more active, or more assertive in the eyes of some Western observers, in defending what it views as its core national interests. While trying to properly resolve potential territorial disputes, Beijing has also endeavored to prevent an America-led coalition against China in the West Pacific, Southeast Asia and Oceania.

The recent crisis between Taiwan and the Philippines over the killing of a Taiwanese fisherman by the Filipino Coast Guard on May 9, 2013, have brought the cross-Strait relationship closer. Taiwan imposed sanctions and conducted two-days of "safety and rescue drills" with its Naval and Coast Guard forces near the waters where the incident occurred, on the grounds that the killing took place within its exclusive economic zone and the Philippine authority's action was in violation of international law. While Manila tries to be evasive, China sent two naval fleets to the region in a drill to support Taipei's efforts to gain justice with Manila. These actions have obvious implications to ASEAN generally, and to the Philippines and Vietnam in particular. If the relationship between China and the United States, as well as cross-strait relations, can be improved, China may exert more pressure on its neighboring countries with whom it has territorial disputes. This may be seen as more assertive in the eyes of some Western observers. While trying to properly resolve potential territorial disputes, Beijing has also endeavored to prevent an America-led coalition against China in the West Pacific, Southeast Asia and Oceania.

Conclusion

As Womack correctly points out, "rethinking the W–B–T triangle is arguably the most important single strategic step that the United States and China can take in order to realign for sustainable leadership in a globalized world." The future prospect of the W–B–T triangle is however, hard to predict. If we try to make it an inclusive triangle and manage to reduce distrust, the triangle may be stabilized and become genuinely mutually beneficial.

For that purpose, Washington and Beijing should commit to regular summitry and upgrade their regular military-to-military dialogues. Washington should consider including China in its planned Trans-Pacific Partnership and encourage peace agreement talk between Beijing and Taipei. The United States should not view its relationship with Taipei as part of a large military presence in the Western Pacific as first chain of island defense perimeter that is preparing for China when China goes global. Likewise, China should learn to behave as a responsible world power, or at least as a responsible regional leader, to smooth the apprehension of other nations in the wake of China's rise. China should also try to be more accommodative to Taipei's desire for more international space, by ensuring that Taiwan independence will not again become a powerful current within Taiwan's domestic politics. Only when cross-strait normalcy is institutionalized so that differences are negotiated within a creative framework, can we indeed hail the replacement of an exclusive, security-based triangle by an inclusive, mature and constructive triangle.

Chapter 5

Rethinking the Triangle: A Japanese Perspective

Takashi Sekiyama

The University of Tokyo

Until very recently, the Taiwan issue was an area where the interests of the United States and those of China clashed the most. Former Chinese leader Deng Xiaoping once said that the issue was a "major obstacle for the China–United States relations, one that could potentially develop into an explosive case in extreme situations."[1] Furthermore, even though the United States–China–Taiwan relationship is characterized as an asymmetric triangle where the constituent members hold significantly different international clout, changes in the domestic political climate in Taiwan, the smallest of the three, have often been seen as swaying the relationship between the bigger powers — the United States and China — since the 1990s.

---

[1] Selected Works of Deng Xiaoping, Vol. 3 (People's Publishing House), p. 97 (in Chinese).

However, we may need to rethink the triangle relationships in the light of present realities and future prospects. The triangle relationships between the United States, the People's Republic of China (PRC, or simply China), and the Republic of China on Taiwan (ROC or simply Taiwan) have become politically stable since 2008, when the *Kuomintang* (KMT's) Ma Ying-Jeou was elected president of the ROC. Economic ties across the Taiwan Strait have significantly strengthened, involving the United States economy. Now, the Washington–Beijing–Taipei (W–B–T) triangle has become an inclusive one in which improvements between any two members benefit the other.[2] Better cross-Strait relations can reduce security risks and may offer a variety of opportunities for the United States. Better relations between the United States and China could be reassuring in terms of the autonomy of Taiwan. Better United States–Taiwan relations could expand China's opportunities.

The idea that economic interdependence promotes international cooperation has been with us since old times.[3] Any disruption in trade due to conflict could translate into high economic cost, giving nations an incentive to avoid conflict.

In United States–China–Taiwan relations, all would be well if the deepening of economic interdependence worked to ease tensions over politics or sovereignty issues among the three parties. China holds the key here. While deepening economic interdependence with neighboring nations, China frequently lets tensions with those neighbors increase. Its relations with Vietnam and the Philippines have been strained over sovereignty issues in the South

---

[2] As for argument on the inclusive opportunity-driven W-B-T Triangle, see Brantly Womack, Rethinking the Washington-Beijing-Taipei Triangle: An American Perspective, presented at University of Virginia, on March 28, 2013.

[3] Liberal school of international relations argues that increased interdependence between countries reduces the chance of them engaging in conflict. For example, see Bruce Russett and John Oneal, *Triangulating Peace: Democracy, Interdependence, and International Organizations* (New York, Norton, 2001).

China Sea. Tensions have been mounting between Japan and China over the sovereignty of the Senkaku Islands, which the Chinese call Diaoyu. Such conflicts between China and neighboring nations cast a shadow over the relationship between China and the United States. Will China really put priority on maintaining economic interdependence over politics or sovereignty matters?

Furthermore, even if economic interdependence overrides sovereignty in the W–B–T triangle, a good three-party relationship will not always be a welcome situation for neighboring nations.

Needless to say, the W–B–T triangle exists not in a vacuum, but within a complex interaction involving many actors in international relations. If the cross-Strait issue no longer poses a major obstacle and the United States develops a highly cooperative relationship with China, such a situation will surely have an impact on other East Asian countries.

In this regard, this paper considers the idea of an inclusive W–B–T triangle from the standpoint of Japan, a major neighbor of China and Taiwan and an ally of the United States.

In the first section, it will be considered whether economic interdependence will really lead to restraint on China. I will go on to conclude that China will likely take, for the foreseeable future, a stance "cooperative to the United States, but hard line against Japan."

If China is to take such a stance against Japan, what kind of impact will a good United States–China–Taiwan relationship have on Japan? It would be worthwhile to consider this question in trying to grasp the W–B–T triangle in larger picture, but the answer has not yet clear. Many studies in English, Japanese and Chinese cover the bilateral relationships between Japan and any of the members of the trilateral relationship. There are also numerous works on the Japan-United States–China and Japan–China–Taiwan relationships.[4] However, very few encompass the relations among Japan, the United States, China and Taiwan.[5]

Thus, in the second section, this paper will go on to consider this question by dividing the four-party relationship into two triangles: the Japan–China–Taiwan relationship and the Japan–United States–Taiwan relationship. From the perspective of either triangle, a good United States–China–Taiwan relationship is a welcome situation for Japan in principle. But in the Japan–China–Taiwan triangle, concern could arise on the part of Japan that China and Taiwan could form a common front against Japan, putting it in a vulnerable spot diplomatically and in terms of national security. Also, in the Japan–United States–China triangle, Japan could have a sense of anxiety that it may be abandoned by the United States. As long as there is a potential conflict smoldering between Japan and China, the United States will face the tough choice of which party to side with. In other words, Japan could take the place of Taiwan as the new "major obstacle" to the development of United States–China relations.

How each party will manage its relationship with Japan will be the key to allowing the United States–China–Taiwan relationship to develop as an inclusive triangle. In the conclusion, this paper will propose that the three parties take a careful stance toward Japan so as not to make it a destabilizing factor in the region.

---

[4] As an Example of the latest English articles on Japan-US-China relations, see Chien-Peng Chung, "Japan's Involvement in Asia-Centered Regional Forums in the Context of Relations with China and the United States," *Asian Survey*, Vol. 51, No. 3, pp. 407–428. As an example of Japan-China-Taiwan relations, see Jing Sun, "Japan-Taiwan Relations: Unofficial in Name Only," *Asian Survey*, Vol. 47, No. 5, pp. 790–810.

[5] Ken Wang's "Taiwan in Japan's Relations with China and the United States after the Cold War" (in *Pacific Affairs*, Vol. 73, No. 3, pp. 353–373) is one of a few good papers on Japan-US-China-Taiwan relations, although it is too out of date.

Will economic interdependence deter China?

Japan–China economic relations

Although in the last four decades, Japan and China built a deep economic interdependence, tensions have been mounting between Japan and China recently. One of the reasons of China's hard line against Japan seems to be related with the recent downgrade of Japan's economic importance in China's trade.

2012 marked the milestone 40th anniversary of the normalization of diplomatic ties between Japan and China in 1972. Between the two countries, private-sector trade had already taken hold at the point of diplomatic normalization. For China in particular, Japan in 1972 was already the largest trade partner, accounting for 12% of exports and 22% of imports.[6] Japan was an indispensable economic partner in the true sense of the phrase.

In the last four decades, Japan and China built a deeply intertwined relationship of economic interdependence. For example, in the two decades between 1991 and 2011, Japan–China bilateral trade grew six-fold,[7] while Japan–United States trade declined by 20% in the same period.[8] Direct investment from Japan to China expanded 60-fold from $230 million in 1991 to $12.65 billion in 2011.[9] As the bilateral economic interdependence deepened, human exchanges grew as well. Japanese visitors to China increased from 170,000 in 1980 to 3.73 million in 2010, while Chinese visitors to Japan expanded from a paltry 20,000 in 1980 to 1.41 million in 2010.[10]

---

[6]*China Statistical Yearbook* 1981 by the National Bureau of Statistics of China.

[7]Calculation in Japanese yen. Ministry of Finance, *Trade Statistics of Japan*.

[8]*Ibid.*

[9]Japan External Trade Organization (JETRO), *Japan's Outward and Inward Foreign Direct Investment.*

[10]Japan National Tourism Organization (JNTO), *Visitor Arrivals and Japanese Overseas Travelers.*

Despite the development of such mutual economic reliance, China is not necessarily seen as putting economic interdependence before sovereignty issues. Will economic interdependence not deter China from showing a belligerent attitude? In order to answer this question, we should take a look at economic interdependence not from a bilateral perspective but from a broader point of view.

With the above point in mind, if we look at the changes in shares of China's trade by country, we can point out that the economic ties between Japan and China have not necessarily been strengthening in relative terms. On the contrary, from China's perspective, the economic importance of Japan has declined compared to the past.

The following graph shows the changes in shares of China's trade by country or region over the six decades between 1950 and 2011 (see Figure 1).

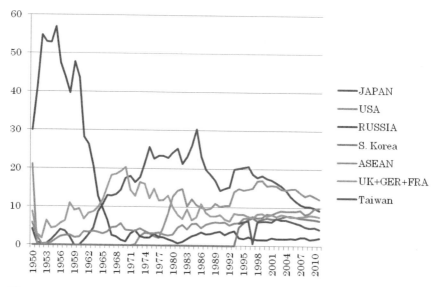

Figure 1:   Changes in shares in China's trade by country (1950–2011)

Sources: *China Statistical Yearbook*, 1981–2011 editions, by the National Bureau of Statistics of China.

Notes: Germany before 1990 is represented by trade data of West Germany. Russia before 1991 is represented by trade data of the Soviet Union.

In the eyes of China, the importance of Japan as a trade partner has decreased gradually since the late 1980s. In 2004, the United States overtook Japan as China's largest trade partner. In 2011, Japan accounted for only 8% of China's exports and 11% of its imports. Japan is now nothing more than the fifth largest export market and the third largest import partner in China's trade.

By contrast, for Japan, China's economic importance has grown rapidly in recent years. This fact is clear to see in Figure 2. For Japan, China started to show growing weight in trade in the mid-1990s, overtaking the United States in 2007 as the largest trade partner. Today, China is Japan's largest trade partner accounting for 20% of its trade volume.

In the last four decades of Japan–China relations, occasional souring of the governmental relationship did not necessarily have a

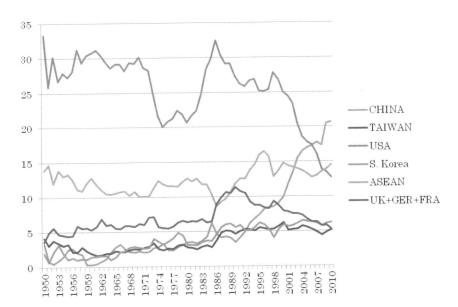

Figure 2: Changes in share of trade with Japan by country (1950–2011)

Sources: Prior to 1978: *Historical Statistics of Japan* by the Ministry of Internal Affairs and Communications, Bureau of Statistics (based on *Monthly Trade Statistics of Japan* by the former Ministry of Finance). From 1979 on: *Trade Statistics* by the Ministry of Finance.

Note: Germany before 1990 is represented by trade data of West Germany.

major impact on the development of bilateral economic ties. One reason is thought to be that neither government wanted the soured political relationship to spill over to the economic side.

However, as Japan's importance as an economic partner wanes for China, the likelihood increases that the Chinese government will cease to make such consideration. In fact, the former Chinese leadership under Hu Jintao had a cooperative stance toward Japan till around 2005, but started to take a particularly hard line around 2010. This timing coincides with Japan's relative decline in terms of its share in China's trade. Even former premier Wen Jiabao, who was widely seen as a leading figure among the group of politicians friendly to Japan, said publicly, "The Diaoyu Islands are an inalienable part of Chinese territory … The Chinese government and its people will make absolutely no concession on issues concerning its sovereignty and territorial integrity."[11]

Furthermore, if Japan now needs China more than China needs Japan, we cannot deny that an incentive could arise on the part of China to take advantage of such asymmetric economic interdependence to achieve its political cnds.[12] In fact, following the 2010 incident in which a Chinese fishing trawler and a Japanese Coast Guard vessel collided off the Senkaku/Diaoyu Islands, it was reported that China restricted exports of rare earth metals to Japan.[13] Also, in 2012, following the nationalization of the Senkaku/Diaoyu Islands by the Japanese government, it was reported that Chinese customs authorities delayed clearance of Japanese imports.[14]

---

[11] Article appearing in Xinhua Net on September 11, 2012. Downloaded from http://jp.xinhuanet.com/2012-09/11/c_131841961.htm on December 6, 2012.

[12] Robert Gilpin of Princeton University says imbalance in trade dependency is often used as a diplomatic leverage. See Robert Gilpin, *The Political Economy of International Relations*, Princeton University Press, 1987.

[13] E.g. China lifts rare earth export ban to Japan: Trader, *Reuters*, September 29, 2010.

[14] E.g. China toughens inspection of Japanese imports amid island row, Yomiuri Shimbun evening edition, September 21, 2012; In a move suspected of economic retaliation, tougher inspection of Japanese imports at customs in Tianjin, China, Asahi Shimbun morning edition, September 21, 2012; China toughens customs clearance for Japanese companies, Sankei Shimbun, morning edition, September 21, 2012.

Needless to say, the decline of Japan's share of China's trade does not necessarily mean the country's economic importance for China has dwindled. China imports core machinery parts from Japan to manufacture goods to export to the United States and Europe. For China, restriction of trade with Japan is a double-edged sword that could boomerang on its own economy.

The problem, however, is that China is seen as becoming more ready to unsheath the double-edged sword despite such drawbacks.

Implications on US–China–Taiwan relations

Similar concerns can be raised regarding the China–Taiwan relationship. In 2011, Taiwan's share of China's trade volume was a mere 4.4% — less than half that of Japan. For China, Taiwan is only the 6th largest trading partner in terms of share in trade volume.[15] On the other hand, Taiwan is becoming increasingly dependent on China economically, the latter accounting for 21.6% of the former's total trade.[16] Given such asymmetric economic interdependence, like the case of Japan–China relations, China may be inclined to use its economic might as political leverage against Taiwan.

In the meantime, China may well take a relatively moderate stance toward the United States, its current largest trade partner. In fact, in its decade in power, the former Chinese leadership under Hu Jintao built a close cooperative relationship with the United States. In particular, since Obama took office with a pledge to emphasize Asia, cooperation between the two powerhouses has deepened, as seen in the United States–China Strategic and Economic Dialogue.

The new leadership under Xi Jinping, which has only recently been fully inaugurated, will likely follow the cooperative stance initiated by the former leaders so as not to be criticized for changing course prematurely. Foreign Ministry spokesman Hong Lei told the

---

[15]National Bureau of Statistics of China, Value of Imports and Exports by Country (Region) of Origin/Destination, *China Statistical Year Book 2012.*

[16]Directorate General of Customs (ROC), *Exports Imports Value by Major Countries-Annual.* https://portal.sw.nat.gov.tw/APGA/GA06E. Accessed August 14, 2015.

press on November 15, 2012, when asked about the foreign policy of the new leadership, "The report made by comrade Hu Jintao at the opening ceremony of the 18th Communist Party Congress totally clarifies our country's view of the international affairs and foreign policy," making public that the new leaders will maintain the cooperative diplomatic stance shown by Hu Jintao.[17]

If China places a premium on the development of the United States–China relationship, it may well exercise restraint toward Taiwan, the "major obstacle" to the development of United States–China relations. From the perspective of a process toward cross-strait integration, it is the most realistic approach to press ahead with socio-economic integration with a view to political unification in the distant future.[18]

In other words, it is very likely that, as a result of China's emphasis on the United States, the trilateral relationship including Taiwan will develop amicably. On the other hand, given that China's stance toward Japan does not warrant optimism, a good United States–China–Taiwan relationship may not necessarily benefit Japan.

Two other asymmetric triangles

What impact would a good W–B–T relationship have on Japan? In considering this question, I would like to divide the relations between the three countries and Japan into two triangles: Japan–United States–China and Japan–China–Taiwan.

---

[17]Hong Lei appeared in a press conference on November 15, 2012. Downloaded on November 30, 2012 from the website of China's Ministry of Foreign Affairs (http://www. mfa.gov.cn/chn/gxh/tyb/fyrbt/jzhsl/t989479.htm).

[18]According to Karl Deutsch's differentiation, "integration" is a psychological policy and institutional consensus, and "unification" is an amalgamation of governments. According to his definitions, "One country, two systems" is a strategy to pursue unification first, and then reach integration under a unified political structure. See Yu-Shan Wu, Theorizing on Relations across the Taiwan Strait: Nine contending approaches, *Journal of Contemporary China*, 9:25 (2000), pp. 407–428.

Japan–China–Taiwan relationships

A good Beijing–Taipei relationship is a welcome situation for Japan as long as Taiwan does not join forces with China to (diplomatically) attack Japan.

In Japan–China–Taiwan trade, there exists international specialization by which Japan exports core parts to Taiwan, Taiwan makes semi-finished products and exports to China, and China assembles finished products.[19] Inasmuch as Japan exports to Taiwan core parts, which Taiwan uses to manufacture semi-finished products to export to China, a stable China–Taiwan relationship and expanding cross-Strait trade will also benefit Japan.

Although it is well known that iPhones are assembled in China by a Taiwanese enterprise Foxconn, few people may know that almost half of the phones' parts are provided by Japanese companies. For example, the LCD on the iPhone 5 is provided by Japan Display, batteries are made by Sony and flash memory is supplied by Toshiba.[20]

In other words, while China is now the largest export market for Taiwan, its exports are supported by imports from Japan. In fact, Taiwan's imports from Japan have been growing in tandem with its exports to China, and Japan is Taiwan's largest import partner. It is not an overstatement to say that Taiwan's economic prosperity depends on a good relationship not only with China but also with Japan.

In this sense, Taiwan, the smallest member of the Japan-China–Taiwan asymmetric triangle, has no choice but keep its emphasis on relations with Japan. It is no wonder that when tensions flared after Japan's nationalization of the Senkaku/Diaoyu Islands in 2012, Taiwan offered to mediate by proposing the East China Sea Peace

---

[19] As for structure of international trade in East Asia, see Ministry of Economy, Trade and Industry of Japan, Structure of international division of labor in East Asia and its change, *White Paper on International Economy and Trade 2012*, pp. 295–316.

[20] Japanese components dominate, *Nihon Keizai Shimbun*, October 19, 2012.

Initiative. Taipei cannot afford to develop cross-Strait relations alone at the expense of a good relationship with Tokyo, but needs to maintain amicable relationships with both Tokyo and Beijing. Taiwan's President Ma Ying-jeou clearly stated that he has no intention to band with China against Japan to claim territorial sovereignty.[21]

Even so, however, as long as a potential flashpoint remains between Japan and China, what would be most troublesome to Japan in terms of the Japan–China–Taiwan relationship is a situation in which China and Taiwan form a common front to keep Japan in check over controversial issues such as the Senkaku/Diaoyu Islands problem.

Japan has a good reason to worry about joint attack from Beijing and Taipei. In fact, it has been reported since around 2008 that China and Taiwan have been discussing joint development of deep-sea oil fields in the waters around the islands. Chinese local media say Beijing looks to join forces with Taipei to weaken the interests of Japan in the contested waters with a view to containing Japan.[22]

On this point, according to polls conducted by Chinese and Taiwanese media in July 2012, 85.3% of Mainland Chinese respondents supported China and Taiwan's joining forces to contain Japan over the Senkaku/Diaoyu Islands issue, while 51.5% of Taiwanese respondents gave an affirmative answer.[23] The Japan side has been wary of such moves between Beijing and Taipei, and every time tension rises over the islands and nearby waters, concerns are raised over a possible coming together of China and Taiwan against Japan.[24]

---

[21] Economy is first priority for Beijing and Taipei, Nihon Keizai Shimbun, July 22, 2011.

[22] *Eastday.com* (东方网), August 28, 2008.

[23] More than 9 out of 10 Chinese say yes to the use of force over Senkakus, Chinese and Taiwanese polls show, *Sankei Shimbun*, July 19, 2012.

[24] Some of the Japanese reports on this issue include: Sense of unity and meeting of interests between China and Taiwan as protests heat up against Japan over Senkakus, *Yomiuri Shimbun*, September 15, 2010; No China–Taiwan unity over Senkakus, *Asahi Shimbun*, September 18, 2010; Taiwan shifts more emphasis to sovereignty, *Asahi Shimbun*, January 25, 2013.

In short, although a good Beijing–Taipei relationship is a welcome situation for Japan especially in terms of economy, there still is a concern that China and Taiwan jointly contain Japan over some political issues.

Japan–US–China relationships

It is desirable for Japan that Taiwan ceases to be an "obstacle" for the United States and China, contributing to a stable United States-China relationship, given that the United States is an ally and China is Japan's largest trade partner.

As long as the United States–China relationship remains stable, Japan will not have to choose between the two nations. Also, from the perspective of Japan–United States–China trade, a stable United States–China relationship and expansion of bilateral trade benefits Japan, too. As I described earlier, there is a mechanism of international specialization in Japan–China trade, and China exports finished products mainly to the United States as well as European Union. Japan exports high-value-added core components directly to China or *via* a third economy such as Taiwan for assembly plants in China.[25] Japan's exports to China consist largely of electrical machinery (23.7% of total exports to China in 2012), including semiconductors and integrated circuits, general machinery (23.2%), such as machine tools and car engines, chemical products (13.9%), including plastic and industrial products (12.3%) like steel and non-ferrous metals.[26] According to data for 2011, 21.8% of China's imports of iron and steel products, 19.6% of machinery, 19.0% of transport equipment, and 10.4% of electrical machinery were directly imported from Japan.[27]

---

[25] *White Paper on International Economy and Trade 2012*, pp. 295–316.

[26] JETRO, Japan–China Trade in 2012.

[27] Calculated based on Japan's exports to China (JETRO) and China's total imports (China Statistical Yearbook, 2012). Classifications based on two-digit Harmonized System codes.

Such cross-border division of specialization brings handsome benefits to Japan only when Chinese exports to final markets remain robust. In this sense, expansion of United States–China trade is a welcome situation for Japan, too.

However, it should be noted that, in the asymmetric triangle of Japan–United States–China relations, Japan is the most vulnerable. As conflict looks set to continue between Japan and China, a robust relationship between the United States and China may lead to a sense of insecurity on the part of Japan, that its ally might "abandon" Japan.

If conflict flares up between Japan and China, which side will the United States take? The Senkaku/Diaoyu Island issue presents the United States with this tough question. The issue will likely be a touchstone for whether the situation will really lead to a sense of "being abandoned" on the part of Japan.

So far, the United States stance regarding the Senkaku/Diaoyu islands issue is clear.[28] In January 2013, Secretary of State Hillary Clinton stated that "we oppose any unilateral actions that would seek to undermine Japanese administration" of the islets. Similarly, United States congressional committees inserted in the FY2013 National Defense Authorization Act a resolution stating that "the unilateral action of a third party will not affect the United States' acknowledgment of the administration of Japan over the Senkaku Islands."

So long as the United States takes the side of Japan in a Japan-China conflict, a good United States–China relationship will benefit Japan, too.

However, as a potential flashpoint continues to exist between Japan and China, the United States will constantly face the tough choice of which side to take every time tension mounts. In other words, Japan might take the place of Taiwan as a new "major obstacle" to the development of United States–China relations.

---

[28] As for United States position on the Senkaku/Diaoyu issue, see Mark E. Manyin, *Senakaku (Diaoyu/Diaoyutai) Ilands Dispute: U.S. Treaty Obligations, CRS Report for Congress*, January 22, 2013.

Conclusion and policy proposals

As I have stated so far, a good United States–China–Taiwan relationship is a welcome thing for Japan in principle. However, a good trilateral relationship might cause, on the part of Japan, a sense of being abandoned by the United States and of insecurity that China and Taiwan might band together to drive Japan into a vulnerable spot diplomatically and in terms of national security.

Such senses of vulnerability might make Japan a destabilizing factor for the region. National security conditions in Northeast Asia are deteriorating, as seen in North Korea's development of nuclear missiles and China's expansionist movement. If Japan were to doubt the reliability of the United States–Japan Security Agreement, the country might be prompted to strengthen self-defense capabilities. Should Japan really move to strengthen defense capabilities, it might lead to an arms race in Northeast Asia involving China and South Korea.

The concern is not a groundless apprehension. With the deterioration of national security conditions surrounding Japan, debates are heating up over whether Japan should bolster its defense capabilities. On February 28, 2013, Prime Minister Shinzo Abe said at a Diet session, "I am debating whether we should continue depending on the United States for the ability to assault enemy territory." At the same time, the ruling Liberal Democratic Party started reviewing the defense plan, with a view to changes including acquisition of offensive equipments such as fighter jets or missiles that have long-range assault capabilities to target enemy lands.[29]

In order not to make Japan such a destabilizing factor in the region, it is desired that the United States, China and Taiwan each

---

[29] The ruling Liberal Democratic Party started reviewing the defense plan, with a view to changes including acquisition of offense capability to target enemy territory. (Sankei Shimbun February 20, 2013) On February 28, 2013, Prime Minister Shinzo Abe said at a Diet session, "I am debating whether we should continue depending on the U.S. for the ability to assault enemy territory."

take a careful stance toward Japan. How each country will manage its relationship with Japan will be the key to allowing the United States–China–Taiwan relationship to develop as an inclusive triangle.

First, it is important for the United States to never forsake Japan in matters such as the Senkaku/Diaoyu Islands issue where the interests of China and Taiwan clash with those of Japan. From the United States perspective, so long as the cross-Strait relationship stays stable, the country can pursue forming cooperative relations with both China and Taiwan, thus building an inclusive triangle. However, once tension rises between Beijing and Taipei, such thinking will only prove an illusion. Therefore, it is important for the United States to keep its military presence in Northeast Asia based on the United States–Japan Security Treaty so as not to allow the cross-Strait tension to intensify, and to maintain the regional power balance by continuing to provide Taiwan with weapons.

As for China, it is desired that the country refrain from provocations such as dispatching aircraft and vessels to the waters near the Senkaku/Diaoyu Islands, or locking fire-control radar on a Japanese navy vessel.[30] When tension mounts between Japan and China, the United States is constantly faced with the tough choice of which side to take, and that may make Japan the new "major obstacle" to the development of United States–China relations. For W–B–T relations to develop as an inclusive triangle, China needs to pursue a stable relationship with Japan.

As for Taiwan, it is desired that it maintains an arm's distance with China diplomatically and in terms of national security while it deepens economic ties, and that it never band with China to contain

---

[30]Chinese vessels and aircraft have repeatedly entered Japan-controlled waters and air-space surrounding the Senkaku/Diaoyu Islands. There have been 10 instances of incursion by Chinese ships in the two months of January and February 2013. (reported by Asahi Shimbun, February 28, 2013, etc.) Also, it was reported that, on January 30, 2013, a Chinese warship locked weapons-guiding radar on a JSDF escort vessel patrolling waters near the Senkaku/Diaoyu Islands. (reported by Asahi Shimbun, February 6, 2013, etc.).

Japan. In an asymmetric triangle of the Japan–China–Taiwan relations, Taiwan cannot afford to develop only cross-Strait relations at the expense of a good relationship with Japan. It is expected of Taiwan to maintain equidistance between Japan and China, and contribute to regional stability as a good middleman.

And of Japan, it is desired that it acts carefully so as not to become a destabilizing factor in the region or a new obstacle to the development of United States–China relations. For matters such as the Senkaku/Diaoyu Islands problem, over which Japan and China cannot meet eye to eye, forcing the United States to make hard choices, it is desirable to shelve such issues so as not to escalate tensions. If Japan succeeds in building politically stable relations with the United States, China and Taiwan respectively, then all the triangles — United States–China–Taiwan, Japan–China–Taiwan and Japan–China–United States — will flourish in a win–win–win relationship as inclusive ones.

Part 3: Background

Triangular Timeline 1885–2015

Compiled by Carl Huang

University of Virginia

	United States	Taiwan	China
1885		Qing Dynasty makes Taiwan a province of China	
1895		Treaty of Shimonoseki cedes Taiwan to Japan	
1913	United States recognition of ROC		United States recognition of ROC
1927			Conflict between KMT and CCP (1927–1949)
1945		Taiwan reverts to control of Chinese government under KMT after Japan surrender	
1945.04	Harry Truman in office		
1945–1949			Chinese Civil War
1945.12	Gen. Marshall's mission to China (1945–1947)		

(*Continued*)

(*Continued*)

	United States	Taiwan	China
1947.02		February 28 uprising and massacre (228 Incident), "White Terror" period begins	
1949.10			Founding of PRC under Mao, end of Chinese Civil War
1950		Korean War	
1950.06	Truman's declaration of Taiwan's status as unsettled		
1953	Dwight Eisenhower in office		
1954	United States–Taiwan Mutual Defense Treaty		
1954–1955		First Taiwan Strait Crisis	
1958		Second Taiwan Strait Crisis	
1969	Richard Nixon in office		
1971	Kissinger's secret visit to Beijing		
1971		UN General Assembly expels the ROC	
1971	Beginning of the Diaoyudao/Senkaku/Diaoyutai territorial disputes between PRC, Japan and Taiwan		
1972			PRC's normalization with Japan
1972	Nixon's visit to Beijing Shanghai Communiqué		Shanghai Communiqué
1975		Death of Chiang Kai-shek Yen Chia-kan becomes President	

(*Continued*)

(Continued)

	United States	**Taiwan**	**China**
1977	Jimmy Carter in office		
1978		Chiang Ching-kuo becomes President	
1979.01	Formally recognizes PRC United States–China 1st Joint Communiqué		United States formally recognize PRC United States–China 1st Joint Communiqué
1979.04	Taiwan Relations Act	Taiwan Relations Act	
1979		Chiang's "Three-Noes Policy"	
1979.12	Termination of United States–Taiwan Mutual Defense Treaty		
1981	Ronald Reagan in office		
1981			Ye Jianying's "Nine Points"
1982	Approves sale of additional F-5E fighter aircraft to Taiwan		
1982	United States–China 2nd Joint Communiqué		United States–China 2nd Joint Communiqué
1982.07	Reagan's Six Assurances to Taipei		
1983	Announces plans to sell $530 million in new arms to Taiwan		
1986.05		Airplane hijacked to Guangzhou leading to first cross-Strait contact	
1986.09		Founding of DPP	
1987		KMT lifts martial law	

(Continued)

(*Continued*)

	United States	**Taiwan**	**China**
1988		Chiang Ching-kuo dies of heart attack; Vice President Lee Teng-hui succeeded Chiang	
1989.01	George H.W. Bush in office		
1989.06			Tienanmen Incident
1989.06	Sanctions against PRC		
1990		Wild Lily Student Movement	
		Founding of Straits Exchange Foundation (SEF)	
1991			Founding of Association for Relations Across the Taiwan Strait (ARATS)
1992		SEF and ARATS met in British Hong Kong, "1992 Consensus"	
1993	Bill Clinton in office		
1993		Wang-Koo summit in Singapore (April 27–29)	
1994	Taiwan Policy Review		
1995.01			Jiang's eight-point for reunification
1995.01		Lee's six-point reply to Jiang	
1995.06		Lee travels to the United States and delivers speech at Cornell University	
1995.07– 1996.03		Third Taiwan Strait Crisis	

(*Continued*)

(*Continued*)

	United States	**Taiwan**	**China**
1996.03		Lee reelected as president	
1997			Transfer of sovereignty over Hong Kong
1998			Clinton–Jiang Summit in Beijing
1999		DPP passed Resolution on Taiwan's Future	
1999.07		Lee's "special state-to-state" relations remark	
2000.03		Chen Shui-bian in office Chen's "Four Noes and One Without" pledge in inauguration	
2000	Clinton declared resolution of the Taiwan question must be peaceful as well as with the "assent" of Taiwan's people		
2001.01	George W. Bush in office		
2001.04	Hainan Island incident between United States and PRC		Hainan Island incident between United States and PRC
2001.04	Bush's "whatever it takes" statement on defending Taiwan		
2001.07			Qian Qichen's "one-China" statement

(*Continued*)

	United States	**Taiwan**	**China**
2002			Hu Jintao in office
2003			Hu's call for "China's peaceful rise"
2003			PRC signed CEPA with Hong Kong
2003		First cross-strait charter flight during Chinese New Year for Taiwanese businessmen in China	
2003.11		Passage of the Referendum Act in Legislative Yuan (11.28)	
2003.12			Wen's visit to Washington
2004		Taiwan's total trade with PRC exceeds total trade with United States	
2004			"Peaceful development"
2004.03		Chen Shui-bian reelected First National Referendum	
2005			Passage of Anti-Succession Law in NPC
		Party leaders' visit to China: Lien Chan in April, James Soong in May, Yu Muming in July	
2006		Chen's new year statement on "new constitution"	

(Continued)

	United States	Taiwan	China
2006.02		Abolition of the National Unification Council & Guidelines	
2006.09		Cross-Strait charter flight for all Taiwan residents	
2006.04		The first Cross-Strait Economic, Trade and Culture Forum between KMT and CPC in Beijing	
2006.10		The second Cross-Strait Economic, Trade and Culture Forum	
2007			PRC tested anti-satellite missile
2007			Hu's "four nevers" statement from 17th Party Congress
2008.03		Ma Ying-jeou becomes president Referendum on Taiwan's UN membership	
2008.04		The Boao Forum For Asia Annual Conference; historical meeting of Vincent Siew and Hu Jintao.	
		Taiwan's KMT chairman Wu Boxiong met with Hu Jintao in Beijing	
2008.06		First Chen–Chiang summit (Beijing)	
2008.08	Bergsten's G-2 article on Foreign Affairs (*A Partnership of Equals*)		Bergsten's G-2 article on Foreign Affairs (*A Partnership of Equals*)

(Continued)

(*Continued*)

	United States	Taiwan	China
2008.11		Chen Yunlin incident and Wild Strawberry Student Movement	
		Second Chen–Chiang summit (Taipei)	
2008.12		Three direct links officially established (flights, shipping, and post)	
2009.01	Barrack Obama in office		
2009.04		Third Chen–Chiang summit (Nanjing)	
2009.11	Obama's first China visit		
2009.12		Fourth Chen–Chiang summit (Taichung)	
2010		Taiwan's total trade with PRC twice of total trade with U.S.	
2010.01	United States Arm Sales to Taiwan		
2010.06		Fifth Chen-Chiang summit (Chongqing)	
		Economic Cooperation Framework Agreement (ECFA) between PRC and Taiwan	
2010.12		Sixth Chen–Chiang summit (Taipei)	
2011	House Foreign Affairs Committee "Why Taiwan Matters" Hearing		
2011		"Taiwan consensus" included in DPP's 10-year party reform	
2011	U.S.–Taiwan Visa Waiver Program		
2011.10		Seventh Chen–Chiang summit (Tianjin)	

(*Continued*)

(Continued)

	United States	Taiwan	China
2011.11	USAID Administrator Rajiv Shah visits Taiwan	Seventh Chen–Chiang summit (Tianjin)	
2012.03		Ma's reelection	
2012.08		Eighth Chen–Chiang summit (Taipei)	
2012.08		Ma's "East China Sea Initiatives"	
2012.09	Japanese's nationalization of disputed Diaoyudao/Senkaku/Diaoyutai territorial disputes and diplomatic crisis		
2012.10		Former DPP Chairman Frank Hsieh's visit to PRC	
2012.12			18th Party Congress, "1992 consensus" written into a Party Congress report for the first time Xi Jinping in office
2013.06		Taiwan, PRC signed the 19th agreement (on trade in services)	
2014.02		Mainland Affairs Council (MAC) Minister Wang Yu-chi met with Beijing's Taiwan Affairs Office (TAO) Director Zhang Zhijun in Nanjing	
2014.04	EPA Administrator Gina McCarthy visits Taiwan		
2014.03		Sunflower Student Movement	

Documents

Except as noted, all documents are full-text. Key passages have been highlighted in some documents.

1. February 27, 1972 United States–PRC Shanghai Communique
   One of the most dramatic turning points of Cold War diplomacy, it marked the beginning of a new relationship with the PRC, and with the ROC on Taiwan as well. The position of the United States shifted from alliance with ROC to pivot between PRC and ROC.
2. January 1, 1979 United States–PRC Normalization Communique
   Since only one government per territory can be recognized, this marked the formal beginning of state–to–state relations between the United States *and PRC, and the end of formal relations with ROC.*
3. January 1, 1979 PRC Message to Compatriots in Taiwan
   This message, simultaneous with United States*–PRC normalization, marked the watershed in PRC cross-Strait policy from liberation to peaceful reunification.*
4. April 10, 1979 United States–Taiwan Relations Act (TRA)
   Since the United States *no longer had diplomatic relations with ROC it had to define its new relationship. In the passage quoted, the TRA went beyond technicalities to claim continuing American security interests in Taiwan.*

5. September 30, 1981 PRC Ye Jianying's Nine Point Proposal on Taiwan

    This was the earliest comprehensive statement of PRC's new Taiwan policy, including the promises that Taiwan could retain its armed forces and that PRC would not interfere in local affairs. The new policy was summarized by Deng Xiaoping as "one country, two systems."

6. August 17, 1982 United States–PRC Joint Communique on Arms Sales

    The mounting tensions over US arms sales to Taiwan were diffused by this promise of reduction and elimination of sales. Continuing arms sales remain a sore point in the relationship.

7. November 3, 1992 PRC–ROC The "1992 Consensus" (Ma Ying-jeou's comments in 2011)

    Perhaps the best expression of the ambiguity of the PRC–ROC relationship is this "agreement to disagree" on the meaning of "China." But as Ma's 2011 statement details, in Taiwan between the KMT and the DPP there is no consensus on the Consensus.

8. January 30, 1995 PRC Jiang Zemin's Eight Points

    While Ye dealt with policies regarding CCP-KMT reconciliation, thirteen years later Jiang had to adjust PRC policy to cope with a multi-party, democratic Taiwan and a more powerful "Taiwan independence" sentiment.

9. July 9, 1999 ROC Lee Teng-hui "Special State-to-State Relations"

    From the mid-1990s Lee Teng-hui articulated an increasingly independent formulation of Taiwan's political identity, causing concerns in the PRC.

10. August 2, 2002 ROC Chen Shui-bian "One Country on Each Side"

    An eloquent statement of the DPP's "deep green" view of Taiwan's status and, from the viewpoint of the PRC, one of Chen Shui-bian's most provocative statements.

Joint Communique
of the United States of America
and the People's Republic of China
(Shanghai Communique)
February 28, 1972

1. President Richard Nixon of the United States of America visited the People's Republic of China at the invitation of Premier Chou En-lai of the People's Republic of China from February 21 to February 28, 1972. Accompanying the President were Mrs. Nixon, United States Secretary of State William Rogers, Assistant to the President Dr. Henry Kissinger, and other American officials.

2. President Nixon met with Chairman Mao Tsetung of the Communist Party of China on February 21. The two leaders had a serious and frank exchange of views on Sino–United States relations and world affairs.

3. During the visit, extensive, earnest and frank discussions were held between President Nixon and Premier Chou En-lai on the normalization of relations between the United States of America and the People's Republic of China, as well as on other matters of interest to both sides. In addition, Secretary of State William Rogers and Foreign Minister Chi Peng-fei held talks in the same spirit.

4. President Nixon and his party visited Peking and viewed cultural, industrial and agricultural sites, and they also toured Hangchow and Shanghai where, continuing discussions with Chinese leaders, they viewed similar places of interest.

5. The leaders of the People's Republic of China and the United States of America found it beneficial to have this opportunity, after so many years without contact, to present candidly to one another their views on a variety of issues. They reviewed the international situation in which important changes and great upheavals are taking place and expounded their respective positions and attitudes.

6. The Chinese side stated: Wherever there is oppression, there is resistance. Countries want independence, nations want liberation and the people want revolution — this has become the irresistible trend of history. All nations, big or small, should be equal: big nations should not bully the small and strong nations should not bully the weak. China will never be a superpower and it opposes hegemony and power politics of any kind. The Chinese side stated that it firmly supports the struggles of all the oppressed people and nations for freedom and liberation and that the people of all countries have the right to choose their social systems according their own wishes and the right to safeguard the independence, sovereignty and territorial integrity of their own countries and oppose foreign aggression, interference, control and subversion. All foreign troops should be withdrawn to their own countries. The Chinese side expressed its firm support to the people of Vietnam, Laos and Cambodia in their efforts for the attainment of their goal and its firm support to the seven-point proposal of the Provisional Revolutionary Government of the Republic of South Vietnam and the elaboration of February this year on the two key problems in the proposal, and to the Joint Declaration of the Summit Conference of the Indochinese People. It firmly supports the eight-point program for the peaceful unification of Korea put forward by the

Government of the Democratic People's Republic of Korea on April 12, 1971, and the stand for the abolition of the "UN Commission for the Unification and Rehabilitation of Korea". It firmly opposes the revival and outward expansion of Japanese militarism and firmly supports the Japanese people's desire to build an independent, democratic, peaceful and neutral Japan. It firmly maintains that India and Pakistan should, in accordance with the United Nations resolutions on the Indo–Pakistan question, immediately withdraw all their forces to their respective territories and to their own sides of the ceasefire line in Jammu and Kashmir and firmly supports the Pakistan Government and people in their struggle to preserve their independence and sovereignty and the people of Jammu and Kashmir in their struggle for the right of self-determination.

7. The United States side stated: Peace in Asia and peace in the world requires efforts both to reduce immediate tensions and to eliminate the basic causes of conflict. The United States will work for a just and secure peace: Just, because it fulfills the aspirations of peoples and nations for freedom and progress; secure, because it removes the danger of foreign aggression. The United States supports individual freedom and social progress for all the peoples of the world, free of outside pressure or intervention. The United States believes that the effort to reduce tensions is served by improving communication between countries that have different ideologies so as to lessen the risks of confrontation through accident, miscalculation or misunderstanding. Countries should treat each other with mutual respect and be willing to compete peacefully, letting performance be the ultimate judge. No country should claim infallibility and each country should be prepared to re-examine its own attitudes for the common good. The United States stressed that the people of Indochina should be allowed to determine their destiny without outside intervention; its constant primary objective has been a negotiated solution; the eight-point proposal put forward by the Republic of Vietnam and the United States on January 27, 1972

represents a basis for the attainment of that objective; in the absence of a negotiated settlement the United States envisages the ultimate withdrawal of all United States forces from the region consistent with the aim of self-determination for each country of Indo-China. The United States will maintain its close ties with and support for the Republic of Korea; the United States will support efforts of the Republic of Korea to seek a relaxation of tension and increased communication in the Korean peninsula. The United States places the highest value on its friendly relations with Japan; it will continue to develop the existing close bonds. Consistent with the United Nations Security Council Resolution of December 21, 1971, the United States favors the continuation of the ceasefire between India and Pakistan and the withdrawal of all military forces to within their own territories and to their own sides of the ceasefire line in Jammu and Kashmir; the United States supports the right of the peoples of South Asia to shape their own future in peace, free of military threat, and without having the area become the subject of great power rivalry.

8. There are essential differences between China and the United States in their social systems and foreign policies. However, the two sides agreed that countries, regardless of their social systems, should conduct their relations on the principles of respect for the sovereignty and territorial integrity of all states, non-aggression against other states, non-interference in the internal affairs of other states, equality and mutual benefit, and peaceful coexistence. International disputes should be settled on this basis, without resorting to the use or threat of force. The United States and the People's Republic of China are prepared to apply these principles to their mutual relations.

9. With these principles of international relations in mind the two sides stated that:

   (a) Progress toward the normalization of relations between China and the United States is in the interests of all countries;

(b) Both wish to reduce the danger of international military conflict;

(c) Neither should seek hegemony in the Asia–Pacific region and each is opposed to efforts by any other country or group of countries to establish such hegemony;

(d) Neither is prepared to negotiate on behalf of any third party or to enter into agreements or understandings with the other directed at other states.

10. Both sides are of the view that it would be against the interests of the people of the world for any major country to collude with another against other countries, or for major countries to divide up the world into spheres of interest.

11. The two sides reviewed the long-standing serious disputes between China and the United States. The Chinese side reaffirmed its position: The Taiwan question is the crucial question obstructing the normalization of relations between China and the United States; the Government of the People's Republic of China is the sole legal government of China; Taiwan is a province of China which has long been returned to the motherland; the liberation of Taiwan is China's internal affair in which no other country has the right to interfere; and all United States forces and military installations must be withdrawn from Taiwan. The Chinese Government firmly opposes any activities which aim at the creation of "one China, one Taiwan", "one China, two governments", "two Chinas", an "independent Taiwan" or advocate that "the status of Taiwan remains to be determined".

12. The United States side declared: The United States acknowledges that all Chinese on either side of the Taiwan Strait maintain there is but one China and that Taiwan is a part of China. The United States Government does not challenge that position. It reaffirms its interest in a peaceful settlement of the Taiwan question by the Chinese themselves. With this prospect

in mind, it affirms the ultimate objective of the withdrawal of all United States forces and military installations from Taiwan. In the meantime, it will progressively reduce its forces and military installations on Taiwan as the tension in the area diminishes. The two sides agreed that it is desirable to broaden the understanding between the people of both the countries. To this end, they discussed specific areas in such fields as science, technology, culture, sports and journalism, in which people-to-people contacts and exchanges would be mutually beneficial. Each side undertakes to facilitate the further development of such contacts and exchanges.

13. Both sides view bilateral trade as another area from which mutual benefit can be derived, and agreed that economic relations based on equality and mutual benefit are in the interest of the peoples of the two countries. They agree to facilitate the progressive development of trade between their two countries.

14. The two sides agreed that they will stay in contact through various channels, including the sending of a senior United States representative to Peking from time to time for concrete consultations to further the normalization of relations between the two countries and continue to exchange views on issues of common interest.

15. The two sides expressed the hope that the gains achieved during this visit would open up new prospects for the relations between the two countries. They believe that the normalization of relations between the two countries is not only in the interest of the Chinese and American peoples but also contributes to the relaxation of tension in Asia and the world.

16. President Nixon, Mrs. Nixon and the American party expressed their appreciation for the gracious hospitality shown them by the Government and people of the People's Republic of China.

Joint Communiqué on the Establishment of Diplomatic Relations between the People's Republic of China and the United States of America

January 1, 1979

The People's Republic of China and the United States of America have agreed to recognize each other and to establish diplomatic relations as of January 1, 1979.

The United States of America recognizes the Government of the People's Republic of China as the sole legal Government of China. Within this context, the people of the United States will maintain cultural, commercial and other unofficial relations with the people of Taiwan.

The People's Republic of China and the United States of America reaffirm the principles agreed on by the two sides in the Shanghai Communique and emphasize once again that:

— Both wish to reduce the danger of international military conflict.
— Neither should seek hegemony in the Asia–Pacific region or in any other region of the world and each is opposed to efforts by any other country or group of countries to establish such hegemony.

Neither is prepared to negotiate on behalf of any third party or to enter into agreements or understandings with the other directed at other states.

— **The Government of the United States of America acknowledges the Chinese position that there is but one China and Taiwan is part of China.**
— Both believe that normalization of Sino–American relations is not only in the interest of the Chinese and American peoples but also contributes to the cause of peace in Asia and the world.

The People's Republic of China and the United States of America will exchange Ambassadors and establish Embassies on March 1, 1979.

Message to Compatriots in Taiwan

(January 1, 1979)

The Standing Committee of the Fifth National People's Congress at its Fifth Plenary Session on December 26, 1978 adopted after discussion a message to compatriots in Taiwan. Following is the full text of the message. — Ed.

Dear Compatriots in Taiwan:

Today is New Year's Day 1979. We hereby extend our cordial and sincere greetings to you on behalf of the people of all nationalities on the mainland of our motherland.

As an old saying goes, "When festival times come round people think all the more of their loved ones." On this happy occasion as we celebrate New Year's Day, our thoughts turn all the more to our kith and kin, our old folks, our brothers and sisters, in Taiwan. We know you have the motherland and your kinsfolk on the mainland in mind too. This mutual feeling of many years standing grows with each passing day. From the day when Taiwan was unfortunately separated from the motherland in 1949, we have not been able to communicate with or visit each other, our motherland has not been able to achieve reunification, relatives have been unable to get together, and our nation, country and people have suffered greatly as a result. All Chinese compatriots and people of Chinese descent throughout the world look forward to an early end to this regrettable state of affairs.

The Chinese nation is a great nation. It accounts for almost a quarter of the world's population and has a long history and brilliant culture, and its outstanding contributions to world civilization and human progress are universally recognized. Taiwan has been an inalienable part of China since ancient times. The Chinese nation has great vitality and cohesion. Throughout its history, foreign invasions and internal strife have failed to split our nation permanently. Taiwan's separation from the motherland land for nearly 30 years has been artificial and against our national interests and aspirations, and this state of affairs must not be allowed to continue. Every Chinese, in Taiwan or on the mainland, has a compelling responsibility for the survival, growth and prosperity of the Chinese nation. The important task of reunifying our motherland, on which hinges the future of the whole nation, now lies before us all; it is an issue no one can evade or should try to. If we do not quickly set about ending this disunity so that our motherland is reunified at an early date, how can we answer our ancestors and explain to our descendants? This sentiment is shared by all. Who among the descendants of the Yellow Emperor wishes to go down in history as a traitor?

Radical changes have taken place in China's status in the world over the past 30 years. Our country's international prestige is rising constantly and its international role becomes ever more important. The people and governments of almost all countries place tremendous hopes on us in the struggle against hegemonism and in safeguarding peace and stability in Asia and the world as a whole. Every Chinese is proud to see the growing strength and prosperity of our motherland. If we can end the present disunity and join forces soon, there will be no end to our contributions to the future of mankind. Early reunification of our motherland is not only the common desire of all the people of China, including our compatriots in Taiwan, but the common wish of all peace-loving people and countries the world over.

Reunification of China today is consonant with popular sentiment and the general trend of development. The world in general recognizes only one China, with the Government of the People's Republic of China as its sole legal Government. The recent conclusion of the China–Japan Treaty of Peace and Friendship and the normalization of relations between China and the United States show still more clearly that no one can stop this trend. The present situation in the motherland, one of stability and unity, is better than ever. The people of all nationalities on the mainland are working hard with one will for the great goal of the four modernizations. It is our fervent hope that Taiwan returns to the embrace of the motherland at an early date so that we can work together for the great cause of national development. **Our state leaders have firmly declared that they will take present realities into account in accomplishing the great cause of reunifying the motherland and respect the status quo on Taiwan and the opinions of people in all walks of life there and adopt reasonable policies and measures in settling the question of reunification so as not to cause the people of Taiwan any losses.** On the other hand, people in all walks of life in Taiwan have expressed their yearning for their homeland and old friends, stated their desire "to identify themselves with and rejoin their kinsmen," and raised diverse proposals which are expressions of their earnest hope for an early return to the embrace of the motherland. As all conditions now are favourable for reunification and everything is set, no one should go against the will of the nation and against the trend of history.

We place hopes on the 17 million people on Taiwan and also the Taiwan authorities. The Taiwan authorities have always taken a firm stand of one China and have been opposed to an independent Taiwan. We have this stand in common and it is the basis for our cooperation. Our position has always been that all patriots belong to one family. The responsibility for reunifying the motherland rests with each of us. We hope the Taiwan authorities will treasure national interests and make valuable contributions to the reunification of the motherland.

The Chinese Government has ordered the People's Liberation Army to stop the bombardment of Jinmen (Quemoy) and other islands as from today. A state of military confrontation between the two sides still exists along the Taiwan Straits. This can only breed man-made tension. We hold that first of all this military confrontation should be ended through discussion between the Government of the People's Republic of China and the Taiwan authorities so as to create the necessary prerequisites and a secure environment for the two sides to make contacts and exchanges in whatever area.

The prolonged separation has led to inadequate mutual understanding between the compatriots on the mainland and on Taiwan and various inconveniences for both sides. Since overseas Chinese residing in faraway foreign lands can return for visits and tours and hold reunions with their families, why cannot compatriots living so near, on the mainland and on Taiwan, visit each other freely? We hold that there is no reason for such barriers to remain. We hope that at an early date transportation and postal services between both sides will be established to make it easier for compatriots of both sides to have direct contact, write to each other, visit relatives and friends, exchange tours and visits and carry out academic, cultural, sports and technological interchanges.

Economically speaking, Taiwan and the mainland of the motherland were originally one entity. Unfortunately, economic ties have been suspended for many years. Construction is going ahead vigorously on the motherland and it is our wish that Taiwan also grows economically more prosperous. There is every reason for us to develop trade between us, each making up what the other lacks, and carry out economic exchanges. This is mutually required and will benefit both parties without doing any harm to either.

Dear compatriots in Taiwan,

The bright future of our great motherland belongs to us and to you. The reunification of the motherland is the sacred mission history has handed to our generation. Times are moving ahead and the situation is developing. The earlier we fulfill this mission, the sooner we can jointly write an unprecedented, brilliant page in the history for our country, catch up with advanced powers and work together with them for world peace, prosperity and progress. Let us join hands and work together for this glorious goal!

Taiwan Relations Act Public Law 96–98 96th Congress

(partial text)

Findings and Declaration of Policy
Section 2.

1. The President — having terminated governmental relations between the United States and the governing authorities on Taiwan recognized by the United States as the Republic of China prior to January 1, 1979, the Congress finds that the enactment of this Act is necessary:

   1. to help maintain peace, security, and stability in the Western Pacific; and
   2. to promote the foreign policy of the United States by authorizing the continuation of commercial, cultural, and other relations between the people of the United States and the people on Taiwan.

2. It is the policy of the United States:

   1. to preserve and promote extensive, close, and friendly commercial, cultural and other relations between the people of the United States and the people on Taiwan, as well as the people

on the China mainland and all other peoples of the Western Pacific area;

2. to declare that peace and stability in the area are in the political, security, and economic interests of the United States, and are matters of international concern;

3. to make clear that the United States decision to establish diplomatic relations with the People's Republic of China rests upon the expectation that the future of Taiwan will be determined by peaceful means;

4. to consider any effort to determine the future of Taiwan by other than peaceful means, including by boycotts or embargoes, a threat to the peace and security of the Western Pacific area and of grave concern to the United States;

5. to provide Taiwan with arms of a defensive character; and

6. to maintain the capacity of the United States to resist any resort to force or other forms of coercion that would jeopardize the security, or the social or economic system, of the people on Taiwan.

3. Nothing contained in this Act shall contravene the interest of the United States in human rights, especially with respect to the human rights of all the approximately eighteen million inhabitants of Taiwan. The preservation and enhancement of the human rights of all the people on Taiwan are hereby reaffirmed as objectives of the United States.

Chairman Ye Jianying's Elaborations on Policy Concerning Return of Taiwan To Motherland and Peaceful Reunification

(September 30, 1981)

Ye Jianying, Chairman of the Standing Committee of the National People's Congress, in an interview with a Xinhua correspondent on September 30, 1981, elaborated on the policy concerning the return of Taiwan to the motherland for the realization of China's peaceful reunification. Following is the full text of his statement. —Ed.

Today, on the eve of the 32ⁿᵈ anniversary of the founding of the People's Republic of China and at the approach of the 70ᵗʰ anniversary of the 1911 Revolution, I wish, first of all, to extend my festive greetings and cordial regards to the people of all nationalities throughout the country, including the compatriots in Taiwan, Xianggang (Hong Kong) and Aomen (Macao), and Chinese nationals residing in foreign countries.

On New Year's Day 1979, the Standing committee of the National People's Congress issued a message to the compatriots in Taiwan, in which it proclaimed the policy of striving to reunify the motherland peacefully. The message received warm support and active response from the people of all nationalities throughout China, including the compatriots in Taiwan, Xianggang [Hong Kong] and Aomen [Macau], and those residing abroad. A relaxed atmosphere has set in across the Taiwan Strait. Now, I would take this opportunity to elaborate on the policy concerning the return of Taiwan to the motherland for the realization of peaceful reunification:

(1) In order to bring an end to the unfortunate separation of the Chinese nation as early as possible, we propose that talks be held between the Communist Party of China and the Kuomintang of China on a reciprocal basis so that the two parties will cooperate for the third time to accomplish the great cause of national reunification. The two sides may first send people to meet for an exhaustive exchange of views.

(2) It is the urgent desire of the people of all nationalities on both sides of the strait to communicate with each other, reunite with their families and relatives, develop trade and increase mutual understanding. We propose that the two sides make arrangements to facilitate the exchange of mails, trade, air and shipping services, family reunions and visits by relatives and tourists as

well as academic, cultural and sports exchanges, and reach an agreement thereupon.

(3) After the country is reunified, Taiwan can enjoy a high degree of autonomy as a special administrative region and it can retain its armed forces. The Central Government will not interfere with local affairs on Taiwan.

(4) Taiwan's current socio-economic system will remain unchanged, so will its way of life and its economic and cultural relations with foreign countries. There will be no encroachment on the proprietary rights and lawful rights of inheritance over private property, houses, land and enterprises, or on foreign investments.

(5) People in authority and representative personages of various circles in Taiwan may take up posts of leadership in national political bodies and participate in running the state.

(6) When Taiwan's local finance is in difficulty, the Central Government may subsidize it as is fit for the circumstances.

(7) For people of all nationalities and public figures of various circles in Taiwan who wish to come and settle on the mainland, it is guaranteed that proper arrangements will be made for them, that there will be no discriminations against them, and that they will have the freedom of entry and exit.

(8) Industrialists and businessmen in Taiwan are welcome to invest and engage in various economic undertakings on the mainland, and their legal rights, interests and profits are guaranteed.

(9) The reunification of the motherland is the responsibility of all Chinese. We sincerely welcome people of all nationalities, public figures of all circles and all mass organizations in Taiwan to make proposals and suggestions regarding affairs of state through various channels and in various ways.

Taiwan's return to the embrace of the motherland and the accomplishment of the great cause of national reunification is a great and glorious mission history has bequeathed on our generation. China's reunification and prosperity is in the vital interest of the Chinese people of all nationalities — not only those on the mainland, but those in Taiwan as well. It is also in the interest of peace in the Far East and the world.

We hope that our compatriots in Taiwan will give full play to their patriotism and work energetically for the early realization of the great unity of our nation and share the honour of it. We hope that our compatriots in Xianggang and Aomen and Chinese nationals residing abroad will continue to act in the role of a bridge and contribute their share to the reunification of the motherland.

We hope that the Kuomintang authorities will stick to their one-China position and their opposition to "two Chinas" and that they will put national interests above everything else, forget previous ill will and join hands with us in accomplishing the great cause of national reunification and the great goal of making China prosperous and strong, so as to win glory for our ancestors, bring benefit to our posterity and write a new and glorious page in the history of the Chinese nation!

United States–PRC
Joint Communiqué
on Arms Sales to Taiwan

August 17, 1982

1. In the Joint Communique on the Establishment of Diplomatic Relations on January 1, 1979, issued by the Government of the United States of America and the Government of the People's Republic of China, the United States of America recognized the Government of the People's Republic of China as the sole legal government of China, and it acknowledged the Chinese position that there is but one China and Taiwan is part of China. Within that context, the two sides agreed that the people of the United States would continue to maintain cultural, commercial, and other unofficial relations with the people of Taiwan. On this basis, relations between the United States and China were normalized.

2. The question of United States arms sales to Taiwan was not settled in the course of negotiations between the two countries on establishing diplomatic relations. The two sides held differing positions, and the Chinese side stated that it would raise the issue again following normalization. Recognizing that this issue would seriously hamper the development of United States–China relations, they have held further discussions on it, during and

since the meetings between President Ronald Reagan and Premier Zhao Ziyang and between Secretary of State Alexander M. Haig, Jr. and Vice Premier and Foreign Minister Huang Hua in October 1981.

3. Respect for each other's sovereignty and territorial integrity and non-interference each other's internal affairs constitute the fundamental principles guiding United States–China relations. These principles were confirmed in the Shanghai Communique of February 28, 1972 and reaffirmed in the Joint Communique on the Establishment of Diplomatic Relations which came into effect on January 1, 1973. Both sides emphatically state that these principles continue to govern all aspects of their relations.

4. The Chinese government reiterates that the question of Taiwan is China's internal affair. The Message to the Compatriots in Taiwan issued by China on January 1, 1979, promulgated a fundamental policy of striving for Peaceful reunification of the Motherland. The Nine-Point Proposal put forward by China on September 30, 1981 represented a further major effort under this fundamental policy to strive for a peaceful solution to the Taiwan question.

5. The United States Government attaches great importance to its relations with China, and reiterates that it has no intention of infringing on Chinese sovereignty and territorial integrity, or interfering in China's internal affairs, or pursuing a policy of "two Chinas" or "one China, one Taiwan." The United States Government understands and appreciates the Chinese policy of striving for a peaceful resolution of the Taiwan question as indicated in China's Message to Compatriots in Taiwan issued on January 1, 1979 and the Nine-Point Proposal put forward by China on September 30, 1981. The new situation which has emerged with regard to the Taiwan question also provides favorable conditions for the settlement of United States–China

differences over the question of United States arms sales to Taiwan.

6. Having in mind the foregoing statements of both sides, the United States Government states that it does not seek to carry out a long-term policy of arms sales to Taiwan, that its arms sales to Taiwan will not exceed, either in qualitative or in quantitative terms, the level of those supplied in recent years since the establishment of diplomatic relations between the United States and China, and that it intends to reduce gradually its sales of arms to Taiwan, leading over a period of time to a final resolution. In so stating, the United States acknowledges China's consistent position regarding the thorough settlement of this issue.

7. In order to bring about, over a period of time, a final settlement of the question of United States arms sales to Taiwan, which is an issue rooted in history, the two governments will make every effort to adopt measures and create conditions conducive to the thorough settlement of this issue.

8. The development of United States–China relations is not only in the interest of the two people but also conducive to peace and stability in the world. The two sides are determined, on the principle of equality and mutual benefit, to strengthen their ties to the economic, cultural, educational, scientific, technological and other fields and make strong, joint efforts for the continued development of relations between the governments and peoples of the United States and China.

9. In order to bring about the healthy development of United States China relations, maintain world peace and oppose aggression and expansion, the two governments reaffirm the principles agreed on by the two sides in the Shanghai Communique and the Joint Communique on the Establishment of Diplomatic Relations. The two sides will maintain contact and hold appropriate consultations on bilateral and international issues of common interest.

President Ma holds press conference to discuss
"1992 Consensus"
2011/08/28

There has been much talk recently about the "1992 Consensus" and the "Taiwan Consensus." I was involved in work associated with the talks that led to the "1992 Consensus" when I was Mainland Affairs Council (MAC) vice chairman. I invited Vice Chairman Kao of the Straits Exchange Foundation (SEF) to attend today's press conference, as Vice Chairman Kao also was a vice chairman of the MAC at that time.

I would like to turn to the history of the "1992 Consensus." The SEF and mainland China's Association for Relations Across the Taiwan Straits (ARATS) were established in 1992, initially to address the issue of verification of documents. At that time, the mainland wanted us to sign an agreement that both sides agreed to a "one China" principle, but our side had a different opinion on this issue. There was no concrete resolution of this issue, so the two sides decided to engage in formal negotiations in Hong Kong in October of that year. On August 1, the National Unification Council, which was headed by then President Lee Teng-hui, held a meeting, during which a consensus was reached as to the meaning of "one China." They felt that we needed to set forth our position and create a bottom line on the issue of "one China," as this issue would arise in the upcoming talks with mainland China, and they came to the decision that "one China" referred to the Republic of China that has been in existence since 1912, and that its sovereignty included all of China, but that its authority to govern was limited to Taiwan, Penghu, Kinmen and Matsu. This was the resolution that was passed at a meeting of the National Unification Council on August 1, 1992 held at the Presidential Office Building and presided over by then President Lee, who also served as the Council's chairperson. I was present at that meeting, which was also attended by Huang Kun-huei, who was then the MAC chairman, in his capacity as a member of the Council.

After this resolution was adopted, the definition of "ROC" set forth therein served as the basis for our discussions in Hong Kong with Mainland China when the issue of "one China" was broached. Ultimately, no agreement was reached and the two sides left Hong Kong at the time without a consensus. However, on November 3 the SEF issued a press release and simultaneously sent a letter to the ARATS via fax that explained its stance on "one China," saying that having obtained the approval of our competent authority, we accept that each side can have its own verbal interpretation (regarding the "one-China" issue). Thirteen days later, on November 16, the ARATS replied in a letter as follows: The formal notification issued by the SEF on November 3 shows that the Taiwan side has agreed that each side can have its own interpretation *via* verbal declaration. The ARATS fully respects and accepts the suggestion by the SEF, and on November 3 phoned Mr. Chen Rong-jye to inform him of this stance. Mr. Chen was then secretary-general of the SEF. This is how the two sides came to agree to accept the "one China, respective interpretations" principle 19 years ago.

Therefore, the meaning of the "1992 Consensus" is quite clear — "one China, respective interpretations." This is a consensus that was reached between the two sides. For us, the so-called "one China" is of course the Republic of China, since at that time prior to the initiation of discussions with Mainland China, the National Unification Council specially convened a meeting and confirmed that the so-called "one China" is the "Republic of China that was established in 1912 and exists to this day." This fact is extremely clear.

Some might comment that although our side was clear as to the meaning, we cannot be sure that Mainland China accepted this arrangement. By examining the letters that were sent between the two sides, we can be clear that authorities on the other side fully respected and accepted our stance. Let's also take a look back at the situation three years ago. I was elected president on March 22, 2008, and on March 26 then United States President George W. Bush and General Secretary of the Communist Party of China Hu Jintao spoke over the phone. During the conversation, Mr. Hu remarked that Mainland China and Taiwan should resume negotiations based on the foundation of the "1992 Consensus. Under the

"1992 Consensus," Mr. Hu explained to then President Bush, both sides acknowledged that there is only one China, but that the definition of it on each side is different. Mr. Hu then described the situation in Chinese and the Xinhua News Agency also released an English press release to this effect. I even remember that this news was the top story in Taiwan's United Daily News.

Not long after I was inaugurated on May 20 of that year, the SEF elected a new chairman and the organization sent a letter to its mainland counterpart stating that it was willing to resume negotiations based on the foundation of the "1992 Consensus." The ARATS also replied that it was willing to do the same. Consequently, the two sides not only accepted the consensus, but were consistent on the content of it. Mr. Hu at the time clearly expressed the state of affairs. As a result, the "1992 Consensus" that we take today as the basis for negotiations between the two sides, does not harm the sovereignty of the ROC, and in fact enables the sovereignty of the ROC to play an important role in the process of reaching agreements between the two sides. The consensus echoes the status between the two sides set forth in the ROC Constitution and it clearly corroborates our standpoint that "one China" refers to the Republic of China.

It is the "1992 Consensus" that has enabled the two sides of the Taiwan Strait to put aside their differences over the issue of sovereignty for the time being. Upon this basis the two sides have been willing, despite the lack of consensus on the issue of sovereignty, to shelve disputes and move ahead with bilateral talks. This is the most important reason why the two sides over the past three years have been able to complete 15 agreements; this is the basis upon which negotiations are made possible. Nineteen years ago it was precisely because of the "1992 Consensus" that the Koo-Wang talks (between the respective heads of the SEF and ARATS) could be held in Singapore, and again in Mainland China the following year, and why four agreements resulted from those talks. Therefore, everyone should understand the enormously important role that the "1992 Consensus" has played in negotiations and cooperation between the two sides.

We have recently seen Democratic Progressive Party (DPP) Chairwoman Tsai Ing-wen repeatedly refer to the "Taiwan Consensus." In fact, to understand what a consensus on Taiwan means, we must first understand the opinions of the people of Taiwan. The people of Taiwan at the present stage favor the policy of "no unification, no independence, and no use of force." That is why, before I took office as President, I advocated a policy under the framework of the ROC Constitution of maintaining the *status quo* in the Taiwan Strait *via* this "three noes" policy. In other words, maintaining the *status quo* reflects the desire of the vast majority of the people in Taiwan. Since its establishment over 20 years ago, the MAC each year has carried out several surveys that clearly show only a minority of people advocate either unification or independence, while an overwhelming majority, nearly 80%, support broadly maintaining the *status quo*. This is the true representation of the will of the Taiwan people, and is the main basis for advocating "no unification, no independence, and no use of force." I call on Chairwoman Tsai to tell the people of Taiwan whether she advocates the "three noes" policy and whether she can communicate her opinion to the majority of the Taiwan public, which supports the "no unification, no independence, and no use of force" policy, and in particular whether she supports the "no independence" portion. Chairwoman Tsai cannot be vague or avoid this question. Rather, she must face the issue. I have been extremely clear in proclaiming that the ROC is our nation, Taiwan is our home, and the blue, white, and crimson flag is the national flag of the ROC. This is a clear fact, and it is something that I should clearly spell out.

Chairwoman Tsai once said that the ROC is a government in exile. I am unaware whether the chairwoman still believes this statement. I am aware that some people in the DPP believe that the ROC national flag cannot represent our nation. There are some political figures from the DPP who when sworn into office have not been willing to face the flag or sing the national anthem. In addition, a very small number of DPP members working as civil servants have even burned the flag. We are quite aware that some members of the DPP maintain the aforementioned attitude towards the nation, the national flag, and the Constitution. Consequently, as Taiwan faces the challenges of the future, I hope that everyone is able to truly understand that the consensus on Taiwan is precisely "no unification, no independence, and no use of force" under the framework of the ROC Constitution. Over the past three years, the government has proven that adoption of this stance can help to create greater room for Taiwan in the international community. This has not only enabled us to engage in discussions with mainland China, but also to have contacts with countries around the world. It is also because of this that we have seen incipient signs of peace emerge in the Taiwan strait, which has helped the two sides to jointly forge peace and prosperity in the Taiwan Strait. I believe that this is the true meaning of the consensus on Taiwan. This is a consensus that enables Taiwan to enjoy peace and prosperity.

If there are some hidden concepts in the "Taiwan Consensus" proposed by Chairwomen Tsai or things that cannot be said, such as "calling for a new constitution using a different title for the nation," I believe that this is not the consensus on Taiwan accepted by the majority of the people, since it would not bring peace and prosperity to Taiwan. Consequently, I hope that Chairwoman Tsai will explain her position and bravely introduce what her "Taiwan Consensus" is. She needs to clearly state whether she supports the "no unification, no independence, and no use of force" policy, and she needs to state whether she believes Taiwan should move in the direction of peace and prosperity.

I believe that the President our people want is a President of the ROC. I love the ROC and my support for the ROC is natural. I have nothing to fear by this and I have no hesitations. I want to shout out that we love the ROC and that we love Taiwan, because the ROC is our nation, Taiwan is our home, and the blue, white, and crimson flag is our national flag. I hope that clarifying this will be a positive factor in forging unity, harmony, and the peaceful development of cross-strait relations. Thank you!

Jiang Zemin's Eight Point Proposal

On January 30, 1995, General Secretary of the Central Committee of the Communist Party of China and President of China Jiang Zemin delivered an important speech entitled "Continuing to Strive Toward the Reunification of China." In his speech Jiang Zemin put forward eight propositions on the development of relations between the two sides of the Taiwan Straits and the peaceful reunification of China on the current stage:

1. Adhering to the principle of one China is the basis and prerequisite for peaceful reunification. China's sovereignty and territorial integrity must never be allowed to suffer division. We must resolutely oppose any statement and action for creating "the independence of Taiwan"; and we must also resolutely oppose the propositions to "split the country and rule under separate regimes," "two Chinas over a certain period of time," etc., which are contrary to the principle of one China.
2. We do not have objections to the development of non-governmental economic and cultural ties between Taiwan and other countries. According to the principle of one China and the characters of international organizations concerned, Taiwan has joined the Asian Development Bank, the Asian–Pacific Economic Cooperation Forum and other international economical

organizations in the name of "Chinese Taibei." However, we oppose Taiwan's activities in "expanding its living space internationally," aimed at creating "two Chinas" or "one China, one Taiwan." All patriotic compatriots in Taiwan and other people of insight understand that instead of solving problems, such activities can only help the forces working for the "independence of Taiwan," and undermine the progress of peaceful reunification. Only after peaceful reunification is accomplished can our Taiwan compatriots and other Chinese truly and fully share the international dignity and honor attained by our great motherland.

3. It has been our consistent stand to hold negotiations with Taiwan authorities on the peaceful reunification of the motherland. Representatives of all political parties and groups from both sides of the Taiwan Straits can be invited to participate in the negotiations for peaceful reunification. I said in my report at the 14th National Congress of the Communist Party of China held in October 1992, "On the premise that there is only one China, we are prepared to talk with the Taiwan authorities about any matter, including the form that official negotiations should take, a form that would be acceptable to both sides." By "on the premise that there is only one China, we are prepared to talk with the Taiwan authorities about any matter," we mean, naturally, that all matters of concern to the Taiwan authorities are included. We have proposed time and again that negotiations should be held on officially ending the state of hostility between the two sides and accomplishing peaceful reunification step by step. Here again I solemnly propose that such negotiations be held. I suggest that, as a first step, negotiations should be held and an agreement reached on officially ending the state of hostility between the two sides under the principle that there is only one China. On this basis, the two sides may bear responsibilities together, maintain China's sovereignty and territorial integrity, as well as plan the future development of the relations between the two sides separated by the strait. As regards the name, place and form of

these political talks, a solution acceptable to both sides can certainly be found so long as consultations on an equal footing can be held at an early date.

4. We shall try our best to achieve the peaceful reunification of China since Chinese should not fight Chinese. We do not promise not to use force. If used, force will not be directed against our compatriots in Taiwan, but against the foreign forces who intervene in China's reunification and go in for "the independence of Taiwan." We are fully confident that our compatriots in Taiwan, Hong Kong and Macao and those residing overseas would understand our principled position.

5. Challenged with world economic development in the 21st century, we shall spare no effect to develop economic exchange and cooperation between the two sides separated by the Taiwan straits so that both sides enjoy a flourishing economy and the whole Chinese nation benefits. We maintain that political disagreement should not impede economic cooperation between the two sides of the Taiwan straits. We shall continue, for an extended period, to implement a policy of encouraging Taiwanese investment on the mainland and carry out the Law of the People's Republic of China on Protecting Investments by Taiwan Compatriots. In any circumstances, we shall protect all legitimate rights and interests of Taiwanese investors in a down-to-earth way and continually encourage exchange and contacts across the Taiwan straits which promote mutual understanding. Since the direct links for postal, air and shipping services and trade between the two sides are the objective requirements for their economic development and contacts in various fields, and since they are in the interests of the people on both sides, it is absolutely necessary to adopt practical measures to speed up the establishment of such direct links. Efforts should be made to promote negotiations on certain specific issues between the two sides. We are in favor of conducting this kind of negotiations on the basis of reciprocity and mutual benefit and signing

nongovernmental agreements on the protection of the rights and interests of industrialists and business people from Taiwan.

6. The splendid culture of 5,000 years created by the sons and daughters of all ethnic groups of China has become ties keeping the entire Chinese people close at heart and constitutes an important basis for the peaceful reunification of the motherland. People on both sides should jointly inherit and carry forward the fine traditions of the culture.

7. The 21 million Taiwan people, whether born there or in other provinces, are Chinese and our own flesh and blood. The lifestyles of our Taiwan compatriots and their desire to be masters of their own country should be fully respected. All their legitimate rights and interests must be protected. All relevant departments in our Party and government, including agencies stationed abroad, must improve their relations with our Taiwan compatriots, listen to their views and requests, show concern for and take care of their interests and do everything they can to help solve their problems. We hope that Taiwan Island enjoys social stability, economic growth and affluence. We also hope that all political parties in Taiwan will adopt a sensible, forward-looking and constructive attitude and promote the expansion of relations between the two sides. We welcome all political parties and personages from different walks of life in Taiwan exchange opinions with us on the relations between the two sides and on peaceful reunification. Their visits to the mainland are also welcome. All personages from various circles who have contributed to the reunification of China will go down in history for their deeds.

8. We welcome leaders of Taiwan to visit the mainland in their proper status. We also are ready to accept invitations to visit Taiwan. We may discuss state affairs or exchange opinions on certain issues first. Even a simple visit to the side will be useful. The affairs of Chinese people should be handled by us, something that does not take an international occasion to accomplish.

People on both sides of the Taiwan straits eagerly look forward to meeting each other and being able to freely exchange visits.

The above eight propositions fully embody the consistency and continuance of the Communist Party of China and the Chinese Government on the issue of Taiwan; they embody their determination and sincerity to develop the relations across the strait and promote the reunification of the motherland. These suggestions have been warmly welcomed by the Chinese people at home and abroad and aroused great attention from the international community. The historical course of reunifying the motherland is irreversible, and the continuously developing relation between the two sides of the Taiwan Straits is in accordance with the general trend and the will of the people. On July 1, 1997 the Chinese Government resumed the exercise of sovereignty over Hong Kong. When the Chinese Government resumes the exercise of sovereignty over Macao on December 20, 1999, the solution to the Taiwan question and the historical mission of realizing the reunification of China will emerge, for the Chinese people, as an even more outstandingly important issue than ever before. At that time the Chinese people on both sides of the Taiwan straits should unite in common efforts toward the reunification of China.

Interview of Taiwan President Lee Teng-hui with Deutsche Welle radio

(partial text)
Taipei, July 9, 1999

Question: Declaring Taiwan an independent state does not seem to be a realistic option, and Beijing's "one country, two systems" formula is not acceptable for the majority of people in Taiwan. Is there any room for compromise between these two lines of policy? And if there is, what does it look like?

Answer: I have already explained very clearly that the Republic of China has been a sovereign state since it was founded in 1912. Moreover, in 1991, amendments to the Constitution designated cross-strait relations as **a special state–to–state relationship**. Consequently, there is no need to declare independence. The resolution of cross-Strait issues hinges on the issue of different systems. We cannot look at issues related to the two sides simply from the perspective of unification or independence.

Progression from an integration of systems to a gradual political integration is the most natural and most suitable choice to guarantee the welfare of all Chinese people. At present, the ROC has become the first democracy in the Chinese community. We would like to take a more active role in the Chinese mainland's modernization process; therefore, we hope that the authorities there can proceed with democratic reform to create favorable conditions for democratic unification. This is the direction of our efforts. We want to maintain the *status quo*, and maintain peace with Beijing on this foundation.

Chen Shui-bian
on Cross-Strait Relations

Full text of speech given via video link by Taiwanese President Chen Shui-bian to the 29th annual meeting of the World Federation of Taiwanese Associations (WFTA), held in Tokyo, Japan on Saturday August 3.

The grand opening of the 29th annual meeting of the World Federation of Taiwanese Associations in Tokyo, Japan, has once again reflected the ardent love of our overseas Taiwanese towards this piece of land, Taiwan, and manifested the strong vitality of the Taiwanese associations in various parts of the world.

[The annual meeting] will surely be able to bring the WFTA to new developments and new horizons and enable it to continue to work wholeheartedly for Taiwan's future.

Over a long period of time, the WFTA has made important contributions to Taiwan's democracy, the opening of its society, and the safeguarding of its human rights.

In the darkest days of the past filled with sufferings, your sacrifices and dedication enabled the flames of Taiwan's democracy to continue abroad.

Safeguarding identity

At the same time, you continued to provide assistance to Taiwan's democratic movement and inspire the general public on the island to earnestly ponder about Taiwan's prospect and its future.

As long as we are united as one, stand firmly in our stride, and master our own direction, I believe we will again open up our own road and carve out the future of Taiwan.

Finally, in the year 2000, with the approach of the new century, we at long last fulfilled your wishes and accomplished the changeover of the ruling party and the peaceful transition of political power, thereby enabling Taiwan to become a completely free and democratic country and to stand before the whole world with this glorious achievement.

At the same time, the WFTA has likewise continued over the years to dedicate its heart and soul to safeguarding Taiwan's identity and letting the international community to hear the heartfelt wishes of the Taiwan people.

In the past, you were not afraid of sacrifice out of your love for Taiwan.

Many fellow Taiwanese were subject to persecution and forced to go into exile, unable to return to the homeland all those years.

Your efforts and sacrifices, however, were not in vain.

Confidence in future

Your long held ideas — that Taiwan's sovereignty and independence can never be deprived of or restricted, that Taiwan's future must be determined by the Taiwan people themselves, that Taiwan's interests must come first, and so on and so forth — have not only become Taiwan's mainstream public opinion but have also won widespread acknowledgment in the international community.

Taiwan is not a part of someone else, not someone else's local government, and not someone else's province.

We must have confidence in ourselves and in the future of Taiwan.

In the past, we were not afraid of the bully of power and with love for our native Taiwan, we insisted on walking down our own road and eventually opened up a road of freedom and democracy for Taiwan.

Today, Taiwan is facing the Chinese communists' armed threats and international suppression.

We must not evade this fact but must not harbur any illusion.

We will open up a new situation for the Taiwan people's dignity and national security as well as the Taiwan society's prosperity and progress.

I again wish that this annual meeting will be successful and sincerely hope that under the leadership of President Kuo and the enthusiastic participation and support of native Taiwanese, the World Federation of Taiwanese Associations will continue to grow and strengthen.

[I hope that they] continue to speak out for Taiwan, actively elevate Taiwan's position in the world, and fully open up the space for Taiwan's survival in the international community.

'Independent state'

Here, I personally wish to make the following few calls and ask everyone to seriously think over them.

In the past few days, I have said that we should think seriously, we should walk down our own road — our Taiwan road — and walk towards our Taiwan's future.

What is walking down our Taiwan road? It is very simple and clear.

Our Taiwan road is "a road of democracy, a road of freedom, a road of human rights, and a road of peace for Taiwan".

Taiwan is our country.

Our country should not be bullied, dwarfed, marginalized and localized.

Taiwan is not a part of someone else, not someone else's local government, and not someone else's province.

Taiwan cannot become the second Hong Kong or Macao because Taiwan is an independent sovereign state.

In short, it must be clearly distinguished that both Taiwan and China are a country on either side of the strait.

People's referendum

China has refused to renounce the option of using force against Taiwan and continued to suppress Taiwan in the international community.

This has greatly hurt the feelings of the Taiwan people.

China's so-called "one China principle" or "one country, two systems" is to change the *status quo* in Taiwan.

It is impossible for us to accept this because whether Taiwan's future and the *status quo* should be changed is an issue not to be decided by any country, government, party, or individual.

Only the great 23 million people of Taiwan have the right to decide on Taiwan's future, destiny, and *status quo*.

How do we make a decision when necessary?

Referendum — it is the ideal and goal we have been pursuing over a long period of time and the common idea of everyone.

Referendum is a basic human right and the 23 million people of Taiwan have this basic human right, which should not be deprived or restricted.

I sincerely call on and encourage all of you to seriously ponder over the importance and urgency of a referendum legislation.

Anti-Secession Law

(Adopted at the Third Session of the Tenth National People's Congress on March 14, 2005)

Article 1: This Law is formulated, in accordance with the Constitution, for the purpose of opposing and checking Taiwan's secession from China by secessionists in the name of "Taiwan independence", promoting peaceful national reunification, maintaining peace and stability in the Taiwan straits, preserving China's sovereignty and territorial integrity, and safeguarding the fundamental interests of the Chinese nation.

Article 2: There is only one China in the world. Both the mainland and Taiwan belong to one China. China's sovereignty and territorial integrity brook no division. Safeguarding China's sovereignty and territorial integrity is the common obligation of all Chinese people, the Taiwan compatriots included.

Taiwan is part of China. The state shall never allow the "Taiwan independence" secessionist forces to make Taiwan secede from China under any name or by any means.

Article 3: The Taiwan question is one that is left over from China's civil war of the late 1940s.

Solving the Taiwan question and achieving national reunification is China's internal affair, which subjects to no interference by any outside forces.

Article 4: Accomplishing the great task of reunifying the mother-land is the sacred duty of all Chinese people, the Taiwan compatriots included.

Article 5: Upholding the principle of "one China" is the basis of peaceful reunification of the country.

To reunify the country through peaceful means best serves the fundamental interests of the compatriots on both sides of the Taiwan straits. The state shall do its utmost with maximum sincerity to achieve a peaceful reunification.

After the country is reunified peacefully, Taiwan may practice systems different from those on the mainland and enjoy a high degree of autonomy.

Article 6: The state shall take the following measures to maintain peace and stability in the Taiwan Straits and promote cross-straits relations:

(1) To encourage and facilitate personnel exchanges across the straits for greater mutual understanding and mutual trust;
(2) To encourage and facilitate economic exchanges and cooperation, realize direct links of trade, mail and air and shipping services, and bring about closer economic ties between the two sides of the straits to their mutual benefit;
(3) To encourage and facilitate cross-Straits exchanges in education, science, technology, culture, health and sports, and work together to carry forward the proud Chinese cultural traditions;
(4) To encourage and facilitate cross-Straits cooperation in combating crimes; and
(5) To encourage and facilitate other activities that are conducive to peace and stability in the Taiwan Straits and stronger cross-straits relations.

The state protects the rights and interests of the Taiwan compatriots in accordance with law.

Article 7: The state stands for the achievement of peaceful reunification through consultations and negotiations on an equal footing between the two sides of the Taiwan Straits. These consultations and negotiations may be conducted in steps and phases and with flexible and varied modalities.

The two sides of the Taiwan straits may consult and negotiate on the following matters:

(1) Officially ending the state of hostility between the two sides;
(2) Mapping out the development of cross-Straits relations;
(3) Steps and arrangements for peaceful national reunification;
(4) The political status of the Taiwan authorities;
(5) The Taiwan region's room of international operation that is compatible with its status; and
(6) Other matters concerning the achievement of peaceful national reunification.

Article 8: In the event that the "Taiwan independence" secessionist forces should act under any name or by any means to cause the fact of Taiwan's secession from China, or that major incidents entailing Taiwan's secession from China should occur, or that possibilities for a peaceful reunification should be completely exhausted, the state shall employ non-peaceful means and other necessary measures to protect China's sovereignty and territorial integrity.

The State Council and the Central Military Commission shall decide on and execute the non-peaceful means and other necessary measures as provided for in the preceding paragraph and shall promptly report to the Standing Committee of the National People's Congress.

Article 9: In the event of employing and executing non-peaceful means and other necessary measures as provided for in this Law, the state shall exert its utmost to protect the lives, property and other legitimate rights and interests of Taiwan civilians and foreign nationals in Taiwan, and to minimize losses. At the same time, the state shall protect the rights and interests of the Taiwan compatriots in other parts of China in accordance with law.

Article 10: This Law shall come into force on the day of its promulgation.

Taiwan's Renaissance

First Inaugural Address by President Ma Ying-jeou
May 20, 2008

Heads of State of Our Diplomatic Allies, Distinguished Guests, Overseas Compatriots, My Fellow Taiwanese, and Dear Friends in front of a Television Set or Computer: Good Morning!

Historical Significance of the Second Turnover of Power

Earlier this year on March 22, through the presidential election of the Republic of China, the people changed the course of their future. Today we are here not to celebrate the victory of a particular party or individual, but to witness Taiwan pass a historic milestone.

Taiwan's democracy has been treading down a rocky road, but now it has finally won the chance to enter a smoother path. During that difficult time, political trust was low, political maneuvering was high, and economic security was gone. Support for Taiwan from abroad had suffered an all-time low. Fortunately, the growing pains of Taiwan's democracy did not last long compared to those of other young democracies. Through these growing pains, Taiwan's democracy matured as one can see by the clear choice the people made at this critical moment. The people have chosen clean politics, an open economy, ethnic harmony, and peaceful cross-Strait relations to open their arms to the future.

Above all, the people have rediscovered Taiwan's traditional core values of benevolence, righteousness, diligence, honesty, generosity and industriousness. This remarkable experience has let Taiwan become "a beacon of democracy to Asia and the world." We, the people of Taiwan, should be proud of ourselves. The Republic of China is now a democracy respected by the international community.

Yet we are still not content. We must better Taiwan's democracy, enrich its substance, and make it more perfect. To accomplish this, we can rely on the Constitution to protect human rights, uphold law and order, make justice independent and impartial, and breathe new life into civil society. Taiwan's democracy should not be marred by illegal eavesdropping, arbitrary justice and political interference in the media or electoral institutions. All of us share this vision for the next phase of political reform.

On the day of Taiwan's presidential election, hundreds of millions of ethnic Chinese worldwide watched the ballot count on TV and the Internet. Taiwan is the sole ethnic Chinese society to complete a second democratic turnover of power. Ethnic Chinese communities around the world have laid their hopes on this crucial political experiment. By succeeding, we can make unparalleled contributions to the democratic development of all ethnic Chinese communities. This responsibility is ours to fulfill.

Mission of the New Era

The new administration's most urgent task is to lead Taiwan through the daunting challenges from globalization. The world economy is changing profoundly, and newly emerging countries are arising rapidly. We must upgrade Taiwan's international competitiveness and recover lost opportunities. The uncertainty of the current global economy poses as the main challenge to the revitalization of Taiwan's economy. Yet, we firmly believe that, with right policies and steadfast determination, our goals are within our grasp.

Islands like Taiwan flourish in an open economy and wither in a closed one. This has been true throughout history. Therefore, we must open up and deregulate the economy to unleash the vitality of the private sector. This will strengthen Taiwan's comparative advantages. Taiwan's enterprises should be encouraged to establish themselves at home, network throughout the Asia–Pacific region, and position themselves globally. Taiwan's labor force must learn to adapt to rapid technological changes and industrial restructuring. Our youth must develop character, a sense of civic duty, global perspectives and lifelong learning capabilities. All forms of political interference in education must be eradicated. In this era of globalization, the government must satisfy the basic needs of the underprivileged and create opportunities for them to develop. While pursuing growth, we must seek environmental sustainability for Taiwan and the rest of the world.

The new administration must also restore political ethics to regain the people's trust in the government. We will endeavor to create an environment that is humane, rational and pluralistic — one that fosters political reconciliation and co-existence. We will promote harmony among sub-ethnic groups and between the old and new immigrants, encourage healthy competition in politics, and respect the media's monitoring of the government and freedom of the press.

The new administration will push for clean politics and set strict standards for the integrity and efficiency of officials. It also will provide a code for the interaction between the public and private sectors to prevent money politics. I hope every civil servant will keep in mind: "Power corrupts, and absolute power corrupts absolutely." The KMT will honor its sincere commitment to accountability in governance. The new government will be for all the people, remain non-partisan and uphold administrative neutrality. The government will not stand in the way of social progress, but rather serve as the engine that drives it.

As President of the Republic of China, my most solemn duty is to safeguard the Constitution. In a young democracy, respecting the Constitution is more important than amending it. My top priority is to affirm the authority of the Constitution and show the value of abiding by it. Serving by example, I will follow the letter and the spirit of the Constitution, especially the separation of powers. We must ensure that the government is based on the rule of law. The Executive Yuan must answer to the Legislative Yuan. The Judiciary must guarantee the rule of law and protect human rights. The Examination Yuan must make the civil service sound. The Control Yuan must redress mistakes by the government and censure malfeasance by civil servants. All told, we must take this opportunity to re-establish a robust constitutional tradition.

Taiwan has to be a respectable member of the global village. Dignity, autonomy, pragmatism and flexibility should be Taiwan's guiding principles when developing foreign relations. As a world citizen, the Republic of China will accept its responsibilities in promoting free trade, non-proliferation, anti-global warming measures, counter-terrorism, humanitarian aid, and other global commons. Taiwan must play a greater role in regional cooperation. By strengthening economic relations with its major trading partners, Taiwan can better integrate itself in East Asia and contribute more to the region's peace and prosperity.

We will strengthen bilateral relations with the United States, our foremost security ally and trading partner. Taiwan will continue to cherish its diplomatic allies and honor its commitments to them. We will expand cooperation with like-minded countries. On top of that, we are determined to defend ourselves, and we will rationalize our defense budget and acquire necessary defensive weaponry to form a solid national defense force. At the same time, we are committed to cross-strait peace and regional stability. The Republic of China must restore its reputation in the international community as a peace-maker.

I sincerely hope that the two sides of the Taiwan Strait can seize this historic opportunity to achieve peace and co-prosperity. Under the principle of "no unification, no independence and no use of force," as Taiwan's mainstream public opinion holds it, and under the framework of the ROC Constitution, we will maintain the *status quo* in the Taiwan Strait. In 1992, the two sides reached a consensus on "one China, respective interpretations." Many rounds of negotiation were then completed, spurring the development of cross-Strait relations. I want to reiterate that, based on the "1992 Consensus," negotiations should resume at the earliest time possible. As proposed in the Boao Forum on April 12 of this year, let's "face reality, pioneer a new future, shelve controversies and pursue a win–win solution." This will allow us to strike a balance as each pursues its own interests. The normalization of economic and cultural relations is the first step to a win–win solution. Accordingly, we are ready to resume consultations. It is our expectation that, with the start of direct charter flights on weekends and the arrival of mainland tourists in early July this year, we will launch a new era of cross-Strait relations.

We will also enter consultations with mainland China over Taiwan's international space and a possible cross-strait peace accord. Taiwan does not just want security and prosperity. It wants dignity. Only when Taiwan is no longer being isolated in the international arena can cross-Strait relations move forward with confidence. We have taken note that Mr. Hu Jintao has recently spoken on cross-strait relations three times: first, in a conversation of March 26 with United States President George W. Bush on the "1992 Consensus"; second, in his proposed "four continuations" on April 12 at the Boao Forum; and third, on April 29 when he called for "building mutual trust, shelving controversies, finding commonalities despite differences, and creating together a win–win solution" across the Taiwan Strait. His views are very much in line with our own. Here I would like to call upon the two sides to pursue reconciliation and truce in both cross-strait and international arenas.

We should help and respect each other in international organizations and activities. In light of our common Chinese heritage, people on both sides should do their utmost to jointly contribute to the international community without engaging in vicious competition and the waste of resources. I firmly believe that Taiwan and mainland China are open minded enough to find a way to attain peace and co-prosperity.

In resolving cross-Strait issues, what matters is not sovereignty but core values and way of life. We care about the welfare of the 1.3 billion people of Mainland China, and hope that Mainland China will continue to move toward freedom, democracy and prosperity for all the people. This would pave way for the long-term peaceful development of cross-strait relations.

The damage from the recent earthquake in Sichuan was shocking. All Taiwanese have expressed deep concern and offered immediate emergency assistance. We offer our deepest condolences to the earthquake victims and pay homage to the rescue workers. May the reconstruction of the affected area be completed at the earliest time possible!

Taiwan's Legacy and Vision

Upon being sworn in, I had an epiphany about the significance of accepting responsibility for the 23 million people of Taiwan. Although I have never felt so honored in my life, this is the heaviest responsibility that I have ever shouldered. Taiwan is not my birthplace, but it is where I was raised and the resting place of my family. I am forever grateful to society for accepting and nurturing this post-war immigrant. I will protect Taiwan with all my heart and resolutely move forward. I will do my very best!

For over four centuries, this island of ours has welcomed waves of immigrants, nurturing and sheltering us all. It has provided us, our children and grandchildren, and the generations to come a safe haven. With its lofty mountains and vast oceans, Taiwan has invigorated us in mind and spirit. The cultural legacies we inherited over time not only survive on this land, but flourish and evolve, creating a pluralistic and vigorous human landscape.

The Republic of China was reborn on Taiwan. During my presidency, we will celebrate the 100th anniversary of the founding of the Republic of China. This democratic republic, the very first in Asia, spent a short 38 years on the Chinese mainland, but has spent nearly 60 years in Taiwan. During these last six decades, the destinies of the Republic of China and Taiwan have been closely intertwined. Together, the two have experienced times good and bad. On the jagged path toward democracy, the ROC has made great strides. Dr. Sun Yat-sen's dream for a constitutional democracy was not realized on the Chinese mainland, but today it has taken root, blossomed and borne fruit in Taiwan.

I am confident about Taiwan's future. Over the years, I have traveled to every corner of the island and talked with people from all walks of life. What impressed me most was that the traditional core values of benevolence, righteousness, diligence, honesty, generosity and industriousness could be seen everywhere in the words and deeds of the Taiwanese people regardless of their location and age. These values have long been ingrained in their character. This is the wellspring of our progress, also lauded as the "Taiwan Spirit."

One can see that Taiwan is blessed with an excellent geographic location, precious cultural assets, a maturing democracy, innovative entrepreneurship, a pluralistic society, active civic groups, patriotic overseas compatriots, and new immigrants from all over the world. We should couple the "Taiwan Spirit" with our comparative advantages and the principle of "putting Taiwan first for the benefit of the people." This way we can transform our homeland — Taiwan, Penghu, Kinmen and Matsu — the envy of the world.

To revive Taiwan requires the efforts of both the government and the people. We need the expertise of the private sector, cooperation among all political parties, and participation by all the people. My dear compatriots, from this moment on, we must roll up our sleeves to build up our homeland. Together, we can lay a solid foundation of peace and prosperity for our children, grandchildren and the generations to come. Let's work hand in hand for our future!

My dear compatriots, please join me:

Long live Taiwan's democracy!
Long live the Republic of China!
Thank you!

Let Us Join Hands to Promote the Peaceful Development of Cross-Straits Relations and Strive with a United Resolve for the Great Rejuvenation of the Chinese Nation

December 31, 2008
Hu Jintao

Speech at the Forum Marking the 30th Anniversary of the Issuance of the Message to Compatriots in Taiwan.

Comrades and Friends,

Tomorrow is New Year's Day of the year 2009. When festive times come round, we think all the more of our loved ones. Accordingly now, on behalf of the people of all ethnic groups on the mainland of our motherland, I would like to extend our sincere greetings and heartfelt felicitations to our compatriots in Taiwan!

On New Year's Day of 1979, the Standing Committee of the National People's Congress (NPC) issued the Message to Compatriots in Taiwan, in which it solemnly announced the major policies and principles for securing the peaceful reunification of our motherland. Thereupon, a new historical chapter opened in the development of cross-Straits relations. The Message to Compatriots in Taiwan expressly declared that reunification of China is consonant with popular will and the general trend of development, and that, in accomplishing the great cause of reunifying the motherland, it is imperative to take the realities into account and to respect the present situation of Taiwan and the opinions of people from all walks of life there and adopt fair and reasonable policies and measures so as to spare the people of Taiwan any adverse effects as a consequence there. The Message clearly proclaimed that we place our hopes in the people of Taiwan and also in the Taiwan authorities. It further explicitly proposed that the state of military confrontation across the Taiwan Straits be ended through consultations and negotiations, the barriers separating the people of the two sides be removed, free travel be facilitated and mail, transport and business links be established and economic and cultural exchanges be promoted. The issuance of the Message to Compatriots in Taiwan heralded the beginning of a new historical era for our theories and practice on the settlement of the Taiwan question.

Since the Taiwan question first came into being in 1949, we have always deemed it our sacred duty to resolve the question and accomplish the great cause of reunifying the motherland, and have made prolonged and unremitting efforts toward this end. In 1978, the Third Plenary Session of the Eleventh Central Committee of the Communist Party of China (CPC) reached its historic decision to shift the focus of the Party and the state's work to economic development and to carry out reform and opening up to the outside world. China's development thus entered into a new era. It was against this important historical backdrop that the Message to Compatriots in Taiwan was issued. Over the past thirty years, we have introduced a series of principles and policies toward Taiwan with the aim to promote the settlement of this question. Comrade Deng Xiaoping, with a view to the development and changes in the international and domestic situations and by proceeding from the fundamental interests of the

Chinese nation and the development strategy for the country, and further based on the thinking of comrades Mao Zedong and Zhou Enlai regarding striving for peaceful resolution of the Taiwan question, creatively put forward his great concept of "one country, two systems," thus making a historic contribution to the principle of "peaceful reunification and one country, two systems." The eight-point proposal put forward by Comrade Jiang Zemin for developing cross-Straits relations and promoting the peaceful reunification of the motherland in the current stage further enriched and developed our principles and policies toward Taiwan. Since the 16th CPC National Congress, we have made major decisions on and arrangements for our work related Taiwan, and put forward a series of new propositions and new initiatives, imparting fresh meaning to our principles and policies toward Taiwan. The enactment and enforcement of the Anti-Secession Law codified into law our policies and principles for the settlement of the Taiwan question, gave expression to our consistent stance and the utter sincerity of our adherence to peaceful reunification and, at the same time, demonstrated the common will and firm resolve of people all over China to resolutely oppose "Taiwan independence" and defend our national sovereignty and territorial integrity.

Since the Message to Compatriots in Taiwan was issued, cross-Straits relations have undergone significant changes thanks to the concerted efforts of our compatriots and people from all walks of life on both sides. At the end of 1987, the longstanding separation between our compatriots was lifted, our interactions became increasingly close and cross-Straits economic cooperation flourished, creating a complementary and mutually beneficial pattern. In 1992, our two sides reached the 1992 Consensus, on the basis of which we held the first Wang Daohan — Koo Chen-fu talks. In 2005, *Kuomintang* (KMT) and CPC leaders actualized a historic meeting and concluded the Common Vision for Cross-Straits Peaceful Development. In March of this year, the situation in Taiwan underwent a positive change and a rare historical opportunity thus presented itself in cross-Straits relations. Since May of this year, in the spirit of forging mutual trust, laying aside disputes, seeking common ground while reserving differences, and jointly creating a win-win situation, cross-Straits consultation has been able to resume and achieve significant fruits on the basis of the 1992 Consensus, and a historic step has been taken toward the two-way, comprehensive and direct three links of mail, transport and business between the two sides. Both sides have resolved a raft of issues in a proper manner. We have sustained momentum in the improvement and development of cross-straits relations, and helped bring about further prospects for their peaceful development. Today, the comings and goings between our compatriots on the two sides are more frequent, our economic ties have become closer, our cultural exchanges are more dynamic and our common interests are of greater breadth than ever before. The Chinese people's cause of safeguarding peace in the Taiwan Straits, promoting the development of cross-Straits relations, and realizing the peaceful reunification of our motherland is increasingly winning over the understanding and support of the international community. The situation wherein countries around the world universally acknowledge one China is being steadily strengthened and developed.

Our practice in developing cross-straits relations over the past thirty years informs us that: To promote the development of cross-straits relations and realize the peaceful reunification of the motherland, what is of the greatest account is adhering to the principle of "peaceful reunification and one country, two systems" and the eight-point proposal for developing cross-Straits relations and promoting the peaceful reunification of the motherland in the current stage, never swaying in adhering to the "one-China" principle, never giving up our efforts to achieve peaceful reunification, never changing the principle of placing our hopes on the people of Taiwan, never compromising in opposing secessionist activities aimed at "Taiwan independence", holding steadfastly to the theme of peaceful development of cross-straits relations, and striving sincerely to secure the blessings of fortune for our compatriots on both sides and peace in the Taiwan straits region, while safeguarding our country's sovereignty and territorial integrity and safeguarding the fundamental interests of the Chinese nation.

Our 30-year practice fully demonstrates that the major policies and principles we have devised for and practiced in our Taiwan work are confluent with the current of the times and in step with the historical trend, aptly serve the fundamental interests of the nation and the core interests of the country, embody the spirit of seeking truth from facts which respects history, reality and the wishes of the people, and mirror a profound understanding of the laws governing the development of cross-Straits relations. These policies and principles have therefore helped bring about historic successes in developing cross-Straits relations. We must continue to maintain and thoroughly implement these policies and principles which have been proven so correct for long into the future and continue to propel the peaceful reunification of our motherland ever onward.

Our 30-year practice further fully attests to the fact that the tremendous progress continuously achieved in the reform, opening up and modernization of the mainland of our motherland is a strong foundation and reliable safeguard for promoting the development of cross-Straits relations and realizing the peaceful reunification of the motherland, and one that determines the essential paradigm for and development orientation of cross-Straits relations.

This 30-year practice has moreover fully proven that Chinese people on both sides of the straits have the ability and wisdom to hold the future of cross-Straits relations in their own hands, strengthen their emotional bonds and augment their common interests through exchanges and cooperation, achieve more consensus and reduce differences through consultations and negotiations, and resolve any issues arising sequentially and at a progressive pace.

This 30-year practice has furthermore fully manifested that the secessionist forces advocating "Taiwan independence" and their secessionist activities harm the common interests of our compatriots on both sides, undermine the fundamental interests of the Chinese nation, and run counter to the inexorable historical trend of China's development. They constitute the most dire threat to the peaceful development of cross-Straits relations and are thus fated to meet with united opposition from our compatriots on both sides. Any attempt by anyone or any force to sever Taiwan from China is doomed to failure.

Comrades and Friends,

Through reform and opening up over the past thirty years, historic changes have taken place to the look of China and our relations with the world. Having traversed stormy and rocky channels, cross-Straits relations have now reached a new starting point in history. Looking back on the nation's journey of uphill struggle in modern times and looking ahead to the bright prospects for the nation's development, we must gaze into the distance from a high eminence, assess the current situation, and carefully consider and practically solve major issues in the development of cross-Straits relations with an awareness of our responsibility to history and to the people, and from the perspective of development of the entire nation, while demonstrating broader vision, deeper wisdom, more stalwart courage and a more pragmatic thought process.

The key to resolving the Taiwan question is the reunification of the motherland. Its purpose is to safeguard and guarantee national sovereignty and territorial integrity, pursue happiness for all the people of the Chinese nation, including our compatriots in Taiwan, and realize the great rejuvenation of the Chinese nation. Reunifying the motherland by peaceful means is most consistent with the fundamental interests of the Chinese nation, including our compatriots in Taiwan. It is also in tune with the trend of the times, namely, aspiring for peace, seeking development and promoting cooperation. We must strive for the peaceful reunification of the motherland with the greatest sincerity and utmost effort. **First of all, it is imperative to**

ensure the peaceful development of cross-Straits relations. This is conducive to our compatriots on both sides strengthening exchanges and cooperation and building greater emotional harmony; it is conducive to the two sides of the straits increasing mutual trust and settling disputes; it is conducive to the economies on both sides developing and prospering together; and it is conducive to safeguarding national sovereignty and territorial integrity and realizing the great rejuvenation of the Chinese nation.

To this end, we must firmly hold to the theme of peaceful development of cross-Straits relations and actively promote it and realize the solidarity, harmony and prosperity of the entire nation. We must take our insistence that the mainland and Taiwan belong to one China as the political foundation for promoting the peaceful development of cross-Straits relations, take deepening exchanges and cooperation and furthering consultations and negotiations as the key approaches to promoting such peaceful development, take strengthening the concerted endeavor of our compatriots on both sides as the strong impetus for promoting it, and strive to open up new vistas in the peaceful development of cross-Straits relations by joining hands to advance and pulling together with hearts united.

1. To firmly abide by the "one-China" principle and enhance political mutual trust. Safeguarding our national sovereignty and territorial integrity is the core interest of the nation. There is only one China in the world, China's sovereignty and territorial integrity brooks no partition. Although the mainland and Taiwan have not yet been reunited since 1949, the circumstances *per se* do not denote a state of partition of Chinese territory and sovereignty. Rather, it is merely a state of political antagonism that is a legacy — albeit a lingering one — of the Chinese civil war waged in the mid- to late-1940s. Nevertheless, this does not alter the fact that both the mainland and Taiwan belong to "one China". **For the two sides of the straits, to return to unity is not the recreation of sovereignty or**

territory, but an end to political antagonism. When both sides of the Straits develop a common understanding and united position on safeguarding the "one-China" framework, which is an issue of principle, this will form the cornerstone on which to build political mutual trust and anything at all will then be open to discussion. The two sides should, with a constructive attitude, actively look to the future, undertake joint efforts, create favorable conditions, and gradually resolve the longstanding issues in cross-Straits relations and any new issues that may arise in the course of development thereof through consultation on equal footing. Continuing to oppose the secessionist activities aimed at "Taiwan independence" is a necessary condition for promoting the peaceful development of cross-Straits relations and is the joint responsibility of our compatriots on both sides. Anything conducive to the peaceful development of cross-Straits relations must be energetically promoted; anything detrimental must be staunchly opposed.

2. To advance economic cooperation and promote common development. Our compatriots on both sides must engage in extensive economic cooperation, expand the three direct links across the straits, cultivate and augment common interests, form close ties and achieve mutual benefits and a win–win situation. We will continue to welcome and support Taiwan enterprises to operate and develop their businesses on the mainland, and encourage and support qualified mainland enterprises to invest and develop their businesses in Taiwan. We look forward to the normalization of cross-straits economic relations and will promote the institutionalization of economic cooperation, so as to lay a more solid material foundation and provide a greater economic impetus for the peaceful development of cross-straits relations. The two sides of the straits may sign a comprehensive economic cooperation agreement to this end and establish a mechanism for economic cooperation which defers to the characteristics of both

sides, so as to maximize the synergy of respective advantages and mutual benefits. Establishing a closer mechanism for cross-straits economic cooperation is conducive to making Taiwan's economy more competitive and expanding the arena for its development, conducive to promoting the common development of the economies on both sides, and conducive to exploring feasible approaches to the dovetailing of the common development of both economies with the economic cooperation mechanism in the Asia–Pacific region.

3. To promote Chinese culture and strengthen spiritual bonds. Chinese culture boasts a long history illuminated by glorious splendors. It is a common and precious asset of our compatriots on both sides and an important link guaranteeing the national emotional bonds between them. Chinese culture has deep roots and luxuriant foliage in Taiwan; Taiwan culture has enriched the substance of Chinese culture. The Taiwan consciousness, which shows the love of our Taiwan compatriots for their home and land, does not equal to "Taiwan independence" consciousness. Our compatriots on both sides should jointly inherit and promote the exquisite traditions of Chinese culture, conduct cultural exchanges in varied forms and enable Chinese culture to be passed down from one generation to the next and enhanced, so as to boost our national consciousness, build up a common will and generate spiritual strength for the joint endeavor toward the great rejuvenation of the Chinese nation. It is of particular necessity to strengthen youth exchanges between the two sides, so as to continuously infuse exuberant vitality into the peaceful development of cross-Straits relations. We will continue to adopt active measures, including our readiness to negotiate an agreement on cross-Straits cultural and educational exchanges, in order to boost such exchanges and cooperation to a new level, where they are more extensive in scope and higher in caliber.

4. **To strengthen two-way visits of people and expand exchanges in various circles.** Our compatriots on both sides should expand

exchanges; various communities on the two sides, and their representatives, should intensify exchanges, strengthen communication in good faith, and enhance mutual understanding. We are willing to respond positively to any constructive opinions conducive to furthering the peaceful development of cross-straits relations. We shall continue to push forward exchanges and dialogue between the *Kuomintang* and the CPC to jointly implement the Common Vision for Cross-Straits Peaceful Development. Regarding the fact that some of our compatriots in Taiwan lack understanding of, or even misunderstand, the mainland of the motherland and have misgivings about developing cross-Straits relations due to various causes, we are not only willing to undo such sentiments and counsel them with the greatest tolerance and patience, but also willing to adopt even more affirmative measures so that more and more of our Taiwan compatriots may enjoy enhanced well-being in the course of promoting the peaceful development of cross-Straits relations. As to those individuals who formerly advocated, engaged in, or pursued "Taiwan independence", we shall also warmly and sincerely welcome them to return to the correct course of promoting the peaceful development of cross-straits relations. We hope the Democratic Progressive Party (DPP) will realize a clear understanding of the tenor of the times, cease carrying out its "Taiwan independence" secessionist activities and stop running counter to the common wish of the entire nation. As long as the DPP changes its "Taiwan independence" secessionist position, we are willing to make a positive response.

5. To safeguard national sovereignty and hold consultations on external affairs. We are consistently committed to safeguarding the legitimate rights and interests of our Taiwan compatriots abroad. Our overseas embassies and consulates should strengthen their ties with our Taiwan compatriots and sincerely aid them in solving their practical difficulties. **We understand our Taiwan compatriots' feelings on the issue of participation in international**

activities and we pay particular attention to solving relevant issues. For the two sides of the straits, to avoid unnecessary internal strife on external affairs is conducive to furthering the overall interests of the Chinese nation. Further consultations can be conducted, as needed, on the prospect of **Taiwan's people-to-people economic and cultural interactions with other countries. Regarding the issue of Taiwan's participation in the activities of international organizations, fair and reasonable arrangements can be effected through pragmatic consultation between the two sides, provided that this does not create a situation of "two Chinas" or "one China, one Taiwan."** Settling the Taiwan question and realizing the complete reunification of the country is an internal affair of China and is not subject to interference by any foreign forces.

6. **To end the state of hostility and reach a peace agreement.** Chinese people on both sides of the straits are duty-bound to jointly end the history of cross-Straits hostility and do their utmost to avoid the recurrence of a clash of arms between consanguine compatriots, so as to grant future generations the chance to join hands and create a better life. In order to facilitate their consultations and negotiations and their arrangements for their interactions, the two sides may make pragmatic explorations in their political relations under the special circumstances where the country has not yet been reunified. In the interest of stabilizing the situation in the Taiwan straits and allaying apprehensions relating to military security, the two sides may at an opportune time engage and exchange with each other on military issues and explore mechanisms for mutual military trust. We hereby renew our appeal: On the basis of the "one-China" principle, we should formally end the state of hostility across the straits through consultation, reach a peace agreement, and build a framework for the peaceful development of cross-straits relations.

Our compatriots on both sides of the straits form a community of common destiny bound by bonds of blood. China, the mainland and Taiwan included, is the common home of our compatriots on both sides, who are thus duty-bound to safeguard and build her well. It takes the joint efforts of our compatriots on both sides to achieve the great rejuvenation of the Chinese nation, our compatriots on both sides must jointly create a new phase in the peaceful development of cross-straits relations, and we will jointly enjoy the fruits thereof. We must persist in putting people first, implement the principle of placing our hopes on the people of Taiwan in our various work related to Taiwan, understand, trust, and care for our compatriots in Taiwan, identify their wishes and appeals, address their concerns and help them overcome difficulties, and exert ourselves passionately to serve their needs. We must protect the legitimate rights and interests of our compatriots in Taiwan in accordance with the law, and unite with them in the broadest sense in promoting the peaceful development of cross-Straits relations. The future of Taiwan hinges upon the peaceful development of cross-straits relations and upon the great rejuvenation of the Chinese nation. On the journey toward these magnificent goals, the compatriots in Taiwan will, together with their compatriots on the mainland, enjoy the dignity and glory of a great country and take pride in being dignified Chinese.

Our compatriots in Hong Kong, Macao and abroad have long identified with the great cause of national reunification and served as an important force opposing "Taiwan independence" and promoting national reunification. We sincerely hope that they will make fresh contributions to promoting the peaceful development of cross-straits relations and realizing the peaceful reunification of the motherland.

For many years, the international community has lent active support to the cause of the Chinese government and people of safeguarding peace in the Taiwan straits, promoting the development of cross-straits relations, and working toward the complete reunification of the country. For this, the Chinese government would like to express its appreciation and gratitude. China's reunification will not impair the interests of any country; to the contrary, it will only serve to promote the prosperity and stability of the Asia–Pacific region and the world and help enable the Chinese people to make new, ever greater contributions to the noble cause of peace and development of mankind.

Comrades and Friends,

The two sides of the straits are bound to be reunified in the course of the great rejuvenation of the Chinese nation. Although there will be further difficulties and obstacles on our way forward, as long as we muster our confidence, work unremittingly, and rely closely on our compatriots on both sides, we will certainly be able to create a new phase in the peaceful development of cross-straits relations and usher in a glorious future for the great rejuvenation of the Chinese nation.

Index